HITLER'S FOLLOWERS

Studies in the sociology of the Nazi movement

Detlef Mühlberger

ROUTLEDGE

London and New York

First published 1991
by Routledge
11 New Fetter Lane, London EC4P 4EE

Simultaneously published in the USA and Canada
by Routledge
a division of Routledge, Chapman and Hall, Inc.
29 West 35th Street, New York, NY 10001

© 1991 Detlef Mühlberger

Typeset in 10/12 pt Baskerville by
Witwell Ltd, Southport
Printed in Great Britain by
TJ Press (Padstow) Ltd, Padstow, Cornwall.

British Library Cataloguing in Publication Data
Mühlberger, Detlef
Hitler's followers: studies in the sociology of the Nazi
movement
1. Germany. Political parties: Nationalsozialistische
Deutsche Arbeiter-Partei
I. Title
324.243038

Library of Congress Cataloging-in-Publication Data
Mühlberger, Detlef.
Hitler's followers: studies in the sociology of the Nazi
movement/Detlef Mühlberger.
p.   cm.
Includes bibliographical references.
1. National socialism–Social aspects.   I. Title.
DD256.5.M75   1990
320.5'33'0943–dc20   90-8455

ISBN 0-415-00802-6

For Sue and Tania

CONTENTS

v

LIST OF MAPS

LIST OF TABLES

viii

ABBREVIATIONS

BA	Bundesarchiv Koblenz
BDC	Berlin Document Center
DHV	Deutschnationaler Handlungsgehilfenverband
DVFP	Deutschvölkische Freiheitspartei
GLAK	Generallandesarchiv Karlsruhe
HA	NSDAP Hauptarchiv (Hoover Institution Mircrofilm Collection)
HHStAW	Hessisches Hauptstaatsarchiv Wiesbaden
HJ	Hitlerjugend
KPD	Kommunistische Partei Deutschlands
Kr.	Kreis (county district)
NHStAH	Niedersächsisches Hauptstaatsarchiv Hannover
NSDAP	Nationalsozialistische Deutsche Arbeiterpartei (Nazi Party)
NSF	Nationalsozialistische Frauenschaft
NSFB	Nationalsozialistische Freiheitsbewegung
NWHStAD	Nordrhein-Westfälisches Hauptstaatsarchiv Düsseldorf
OG	Ortsgruppe (Nazi Party branch)
Reg.-Bez.	Regierungsbezirk (administrative sub-division of a Prussian province)
RM	Reichsmark
SA	Sturmabteilung
SPD	Sozialdemokratische Partei Deutschlands
SS	Schutzstaffel
StAB	Staatsarchiv Bremen
StAD	Staatsarchiv Darmstadt
StAF	Staatsarchiv Freiburg
Stadtkr.	Stadtkreis (urban district)
StAL	Staatsarchiv Ludwigsburg

StAM	Staatsarchiv Münster
StDR	*Statistik des Deutschen Reichs*
StJDR	*Statistisches Jahrbuch für das Deutsche Reich*
StJFP	*Statistisches Jahrbuch für den Freistaat Preußen*
VB	*Völkischer Beobachter*

ACKNOWLEDGEMENTS

Many individuals and institutions have given me assistance in the preparation of this book. I am most grateful for the invaluable help and guidance provided by the staffs of the *Bundesarchiv*, Koblenz; the *Generallandesarchiv*, Karlsruhe; the *Hessisches Hauptstaatsarchiv*, Wiesbaden; the *Niedersächsisches Hauptstaatsarchiv*, Hanover; the *Nordrhein-Westfälisches Hauptstaatsarchiv*, Düsseldorf; and of the *Staatsarchive* at Bremen, Darmstadt, Freiburg, Ludwigsburg and Münster. For access to the Hoover Institution NSDAP *Hauptarchiv* Microfilm Collection at St Antony's College, Oxford, I am indebted to the Librarian, Ms Rosemary Campbell. The Inter Library loan department at Oxford Polytechnic took a great deal of trouble to meet my many requests, as did the staff of the Bodleian Library.

I am also very grateful for the financial assistance provided by the Research Committee of Oxford Polytechnic, which permitted my lengthy stays in Germany in 1987 and 1988 to pursue research on the sociology of Nazism. My thanks also go to Mr Richard Stoneman of Routledge for his help and encouragement in the completion of the present work.

To my wife, who has tolerated my lengthy absences abroad and who has given me constant encouragement over the years, I owe a special thanks.

Detlef Mühlberger

INTRODUCTION

It was the startling success of the Nazi Party in the *Reichstag* election on 14 September 1930 and its transformation from marginal to major factor in Weimar politics which first prompted contemporary observers and political analysts to look more closely than before at the question of *who* were the carriers of Nazism. Much speculation on the social basis of Nazism took place in the 1930s, while the revelation of the full extent of German barbarism at the end of the Second World War gave renewed impetus to diagnosing which social group or groups had provided Nazism with its mass base. A variety of hypotheses about the social background of the supporters of the Nazi Party were advanced from the early 1930s which had one major feature in common: they were based on very little, if any, empirical evidence relating to the rank and file membership of the Nazi Party or its major specialist organizations, such as the SA or SS.

It is only since the late 1960s that the question of which social types were attracted to Nazism[1] gradually began to be based on hard evidence relating to the membership of the Nazi Party, while methodological and interpretational problems involved in using the available data also attracted the critical attention of social scientists and historians. Yet despite the fact that, compared to the dearth of such studies in the past, there has been what seems like a veritable explosion in the publication of empirical data relating to the social basis of the Nazi Movement in the last decade or so, our knowledge of the social structure of the party and of its major auxiliary organizations is at present still relatively limited, and more time is now being spent on providing résumés of what has been written on the subject, on arguing about methodological problems involved in handling

1

data, and on offering useful (and not so useful!) advice on how to proceed in the future.[2] Though valuable in their own way, these works do nothing to actually expand the available, somewhat restricted data base around which much of the debate about the sociology of Nazism revolves.

The use of sophisticated quantitative methods in analysing data with the aid of computer technology has undoubtedly led to significant results in recent years, especially the establishment of two important sets of membership data dealing with the broad social contours of the Nazi Movement at the macro level, one relating to the period 1925 to 1945, the other to the years 1919 to 1932.[3] Based on individuals joining the NSDAP in these periods, neither set can - given the massive fluctuations in membership before 1933 - be precise about the social structure of the membership of the NSDAP at specific moments in time, since the social types leaving the party cannot be taken into consideration. Nor can the profile of the NSDAP newcomers at the national level say anything specific about the Nazi Party at the regional - never mind the local - level. The macro analysis cannot provide any insight into the undoubted regional variations in the sociology of Nazism. Except for the work on the formative phase of the NSDAP's development when it was still primarily a Bavarian phenomenon,[4] and a few regional and local studies,[5] virtually nothing specific is known about the structure of the NSDAP at the regional level, beyond the evidence the Nazis themselves provided in the form of the *Partei-Statistik*.[6] One way forward to reconstruct the social characteristics of the Nazi Movement at the regional and local level is, of course, a full evaluation of the material in the Berlin Document Center (the computerization of its contents was apparently once considered, but rejected on the grounds of cost). This contains the biographical details of almost the entire Nazi membership in two sets of card files, one listing the members alphabetically (this has large gaps and contains 5,772,200 cards) and another in which the membership is listed according to the Nazi *Gaue* (which has 9,052,200 cards).[7] To work through this massive amount of material (which records probably 80 per cent of the total Nazi membership[8]) would be a mammoth task, but would allow an almost accurate breakdown of the NSDAP's membership over time at the national, regional and local level. Undoubtedly this will one day be done by a team of well-funded and dedicated historians!

The alternative to discovering the nature of the Nazi Party at the level of the community or region, is to work through material on the party's membership held in the numerous *Länder* archives, an approach which has paid little dividend until recently.[9] Provided a sufficiently large cluster of branches in a particular area for a specific time-span can be found, the approach at the grassroots level has the major advantage of allowing one to set the social structure of the Nazi Party within the specific socio-economic, confessional and political context in which it developed. The impact on the social structure of the NSDAP of local and regional factors can thus be more accurately reflected, and considerable detail added to the generalized macro picture currently available on the social contours of Nazism.

There is a surprisingly extensive array of such data available in the numerous archives of the Federal Republic, as the material on which the present work is based demonstrates. Some of the archive material used in this study is astonishing, and even more astounding is the fact that very little, if any, of the data has been utilized before. The authors who produced the regional studies of the Nazi Party in Hesse, Lower Saxony and the Ruhr in the early 1970s were probably either unaware of the existence of the material on the membership of the Nazi Party in the archives which they used or they were denied access to it at that time.[10] But the very little use of membership lists for the Nazi Party, the SA and the SS by the numerous contributors to the collection of essays on the NSDAP's development in various localities of Hesse[11] which appeared in the early 1980s is puzzling, especially since it is clear from some of the contributions to the volume that a number of authors did tap the quite extensive material on the membership of the Hessian NSDAP in the *Hessisches Hauptstaatsarchiv* Wiesbaden, as well as the more limited material available at the *Staatsarchiv* Darmstadt.[12]

While gathering the material which forms the basis of this series of case studies on the social profile of the Nazi Movement in various regions of Germany, ominous noises about changes in data protection laws and their (possible) application to the type of material I was looking at were being made in some of the archives which I visited. Access to the material held by some archives (despite securing the required clearance) was not always easy and straightforward, given the severe restraints which are (it seems) imposed on the archival authorities by some *Länder* governments (whose policies on what can and cannot be seen seem to be anything but consistent) to whom they are responsible. Whereas the archivists of the bulk of the archives I visited were most helpful and went out of their way to meet my requests, in one archive everything I used seemed to have been subjected to scrutiny beforehand and a number of requests to see SS files appeared to be consistently stonewalled, though I was never actually told that I would not be allowed to see them. Another archive did not allow any access to the extensive collection of *Gau* membership files of the NSDAP under their control (the files had previously been in the Berlin Document Center and were given to the archive in 1978). In one archive, which in the event I did not use, I would not have been able to see the files I wanted at all and would only have been furnished with photocopies of the relevant membership lists after the names of the individuals had been removed. Finally, in another archive I was able to see some files, but denied others of an almost identical nature, an inconsistency which I never did – and still cannot – fathom out, especially since I know that a colleague in Israel working on a related theme to my own had had access to the very same set of files some two years previously. Fortunately, such restrictions were not enforced in most of the archives visited which, as far as I could see, allowed access to anything which they had without reference to new laws relating to data protection! I fear that in future, changes in the application of laws relating to data protection made urgent by the appearance of computerized data banks may be used by some of the political masters of *Länder* archives to prevent access to personal files on members of the NSDAP, the SA, the SS, and so on, a possible development which the academic community must challenge and resist collectively.

1

HISTORIOGRAPHICAL AND METHODOLOGICAL ASPECTS

To set the current debate on the social basis of Nazism in context, a brief historiographical review of the main conclusions reached on the subject suggests itself.[1] Virtually all the main theories attempting to explain the social characteristics of Nazism emerged in the late 1920s and early 1930s.[2] The early efforts made by political scientists, historians and political commentators to answer the question of which social types were being attracted to Nazism were based largely on impressionistic assertions not substantiated by any meaningful empirical evidence. Before 1933 the usual route taken by most analysts grappling with the problem of the social make-up of the supporters of Nazism concentrated on identifying the Nazi electorate.[3] On the basis of this approach the conclusion was reached in the early 1930s, strongly reinforced by Theodor Geiger's seminal work on the structure of German society published in 1932,[4] that the NSDAP was a middle-class party (*Mittelstandspartei*) or class party (*Klassenpartei*), or more often specifically a lower-middle-class movement. The 'middle-class image' of Nazism became strongly entrenched in the literature on the NSDAP long before the collapse of the Nazi regime, and the view was further strengthened in the post-1945 period,[5] and has continued to dominate the debate on the nature of Nazism until the early 1980s. The counter-argument, which suggested that the Nazi Party was a mass movement, a *Volkspartei* or people's party based on support drawn from all social groupings, a hypothesis also first developed in the 1930s[6] and one which also basically rested only on observations relating to the electoral performance of the NSDAP in the end-phase of the Weimar period, found few supporters at the time and has remained very much a minority

5

view in the debate on the social structure of Nazism.[7] Various attempts to develop other theories on the nature of Nazism have also been made from time to time. One such is the 'Marginal Man' theory, based on the idea that the Nazi members were essentially 'failures' or 'marginal' types, an idea first suggested by Konrad Heiden,[8] which was pushed to an absurd level by Daniel Lerner[9] in the post-war period, and one which still surfaces from time to time.[10] An alternative to the usual 'class' approach which dominates the theoretical works on the nature of the membership of the Nazi Party is the 'Generational Revolt' hypothesis, the view that youth played the most critical role in mobilizing support for Nazism, a thesis most persuasively argued by Peter Loewenberg and Peter Merkl.[11] The notion that the Nazi Party represented a sort of 'green revolt', that it was essentially a small-town and rural affair, has also been advocated over the years by a number of historians.[12] All these efforts have had little fundamental impact on the dominance of the 'middle-class theory', the orthodox interpretational line to be found in the major studies on Nazism.[13]

I

Given the almost universal acceptance of the thesis that the Nazi Party was essentially a middle-class movement, the main thrust of research from the 1930s onwards was centred on explaining why the *Mittelstand* was so attracted to Nazism,[14] rather than on providing a firm empirical base on which to base the theory. Admittedly not all the theoretical works postulating the 'middle-class theory' of Nazism were based entirely on educated guesswork, for some statistical evidence originated in the 1930s, which was used to underpin the theory. The first set of data was contained in Theodore Abel's interesting study[15] compiled in the early 1930s with the co-operation of the Nazi Party, which was based on an essay competition advertised in the Nazi press in 1933 on the theme of 'Why I became a Nazi', to which 687 Nazi members responded. The other source was the census of Nazi Party members undertaken by the Nazis themselves in 1934, the *Partei-Statistik*, published in three volumes in 1935.[16] This latter source was first used in an abbreviated form by Volz[17] in his account of the development of the Nazi Party which appeared in 1938. The *Partei-Statistik* data, as filtered through the *Berliner*

6

Tageblatt of 1 April 1937 and *Der Schulungsbrief* of 1938, was also the basis of an analysis of the Nazi Party membership and leadership produced by Hans Gerth[18] in 1940. Given the absence of any other material on the structure of the NSDAP for a considerable time-span in the post-war years, the *Partei-Statistik* has been used, though almost invariably with reservation and often with considerable misgivings, by numerous scholars attempting to grapple with the sociology of Nazism at the national[19] or regional level.[20]

For long attacked by many scholars[21] as an unreliable guide to the social structure of the Nazi Party, the utility of the *Partei-Statistik*, if used carefully in view of its undoubted limitations, is now being pointed to by a number of historians.[22] It cannot simply be dismissed as a piece of propaganda or the reflection of wishful thinking on the part of the Nazi leadership, given that the collated data was only to be used for internal party purposes and was also designed to provide a guide to future recruitment policy.[23] The Nazis were well aware of the fact that the party membership mirrored the social structure of German society imperfectly, and that workers and farmers were under-represented in the party and were thus to be encouraged to join it, whereas occupational groups such as civil servants and the self-employed, already over-represented in the movement, were not to be given easy access to the party. If the *Partei-Statistik* does indeed – as more than one critic has suggested – represent an attempt by the party hierarchy to project the NSDAP as a *Volkspartei* by inflating the size of the working-class membership within its ranks, it does a very inadequate job. The real problem with the *Partei-Statistik* is that it can only show the make-up of the membership as on 1 January 1935. It cannot be used to give an *accurate* picture of the social characteristics of the party's membership in the three time-spans for which breakdowns are provided, namely the period from 1925 to 14 September 1930, that from 15 September 1930 to 30 January 1933, and that from 30 January 1933 onwards, because it records only those members who had joined the Nazi Party in 1925 or thereafter and who had never left it until the census was taken (some time in 1934 presumably). Given that we know that the party experienced very significant membership fluctuations before January 1933, involving a membership loss of probably 40 to 50 per cent between 1925 and 1933[24] (it is unlikely that

7

members left the party in any great number immediately after the Nazi seizure of power), it is clear that the *Partei-Statistik* cannot provide any clue to the social profile of a sizeable element of the membership which had joined the party at some stage and left it subsequently. Despite its limitations, however, it can be used to illustrate the often marked regional variations in the social profile of the party at the *Gau* level,[25] and the data can be used to compare the sociology of the Nazi membership with that of the working population of Germany, given that the occupational categories used in the *Partei-Statistik* are similar to those employed in the censuses of 1925 and 1933, and are not as vague as some authorities were still suggesting in the 1980s.[26]

The move away from using Abel's limited data or the material provided in the *Partei-Statistik* and to get to grips with the problem of who joined the NSDAP by analysing new empirical evidence came in the early 1960s, when first Georg Franz-Willing and then Werner Maser made rather unsatisfactory attempts to throw some light on the social background of Nazi members in the pre-1923 period by evaluating fragments of Nazi membership lists.[27] Both authors concluded that the Nazi Party was essentially a *Mittelstandsbewegung* in its formative stage of development. The first modern study on the social characteristics of the NSDAP's membership came in 1971 with the publication of Michael Kater's article on the sociography of the pre-1923 Nazi Party.[28] Based on sophisticated quantitative techniques involving computer data analysis, this essay heralded the beginning of a series of important studies by the same author which broke new ground in several directions, with essays which underlined the massive potential of the use of the material in the Berlin Document Center, which explored the methodological problems surrounding work on the social structure of the Nazi Movement, and which pointed to the need to include the more important auxiliary organizations in the study of the sociology of Nazism as a whole.[29] In all of his work on the sociology of Nazism since the early 1970s, Michael Kater has consistently argued that Nazism was a *Mittelstand* phenomenon, irrespective of whether one is looking at the party itself, or the SA, or the SS. Not even a very significant change in the late 1970s in the classification model employed by him, when he abandoned his narrow concept of the occupational groups which composed the German working class and started to include skilled workers and apprentices in the lower class,[30] has led Michael Kater to change his views on the sociology of Nazism, despite the marked increase in the working-class presence in the Nazi Party which the adoption of his more realistic class model has resulted in. In his recent study summarizing the results of his extensive research on the social basis of Nazism, Michael Kater concludes that 'judged from the point of view of party membership (both rank and file and leadership corps), the National Socialist movement was indeed a pre-eminently lower-middle-class phenomenon'.[31]

The pioneering work on the social basis of Nazism by Michael Kater in the 1970s has undoubtedly stimulated research on the subject in the last decade or so. The social characteristics of the early NSDAP membership have been subjected to further analysis by Donald Douglas and Paul Madden.[32] A few studies on the sociology of the NSDAP beyond its Bavarian context, and dealing with the later phases of its development, have also begun to appear.[33] In the late 1970s and early 1980s significant work on the social make-up of the SA's rank and file and leadership was also published.[34] The results of the research on the social characteristics of the followers of Nazism was summarized in my contribution to *The Social Basis of European Fascist Movements* which appeared in 1987, in which additional new material was also presented on the NSDAP, the HJ and the SA.[35]

The growing volume of literature on the sociology of Nazism based on empirical evidence which has appeared since the 1970s has been accompanied by challenges to the deeply entrenched middle-class thesis of Nazism. Leaving aside the data in the *Partei-Statistik*, which contained statistical material suggesting that the party had succeeded in extending its social base well beyond the lower-middle class before the *Machtergreifung* of 1933,[36] evidence was beginning to appear from the late 1960s onwards which indicated that the party was drawing support from various social groups, and that at least in some areas of Germany it was proving problematical to apply the conventional *Mittelstand* thesis to the NSDAP's membership. In his collection of documents on the NSDAP in the Mainz-Koblenz-Trier area, Franz Josef Heyen published a number of reports made in the early 1930s by the *Regierungspräsident* of Koblenz in which the often stark differences in the social structure of the branches of the NSDAP in this predominantly Catholic region (including strong support from the lower class in some parts) was noted.[37] A more overt attack on the notion that the NSDAP was little more than a *Mittelstandsbewegung*, at least in its infancy, was made by Harold Gordon who, on the basis of occupational data relating to 1,126 individuals who joined the NSDAP in 1923, concluded that the membership of the NSDAP was 'a heterogeneous mixture of people of all classes and all professions and trades'.[38] In his doctoral thesis submitted in 1976 Paul Madden, on the basis of a representative sample of 40,101 members (drawn primarily from the NSDAP Master File in the Berlin Document Center) who had joined the NSDAP between 1919 and 1930, argued that 'National Socialism cannot be characterized as a class movement because of the presence in its adherents of representatives of all strata of German society in large numbers'.[39] My summary in 1980[40] of much of the available material on the social basis of Nazism led me to very similar conclusions, and the conviction that the NSDAP could not be viewed as a *Mittelstandsbewegung* was strengthened by further work on the theme subsequently.[41] In a recent article Paul Madden has, on the basis of a sample of 55,582 persons who joined the NSDAP between 1919 and 1932, reiterated his argument that the Nazi Party cannot be viewed as consisting overwhelmingly of *Mittelstand* types, and that 'Nazis before 1933 came from all segments of German society from the proletariat to the nobility'.[42]

No unanimous view has emerged to date among the social scientists and historians who have worked on the social background of the Nazi Party membership. We are now in the very odd situation in which Michael Kater, one of the strongest current advocates of the *Mittelstand* thesis of Nazism, has produced statistical evidence which shows that 41.1 per cent of persons joining the Nazi Party between 1925 and 1932 were from the working class, 49.6 per cent from the lower-middle class, and 9.2 per cent from the upper-middle class,[43] who has demonstrated that in quite a few Nazi branches scattered throughout Germany the working class represented over 40 per cent of the membership, and in some instances even formed the absolute majority,[44] and has reworked data furnished by Madden, a consistent critic of the middle-class thesis of Nazism, to show that the working class accounted for between 36.6 per cent and 45.9 per cent of Nazi recruits in the period 1925 to 1930.[45] In contrast Paul Madden has argued that one cannot view the NSDAP as a *Mittelstand* phenomenon on the basis of his set of data, in which working-class persons joining the Nazi Party do not provide more than 27.7 per cent of the new members in any year before 1924, 31.3 per cent in any year before 1930, and 33.6 per cent in any year before 1933. On the basis of the data on which they rest their conflicting conclusions, it would perhaps make more sense if the respective positions taken by Kater and Madden were reversed!

II

The growth in the volume of literature based on empirical evidence which has appeared since the early 1970s has been accompanied not only by interpretational disputes, especially the questioning of the 'traditional' middle-class thesis of Nazism, but also by lively debates about methodological problems involved in handling data of variable quality and diverse provenance, and by differences among scholars in the assignment of occupational categories to social class groupings.

There are limitations inherent in the very nature of the bulk of the available source material from which conclusions about the social characteristics of Nazism are drawn. Virtually all the analyses which have been made to date depend on membership lists and party cards which involve self-assigned occupational descriptions, on the basis of which the individual's position in social space has to be determined. The problem here is that some of the job descriptions, such as 'worker' or 'businessman', which appear quite frequently in the source data, are terminologically imprecise, and can at times be far removed from objective reality.[47] The fact that one has to establish the social structure of the Nazi membership on the basis of the occupational information almost invariably provided by the members themselves results inevitably in a degree of imprecision.[48] Another limitation which applies to the majority of the available material is that except for information on the occupation of members (and usually also their name, age and place of residence, sometimes also their marital status and religion), there is generally no data on the family background, education, income level and financial status of the individuals involved, in short the lack of the sort of comprehensive information which is normally required for contemporary social class analysis.[49] If additional information on, say, the income of Nazi members were at hand, it would probably further confuse, rather than necessarily solve, the

11

problem of occupational stratification in status terms. Even a cursory look at the information that we have on average income levels of selected occupational groups in the 1920s underlines the complexity of the problem one would face, given that unskilled workers in one industry often had much higher incomes than skilled workers in other industrial branches,[50] and that quite a few groups of skilled blue-collar workers had incomes considerably higher than those enjoyed by some white-collar employees.[51] It is an unfortunate fact that except in rare instances where full data on Nazi members is available (and this is primarily restricted to the leadership corps), the goal of absolute precision is not attainable, and in the absence of the sort of detail one would like, one is forced to fall back on the data presented in the membership lists and cards, which do provide the most important clues on which to base the analysis of the social background of the membership of the NSDAP and its auxiliary organizations. It is probable that even if all the desired information on the Nazi rank and file were at hand, it would still not resolve the problem of translating occupational categories into social class groupings to the satisfaction of everyone working on the question of the sociology of Nazism. Given the understandable revulsion against Nazism, interpretations of the phenomenon have been strongly coloured not only by moral but also political standpoints, reflected especially in the tendency of socialist historians to dissociate the working class from Nazism.

Quite critical in determining the different results secured by various scholars who have undertaken statistical analysis of the Nazi Movement's membership is not only the type of data which they have evaluated but, more crucially, what kind of system they have employed in the assignment of various occupations to specific occupational groups and to which social class the latter have been assigned in turn. Disagreements and problems surrounding the utility and reliability of the available data, and the difficulty of reaching agreement on the definition of terms employed in analysing statistical evidence, are central to the theoretical and conceptual conflicts involved in the debate. A basic problem, and one which continues to bedevil the analyses of the social characteristics of the Nazi Movement, is the lack of an agreed class model to which all scholars could subscribe. Given the many objective and subjective determinants which social scientists have suggested are involved in defining class groupings and class boundaries, there is more than the usual amount of room for disagreement. Yet it is clear that even slight differences in the method used can produce quite different results from the same set of data.[52] Especially problematical is the issue as to where to draw the boundary between the lower and middle classes, and which occupational categories should be assigned to these social class groupings.[53] Michael Kater in his earlier work on the sociology of Nazism obtained very low percentage values for working-class members in the NSDAP and SA because he only included unskilled workers in his lower-class category, placing dependent skilled (craft) workers and apprentices into the *Mittelstand,* a classification which inflated the lower-middle-class support supposedly enjoyed by the NSDAP.[54] Fortunately Kater subsequently moved away from such a narrow concept of the occupational groups which composed the German working class during the Weimar era.[55] A somewhat inflated view of which occupational categories can be assigned to the *Mittelstand* is still evident in the work of Paul Madden, who does not distinguish between dependent and independent artisans and places all artisans into the middle class.[56] Also unsatisfactory from the methodological viewpoint is the reverse process of expanding the lower class by blurring the differences between manual workers, skilled craftsmen and white-collar employees (*Angestellte*), by including the latter in the lower class, an approach used by Harold Gordon and Max Kele.[57] Another unsatisfactory variant is that employed by Donald Douglas, who puts some white-collar workers (such as retail store sales clerks and clerical workers) into the working class, but places artisans (fitters, machinists, metal smiths, printers, electricians, mechanics) into the *Mittelstand.*[58]

The differences in the classification models which have been employed in the attempts to determine the social composition of the Nazi Party have restricted the direct comparison of the data produced by various scholars. One way round this problem, suggested by Andrews, is to encode data in what he calls its 'hardest' form, that is to provide as fine a differentiation as is possible, which would allow 'for the possibility of fitting data into different models for the purpose of comparing their validity or for juxtaposing various subgroups'.[59] This is an ideal objective and feasible if one is working with a small data base, but I can see practical problems arising with publishers if huge chunks of data threaten to totally swamp the text! Another way forward to overcome the problem is for those involved in analysing the social structure of the NSDAP to establish a class model on which at least non-Marxists could agree.

There is general consensus on the broad division of German society in the 1920s and 1930s into three social class groupings: an upper class (elite) or upper-middle class and upper class (in view of the difficulty of clearly differentiating between the upper-middle class and the upper class); a middle class (or *Mittelstand*) or lower- and middle-middle class (which signals the space which exists in status terms between, for example, low- and middle-grade employees, or farmers with small and medium-sized holdings); and a lower class (or working class).[60] In the literature dealing with the social characteristics of the Nazi Party the parameters of these three social class groupings are generally identified on the basis of ascribing specific occupational subgroups to them. As noted above, it is at this stage that there are some significant differences among scholars in their approach as regards which occupational subgroups should be assigned to which class grouping, and which occupations should be assigned to which occupational subgroup. In these two processes it seems advisable to take note of the extensive information and guidelines on occupations and their position in social space provided by the statisticians involved in the occupational censuses of 1925 and 1933.[61]

The assignment of unskilled, semi- and skilled workers, and (household) servants to the lower class is now a common feature of the occupational and class models employed in the analysis of the Nazi Movement. Whether or not one should also assign blue-collar workers in the public sector to the lower class is more problematical.[62] In this study blue-collar workers in the public sector, such as those employed in the postal, railway and telephone services, as well as workers employed in municipal enterprises, are included in the lower- and middle-grade civil servants subgroup. Although many of these manual workers in the public sector performed jobs of a routine and menial nature, various legislative acts passed during the Weimar period did elevate many public employees from wage-earners to salaried employee status, and they were generally regarded as of lower-middle-class status at the time.[63] It is on the question as to which class grouping one should assign artisans and artisanal apprentices that significant variations in approach are employed by scholars. Both Donald Douglas and Paul Madden place artisans (covering such occupations as *Maurer, Maler, Dachdecker, Weber, Zimmerer, Metzger, Schmied, Maschinist, Drucker, Mechaniker*) into the *Mittelstand*,[64] while Kater (who did the same in his earlier work on the sociology of Nazism) now employs a formula which allocates 63.4 per cent of all skilled craft workers to the working class, placing the rest into the master craftsmen subgroup (which forms part of the lower-middle class in his social class model) on the assumption that they were of independent status.[65] The placement of all artisans in the *Mittelstand* is not tenable and is inappropriate for the Weimar era. First of all, it ignores the fact that dependent artisans were included in the working class in the censuses of 1925 and 1933, being perceived as of lower-class status at the time.[66] In the second place such a transfer would mean that both the SPD and the KPD would have drawn a sizeable section of their membership from the (lower) *Mittelstand* during the Weimar period![67] Artisanal occupations (such as *Schloßer, Maurer, Schuhmacher, Zimmerer, Tapezierer, Schreiner, Seiler, Dachdecker, Schmied, Weber, Pflasterer* and so on) occur quite frequently among the job descriptions of members and leaders of the KPD during the 1920s and early 1930s, and were also prominent among the Communist resistance movement in various parts of Bavaria after 1933, while the category 'artisans/skilled workers' accounted for just over 50 per cent of the 985 persons identified by the *Gestapo* as having belonged to the SPD in Lower Franconia in the period 1925 to 1933.[68] Kater's solution to the problem of differentiating between dependent and independent artisans by placing 36.6 per cent of all artisans automatically into the lower-middle class looks at first glance to be a neat solution to a tricky problem, but the difficulty here is that this percentage is much too high for many artisanal groups, and this method places too many workers in the middle class by inflating the master craftsmen subgroup. That this is probably so one can deduce from a comparison between the returns of the census figures of 1933 and the percentages of a number of occupational subgroups calculated by Kater on the basis of the 1933 census returns. According to the 1933 census, those deemed to be 'independent' (which included members of the liberal or free professions, higher-grade civil servants and high-ranking officers, farm proprietors and tenant farmers, white-collar workers in leading positions, proprietors and owners of shops, and master craftsmen) accounted for 16.4 per cent of the gainfully employed population.[69] According to Kater, three subgroups in the lower-middle class alone accounted for an independent element within the gainfully employed population of 23.26 per cent (Kater's calculations suggest that 9.56 per cent were independent master craftsmen, 6 per cent were self-employed merchants, and 7.7 per cent were self-employed farmers).[70] Important also is the fact (and this is pointed out in the 1933 census) that the chances of artisans becoming independent (or self-employed) differed widely between the various artisanal occupations, depending on such variables as the age structure of those in the occupation, the capital requirements to set up an independent business, and the extent of consumer demand.[71] Thus whereas 57.7 per cent of all cobblers (*Schuhmacher*), whose capital outlay to set up a shoe repair business was very low, were of independent status according to the 1933 census, only 4.1 of all locksmiths (*Schloßer*), including mechanics or fitters (*Maschinenschloßer*), were independent, given that their capital outlay to secure that status was very high, and their chance of becoming independent therefore very limited. Thus some occupations, such as hairdressers, clock-repairers, tailors, butchers, and millers had a one in two or one in three chance of securing independent status, while brewers, bricklayers, coppersmiths, bookbinders, and carpenters had a one in ten to one in twenty chance of setting up on their own. Crucial therefore, given the widely differing possibilities open to artisans of becoming independent, is the frequency of these artisanal occupations within the working population, and the frequency of their appearance in the Nazi membership. It would need a sophisticated computer programme to do justice to this frequency aspect. But even if we accept that Kater is right to assume that 36.6 per cent of all artisans in gainful employment were independent, another problem emerges when this percentage is applied to the Nazi membership. It leads to distortion in that the age of those *Schloßer, Bäcker, Fleischer, Schmiede, Maurer, Maler, Schuhmacher* and so on, assigned by Kater to the master craftsmen (independent) subgroup, is critical. Material presented in the 1925 census shows that relatively few bakers, butchers, locksmiths, painters, cobblers, carpenters etc., under the age of thirty were independent, though the percentage rises when the thirty to forty year age group is considered as far as bakers, butchers, carpenters and cobblers are concerned.[72] Since there is general agreement about one aspect of the Nazi Movement, the relative youthfulness of its membership,[73] it would follow that the bulk of the artisans attracted to Nazism were probably also from the younger age groups (forty years and under); relatively few of these would have been independent. Given all these problems, it does not seem advisable to follow Kater's method of differentiating between dependent and independent artisans. The approach used here rests upon the hierarchic issue of whether or not an artisan had acquired his master (*Meister*) title: those artisans without master status are assigned to the lower class, while those who described themselves as masters or indicated their independent status in some other way (for example, by describing themselves as a proprietor) are assigned to the lower-middle class.[74]

Obviously if an error is made in the assignment of an individual occupation to one subgroup rather than another within the same social class it is not as critical as if mistakes are made in assigning a particular occupation to a subgroup which involves a change of class.[75] Thus the undoubted fact that quite a few Nazi members who described themselves as merchants (*Kaufmann*) when their age would suggest that they were not independent and probably commercial employees (*Handlungsgehilfen*), distorts to some extent the overall percentages of the lower- and middle-grade employees subgroup and of the merchants subgroup, but does not affect the overall percentage of the lower- and middle-middle-class component active in the Nazi Movement. It would also seem highly likely that given the youth of many Nazi members who described themselves as farmers (*Bauer* or *Landwirt*), subgroup eleven probably contains some who were sons of farmers, who were (more accurately) assigned to the 'assisting family members' category in the censuses of 1925 and 1933. Although again the inclusion of sons of farmers in the lower- and middle-middle class is broadly acceptable in social class terms, it does create a problem when the census returns on the social profile of the gainfully employed in German society are compared with the social structure of the Nazi membership. The probability that one is not exactly comparing like with like has to be borne in mind.

Although the census statisticians provide a percentage figure for '*Arbeiter*', and give considerable guidance on the identification of this social group, there is no separation in either the 1925 or 1933 censuses of the *Mittelstand* from the elite component of society in a straightforward statistical sense. The criteria used to identify the economic, cultural and social *Oberschicht* in German society by the 1920s and 1930s combined in diverse patterns wealth, income, prestige or esteem (of occupation or rank held), and education.[76] There are important clues in the 1925 and 1933 censuses as to what the upper-middle class and upper class (the elite stratum) involved in occupational terms.[77] In the assignment of managers, senior officials, and members of the professions to the upper-middle class and upper class, I have accepted the reasoning conditioning Michael Kater's approach, rather than using the restricted 'elite' concept employed by Paul Madden, who places these elements in the *Mittelstand*.[78] I have not, however, adopted Kater's formula by which he assigns 2.2 per cent of all merchants, farmers, owners and lease-holders to the elite on the assumption that these were in the highest income bracket and that a small percentage of farmers involved in the transfer were in reality estate owners.[79] It is unlikely that farmers who were in reality estate owners would not have indicated their superior status, and likewise merchants who were in reality wholesale merchants usually indicated this fact by describing themselves as *Großhändler*.

One other grouping which presents special difficulties and involves diverse approaches in classification among scholars is the student category. While Madden places all students in the *Mittelstand*,[80] Kater argues for their inclusion in the elite component of German society on the basis that 'upper-school and university students customarily belong to the social elite' and 'because of the prestigious and well-paying professions they may look forward to after graduation'.[81] The latter assumption is questionable during the Weimar period, given the problem of unemployment among graduates in the 1920s even before the massive unemployment problem affected Germany in the early 1930s. Nor was it inevitable that a grammar school pupil would necessarily go on to attend university, given the serious financial situation affecting many middle-class parents in the post-1918 period.[82] Given Kater's own differentiation between engineers trained at polytechnic-type institutions (whom he assigns to the non-academic professional subgroup which formed part of the *Mittelstand*) and those who attended a university (whom he includes in the academic professional subgroup which formed part of the elite), it would seem unwise to lump all students together. It would seem sensible to use a classification model which separates university and non-university students, and the method employed in this study is to assign only those students who clearly indicated their 'university status' by describing themselves as *stud. phil.* or *cand. med.* to the university students subgroup, while those who described themselves as *Schüler, Gymnasiast,* or simply as *Student,* are assigned to the non-university students subgroup. Although admittedly a rough and ready differentiation, it does guard against the artificial inflation of the elite element among some Nazi branches in non-university towns in which 'students' often formed a sizeable section of the membership.

The social and occupational classification model employed in this study involves the conventional triple division of German society into a lower class (*Unterschicht*, working class, proletariat), a lower- and middle-middle class (*Mittelschicht, Mittelstand*), and an upper-middle class and upper class (*Oberschicht*, elite). Five occupational subgroups comprise the lower class (agricultural workers, unskilled and semi-skilled workers, skilled craft workers, other skilled workers, and domestic workers),[83] six occupational subgroups make up the lower- and middle-middle class (master craftsmen, non-academic professionals, lower- and middle-grade white-collar employees, lower- and middle-grade civil servants, merchants, and farmers), and five occupational subgroups form the upper-middle class and upper class (managers, higher-grade civil servants, university students, academic professionals and entrepreneurs). In order to provide as comprehensive a picture of the overall structure of the sociology of the Nazi Movement as is possible, it is also important to include those members who cannot straightforwardly be assigned to any particular social group. These are listed in an additional 'status unknown' category (comprising the subgroups non-university students, pensioners/retired, wives/widows, military personnel, and illegible/no data). The few Nazis listed under subgroup twenty (military personnel) could have been assigned in part to subgroup nine (lower- and middle-grade civil servants) in the case of NCO's and enlisted men, and in part to subgroup thirteen (higher civil servants) in the case of officers, given that in the census of 1933 the official statisticians point to the 'civil service status' of at least the higher ranks of the military.[84] I have not followed Herbert Andrews' suggestion[85] of putting those who described themselves as 'retired' and gave their former occupations into the subgroups which their pre-retirement occupation associates them with, nor have I placed those who described

19

themselves as *Ehefrau, Gattin, Hausfrau,* or *Witwe* into the occupational category (where this could be established) of their husband or deceased partner. Had I done so, the changes in the various occupational subgroups and the overall impact on the class structure of the Nazi Movement would have been very marginal. In the assignment of particular occupations to specific occupational groups, and the placement of these in social class terms, I have generally followed the suggestions contained in the 1925 and 1933 censuses. Checking into which group the census statisticians placed the numerous occupations which Nazis assigned themselves when filling in their membership forms involved a laborious process, but one worthwhile in the attempt to be as accurate as is possible. Although lack of space prevents the listing of the thousands of occupational descriptions encountered in the membership files under the specific occupational subgroups to which they are assigned, the following is designed to give some insight into the types of occupations which are 'typical' of the specific subgroups used in this study:

Subgroup 1 (Agricultural workers)

Includes blue-collar workers in agriculture, horticulture and forestry performing menial tasks which did not involve any significant skill or training, such as *Ackerer, Ackergehilfe, Anlagengärtner, Baumfäller, Blumenbinder, Butterbereiter, Chaluppner, Drescher, Dreschmaschinenarbeiter, Erntearbeiter, Feldarbeiter, Feldhüter, Forstarbeiter, Futtermann, Gartenarbeiter, Gärtner* (numerous prefixes), *Gespannführer, Gutstagelöhner, Hirte, Hofmann, Hoftagelöhner, Holzarbeiter, Inste, Käser, Knecht* (several prefixes), *Landarbeiter, Landhelfer, Melker, Pferdepfleger, Pflüger, Rebarbeiter, Schäfer, Stallbursche, Viehpfleger, Waldarbeiter, Wiesenwärter.*

Subgroup 2 (Unskilled and semi-skilled workers)

Includes blue-collar workers in the non-agrarian sectors of the economy who performed basic tasks not requiring any significant skill-level or training, such as *Abschlepper, Arbeiter* (innumerable prefixes), *Aschelader, Ausfeger, Bergmann, Bügler, Dosenfüller, Garnwieger, Härter, Hauer* (various prefixes), Heizer, *Helfer, Kellner, Kohlenwäscher, Kraftwagenführer,*

20

Kutscher, Leimer, Maschinenputzer, Mitfahrer, Packer, Pressehelfer, Reiniger (several prefixes), *Säuberer, Stapler, Tongräber, Verlader* (various prefixes), *Wächter, Wagenfüller, Zuschläger, Zuträger.*

Subgroup 3 (Skilled craft workers)

Includes dependent skilled blue-collar workers and apprentices in occupations which were artisanal in character in pre-industrial times or assumed artisanal character during industrialization such as *Bäcker, Böttcher, Brauer, Buchdrucker, Dachdecker, Drechsler, Dreher, Färber, Fleischer, Former, Friseur, Gerber, Glasbläser, Graveur, Gürtler* (several prefixes), *Hutmacher, Korbmacher, Klavierbauer, Klempner, Konditor, Lithograph, Maler* (several prefixes), *Maurer, Mechaniker, Metzger, Monteur, Müller, Musikinstrumentenmacher, Orgelbauer, Portefeuiller, Sattler, Schildmaler, Schleifer* (various prefixes), *Schloßer* (various prefixes), *Schmelzer, Schmied* (several prefixes), *Schneider, Schriftsetzer, Schuhmacher, Spinner* (various prefixes), *Steinmetz, Tapezierer, Tischler* (various prefixes), *Töpfer, Uhrmacher, Weber, Werkzeugmacher, Ziegler, Zigarrenmacher, Zimmermann.*

Subgroup 4 (Other skilled workers)

Includes skilled blue-collar workers in 'newer' industrial processes not traditionally associated with artisanal occupations such as *Auto-* and *Flugzeugmechaniker, Chemigraph, Elektriker, Elektromonteur, Galvaniseur, Motorschlosser, Oxydierer, Schreibmaschinenmechaniker, Schweißer, Vulkaniseur.* There is a degree of artificiality in the separation of subgroups 3 and 4, which could have been combined under one 'skilled workers' subgroup, given that by the 1920s the line of demarcation between skilled workers in crafts and industry became increasingly blurred.[86]

Subgroup 5 (Domestic workers)

Where to place *Hausangestellte* in social class terms is problematic, though some guidance as to which domestic employees can be assigned to the lower class are made by the statisticians

21

involved in compiling the 1933 census returns.[87] Included in this subgroup are *Aufwärter, Ausläufer, Dielenfrau, Hausbursche, Haushilfe, Hausmädchen, Pförtner, Privatgärtner, Putzfrau, Wochenfrau.*

Subgroup 6 (Master craftsmen)

Includes those independent craftsmen and tradesmen who had either acquired their *Meister* (master) title, such as *Bäckermeister, Klempnermeister, Malermeister, Müllermeister, Schreinermeister, Tischlermeister, Tünchermeister,* or described themselves as independent (*selbstständig*) craftsmen.

Subgroup 7 (Non-academic professionals)

Included in this subgroup are various types of professionals who had gone through specialist training usually in the form of higher (but non-university) education, such as *Chemiker, Dentist, Drogist, Fotograf, Heilpraktiker, Ingenieur* (various prefixes), *Journalist* (or *Korrespondent* or *Reporter*), *Laborant, Masseuse, Optiker, Schriftleiter, Zeichner* (various prefixes). Agricultural specialists, such as *Baumwart, Eleve, Förster, Jagdaufseher, Milchviehkontrolleur,* are also included in this subgroup. Also part of this subgroup are artists and writers, such as *Bildhauer, Künstler, Musiker, Sänger, Schauspieler, Tänzer.*

Subgroup 8 (Lower- and middle-grade white-collar employees)

Includes salaried white-collar employees (*Angestellten*) in lower and intermediary positions, such as *Bankbeamter, Buchhalter, Bücherrevisor, Expedient, Handlungsgehilfe, Hüttenbeamter, Kassengehilfe, Kontorist, Lagerist, Matrose, Reisender, Reklamefachmann, Revisor, Schreibgehilfe, Sekretär* (numerous prefixes), *Techniker* (various prefixes), *Telefonist, Verkäufer, Volontär, Versicherungsangestellter,* as well as supervisory staff in industry, commerce and trade, such as *Abteilungsleiter, Aufseher, Betriebsführer, Bruchmeister, Bürovorsteher, Fabrikmeister, Filialleiter, Inspektor, Kellermeister, Lampenmeister (Bergbau), Revisionsmeister, Schachtmeister (Bergbau), Steiger, Werkmeister.*

Subgroup 9 (Lower- and middle-grade civil servants)

Includes blue-collar workers in the public sector, such as *Bahnarbeiter, Güterbodenarbeiter, Lokomotivheizer, Posthelfer, Rangierarbeiter, Telegraphenarbeiter, Weichenwärter,* and civil servants in lower and intermediary grades, such as *Amtmann, Arbeitsamtsekretär, Bahnmeister, Bauamtmann, Eichwart, Gefängnisaufseher, Gemeindesekretär, Gerichtsgehilfe, Jugendleiter(in), Kanzleiassistent, Kindergärtnerin, Krankenkasseninspektor, Krankenpfleger* and *Krankenschwester, Lehrer (Berufs-, Mittel-, Real-* and *Volksschule), Lokomotivführer, Magistratsassessor, Ministerialamtmann, Polizeiwachtmeister, Präsidialsekretär, Regierungssekretär, Reichsbahntechniker, Schaffner, Staatsförster, Stadtgehilfe, Steueramtmann, Steuersekretär, Versorgungsanwärter, Vollziehungsbeamter, Wohlfahrtspfleger(in), Zollassistent, Zollinspektor, Zollsekretär.*

Subgroup 10 (Merchants)

Includes *Cafe Besitzer, Geschäftinhaber* (various prefixes), *Händler* (various prefixes), *Kaufmann, Restauranteur, Wirt.*

Subgroup 11 (Farmers)

Includes individuals who were self-employed or of an independent status active in agriculture, horticulture, forestry and fishing, such as *Bauer* (various prefixes), *Erbpächter, Fischereibesitzer, Gartenbaubesitzer, Gütler, Hofbesitzer, Kräutereibesitzer, Landwirt, Obstler, Ökonom, Weinbauer* or *Winzer.*

Subgroup 12 (Managers)

Includes salaried white-collar employees in managerial positions in the private sector, such as *Baumeister, Betriebsvorsteher, Direktor* (various prefixes), *Prokurist, Verwalter* (various prefixes).

Subgroup 13 (Higher civil servants)

Includes *Amtsgerichtsrat, Archivdirektor, Bergrat, Finanzamtsdirektor, Gemeinderat, Generalstaatsanwalt, Gewerberat,*

Hochschullehrer, Kreisrat, Landrat, Magistratsrat, Minister, Polizeidirektor, Postdirektor, Professor, Reichsbahnrat, Studienrat, Rektor.

Subgroup 14 (University students)

Includes those who could be positively identified as attending university, namely those individuals described as *cand.* or *stud. arch., chem., ing., jur., med., med. dent., pharm., phil., rer. pol., theol..*

Subgroup 15 (Academic professionals)

Includes the academically (university) trained, usually self-employed professionals, such as *Apotheker, Architekt, Arzt, Rechtsanwalt, Tierarzt, Zahnarzt.* All those with a doctorate (for example those listing their occupation as *Chemiker, Ingenieur, Volkswirt*) are also included in this subgroup.

Subgroup 16 (Entrepreneurs)

Includes those who described themselves as *Bankier, Fabrikant, Großhändler* (various prefixes), *Gutsbesitzer, Unternehmer* (various prefixes).

Subgroup 17 (Non-university students)

Includes those described as *Gymnasiast, Oberrealschüler, Schüler, Student.*

Subgroup 18 (Pensioners/retired)

Includes all those who indicated their retired status by entering *a.D. (außer Dienst)* or *i.R. (im Ruhestand)* under *Stand* or *Beruf,* or added *a.D.* or *i.R.* to their former occupation, as well as those described as *Invalide, Kriegsbeschädigter, Rentner* (various prefixes).

24

Subgroup 19 (Wives/widows)

Includes all those who described themselves as *Frau, Gattin, Hausfrau, Witwe.*

Subgroup 20 (Military personnel)

Includes those listed as *Militäranwärter, Offizier, Soldat.*

Subgroup 21 (Illegible/no data)

Individuals with no entry under *Stand* or *Beruf* form the bulk of the members recorded in this subgroup. A small number of illegible entries were contained in a number of handwritten membership lists. This subgroup also includes a handful of individuals who provided occupational titles which are not listed in the alphabetical lists of occupations given in the 1925 and 1933 censuses, as well as a few individuals who did not indicate their occupational status but described themselves as unemployed (*erwerbslos*).

2

THE WESTERN RUHR
1925-6

The history of the Nazi Party in the Ruhr region[1] can be traced back to the spring of 1920, when the first Nazi branch was formed at Dortmund in the eastern Ruhr, probably the first Nazi branch founded outside of Bavaria, certainly the first established north of the Main.[2] The subsequent history of the NSDAP in the Ruhr is characterized by its constant struggle to make an impression on an area in which, from the Nazi point of view, both social and religious factors worked strongly against it. Throughout the Weimar period the Nazi Party fared badly electorally in both the western and eastern parts of the Ruhr. In the electoral districts of Düsseldorf-East and Düsseldorf-West and of Westphalia-North and Westphalia-South, in which the Ruhr was situated, the Nazi Party consistently recorded a vote below (usually well below) its national average in every election from May 1924 (when it first participated in the shape of the *Völkisch-Sozialer Block*) until the last so-called 'free' election of March 1933.[3]

Concentration in this essay will fall on the social make-up of a number of Nazi branches situated in various towns in the western Ruhr (see Map 1) and on the years 1925 to 1926, a period following the re-formation of the Nazi Party and its first real penetration into the Ruhr region to the point where it became a growing irritant to the established political forces active in the area.[4] It is only for this period that comparatively detailed information on the membership of a number of Nazi branches situated in the western half of the Ruhr has survived, data which either captures the social structure of particular branches at a specific moment in time, or provides a series of lists which monitor the gains and losses of some branches, thus also giving an insight into their recruitment pattern over time.[5] Comparable

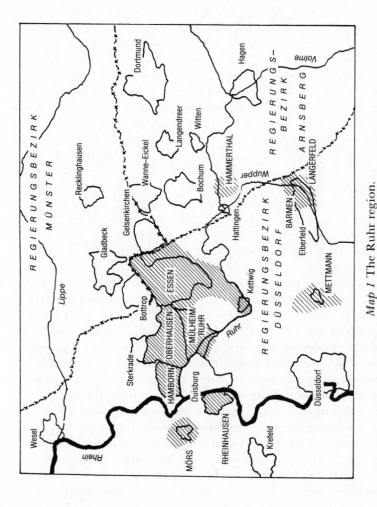

Map 1 The Ruhr region.

Note: Nazi Party branches with information on their social structure are in capitals. Shaded area indicates the catchment area of the branches.

material on the Nazi Party in the Ruhr is lacking for the 1920 to 1925 and 1926 to 1933 periods. Such evidence as there is on its social structure in these years needs to be treated with caution. It is nevertheless adequate to outline the social make-up of the NSDAP in the region for the period 1920 to 1933 as a whole.

In the Ruhr the Nazis operated in a heavily populated,[6] highly urbanized,[7] and predominantly industrialized region (see Table 2.1), an area in which the lower class was by far the dominant social element. In the *Regierungsbezirk* Düsseldorf as a whole, which included the western part of the Ruhr, the lower class accounted for some 60 per cent of the working population (see Table 2.3, column 10b). Given that the *Regierungsbezirk* also included such less industrialized, agrarian counties as Cleve, Geldern, Mörs, Rees and Dinslaken, it is almost certain that the lower-class element of the population in the western Ruhr was considerably higher, probably in the 65 to 75 per cent range.[8] The 'proletarian' nature of the working population in the western Ruhr is shown in the data presented in the b columns in Table 2.3, in which those towns are listed for which Nazi branch membership details are available. In Hamborn, the economy of which was dominated by mining and heavy industry, unskilled workers alone accounted for almost 50 per cent of the working population in the 1920s.[9] Coal mining and the iron and steel industry employed the majority of the working population in the secondary sector in such towns as Essen, Oberhausen, Mülheim/Ruhr, and Rheinhausen.[10] In Mörs coal-mining was the premier industry, employing just over one-third of the working population, while in Mettmann the manufacture of metal goods in numerous small and medium-sized concerns was by far the most important branch of local industry.[11] It was only in Barmen that 'coal and iron' did not dominate economic activity. Here the textile industry, which employed around one-third of the workforce, was by far the most important economic sector.[12] Some of the larger cities which had important administrative, commercial and trading functions, such as Essen, did contain districts in which the lower class was less conspicuous and in which middle-class and upper-class elements accounted for a more sizeable percentage of the population.[13]

Given the socio-economic stucture of the region, the 'proletarian milieu' of the urban areas was one of the major determinants which conditioned the politics of the Ruhr. In electoral districts

Table 2.1 The breakdown of the working population according to economic sectors in 1925 in selected Ruhr towns and in the Rheinprovinz and Westphalia (by row %)[14]

	Agriculture & forestry	Industry & crafts	Trade & transport	Other
Barmen-Langerfeld	0.9	68.6	19.4	11.1
Essen	1.2	62.1	21.9	14.8
Hamborn	0.7	77.0	11.2	11.1
Mettmann	12.0	61.7	13.7	12.6
Mörs	7.2	60.9	18.5	13.4
Mülheim/Ruhr	2.4	61.5	23.5	12.6
Oberhausen	0.7	67.4	19.4	12.5
Rheinhausen	4.3	75.3	13.1	7.3
Reg.-Bez. Düsseldorf	7.7	60.7	19.2	12.4
Reg.-Bez. Arnsberg	10.8	61.4	16.2	11.6
Reg.-Bez. Münster	27.1	49.5	11.8	11.6
Rheinprovinz	19.3	50.0	18.6	12.1
Westphalia	19.8	54.8	14.2	11.2
Prussia	29.5	40.9	17.1	12.5
Germany	30.5	41.4	16.5	11.6

Düsseldorf-East and Westphalia-South, which covered the bulk of the Ruhr towns, the major left-wing parties, the SPD and KPD, attracted 30 to 40 per cent of the vote between them in all of the *Reichstag* elections of the 1920s and early 1930s.[15] This share of the vote is perhaps lower than one would expect, given the sizeable lower-class presence in the area, even when one makes due allowance for the rural areas also contained within these electoral districts.[16] Of the two left-wing parties operating in the Ruhr during the Weimar period, it was the KPD which developed a particularly active, aggressive profile, especially in the western Ruhr, where it established a dominant position over the SPD in electoral terms from the early 1920s. In electoral district Düsseldorf-East the KPD outpolled the SPD in all elections from May 1924 to March 1933, securing double the support enjoyed by the SPD in the elections of the early 1930s. In the eastern half of the Ruhr the KPD, with the exception of the May 1924 *Reichstag* election, did not surpass the SPD vote until the elections of 1932. The strong presence of the KPD in the Ruhr created not only problems for the SPD, but also for the Nazi Party as it gradually entrenched itself in the region in the course of the 1920s. The Communists took the motto 'Slay the fascists where you find them' often quite literally!

Beyond the social factor which worked against an easy Nazi penetration of the Ruhr, a second major problem confronting the Nazi Party (and one which also reduced the size of the left-wing vote) was the strength of political Catholicism in the region.[17] In the western Ruhr Catholicism was the majority faith. According to the 1925 census, 55 per cent of the population of *Regierungsbezirk* Düsseldorf was Catholic. In the eastern Ruhr the situation was reversed, for the *Regierungsbezirk* Arnsberg had a small Protestant majority (52.3 per cent).[18] It has been estimated that some 60 per cent of the Catholic population in *Regierungsbezirk* Düsseldorf was still voting for the Centre Party by the time of the December *Reichstag* election of 1924. In the larger eastern Ruhr towns in which the Catholics were in the majority, namely Essen, Oberhausen and Hamborn, the percentage of Catholics still voting for the Centre Party by the time of the 1928 *Reichstag* election was 53.4 per cent, 52.9 per cent and 33.2 per cent respectively.[19] The strength of the Centre Party in the Ruhr, as in other regions of Germany with a significant Catholic presence, rested not only on its ability to transcend the class divide and to mobilize support from Catholics of all classes, but also on its ability to hold onto its electorate relatively successfully throughout the Weimar era. Such detailed studies of the region that we have all emphasize the tough time the Nazis had in penetrating into the Catholic communities of the Ruhr.[20]

I

There is very little available information which might provide an insight into the social types attracted to Nazism in the Ruhr in the period before 1925. There is not even any precise data on how many members the various Nazi branches which were established in the area were able to attract. The early history of Nazism in the Ruhr before 1922 revolves primarily around the existence of one branch, that formed at Dortmund in the eastern Ruhr, which had 23 members on 1 May 1920,[21] and about 100 by March 1922.[22] Although attempts were made to found further branches in a number of Ruhr towns, these efforts amounted to very little in organizational terms.[23] It was only in the course of 1922 that the

Nazis were able to firmly establish a few further branches, namely those established at Hagen (with 45 members at its formation) and at Wanne-Eickel in March, at Bochum and Westerfilde (near Dortmund) in May, at Mengede (also near Dortmund) in June, at Essen in August, at Hattingen in October, and at Recklinghausen in November.[24] This limited organizational activity was halted by the ban imposed on the NSDAP by the Prussian authorities in mid-November 1922.[25] After November the Nazis continued their activities illegally, or re-emerged in the shape of athletic associations, or as anti-Semitic clubs, or as 'Reading Societies of the *Völkischer Beobachter*'.[26]

Little is known about the strength of the Nazi movement at this time. Böhnke suggests that there were about 100 Nazis scattered around the Ruhr by 1922, and about 500 by the time the ban was placed on the party in Prussia in mid-November 1923.[27] These 'guestimates' are undoubtedly on the conservative side and much too low given that the Hagen branch alone appears to have had around 300 members by May 1922.[28] On the social make-up of these members there is also only very limited information. Karl Kaufmann, who later emerged as *Gauleiter* of Rhineland-North before being elected to head *Gau* Ruhr in 1926, was to claim some fifty years later that half of the early Nazi membership in the Ruhr was made up by working-class elements, the other half being drawn from the ranks of the *Mittelstand*.[29] A few police reports of the period which touch on the social profile of the party membership, suggest that the Ruhr NSDAP had a fairly broad social base in its formative phase. Thus a police report on the Hagen branch written in May 1922 spoke of '304 members drawn from working-class and middle-class circles, with skilled workers and office employees predominating'.[30] According to a report by the *Landrat* of county Dortmund, the small branch established at Westerfilde consisted of 'a dozen or so miners', while a similarly small membership of 'miners, farmers and petit-bourgeois elements' were active in the Mengede branch.[31] A further limited clue as to the social types attracted to Nazism in the region is provided by the composition of the leadership of the Dortmund branch. Until 1922 five civil servants and one miner formed the branch committee, which was replaced by a committee composed of two fitters and a turner in late 1922, a change which suggests perhaps a significant influx of lower-class types into the branch if one assumes that the election of the new party committee reflected the social structure of the branch member-ship.[32] One further source, although again of limited value, are the early membership lists of the party drawn up at the Munich party headquarters. In the list 'Adolf Hitler's *Mitkämpfer*, 1919–1921', in which 2,548 members who had joined the Munich organization by August 1921 are recorded, there are three entries for members resident in the Ruhr, namely a 'typographer' in Duisburg, a 'miner' in Mengede, and an 'electrician' in Dortmund.[33] In the largest membership list relating to the pre-1923 NSDAP that has survived, in which 4,786 members enroll-ing in the Nazi Party on the eve of the Munich Putsch are recorded, there are entries for 35 recruits resident in the Ruhr region (with clusters of members in Hagen and Elberfeld-Barmen, and a few resident in Essen, Hamborn, Gladbeck and Recklinghausen).[34] Of these 25.6 per cent were from the lower class, 62.4 per cent from the lower- and middle-middle class, and 5.7 from the upper-middle class and upper class.[35] There is no way of knowing how representative this class breakdown is of the pre-1923 Nazi membership in the Ruhr.

II

In comparison with the sketchy information on the early years of the Nazi Party in the Ruhr, there is much more data on which to evaluate its social make-up in the post-1925 period. Following the removal of the ban on the NSDAP in Prussia in December 1924 and the re-formation of the party by Hitler in February 1925, Nazi supporters in the Ruhr were able to establish a much more noticeable presence in the region in the course of 1925. This is reflected not only in the larger number of branches established by 1926, but by the often quite sizeable membership which these attracted, especially in large cities such as Essen, Bochum, Gelsenkirchen, Duisburg, Elberfeld and Barmen, as well as in the small town of Hattingen, a major centre of expansion for the party from 1925 onwards.[36] The growth rate of a number of branches was quite striking, as in the case of Essen, where the Nazis were able to record a nine-fold increase in membership between July 1925 and March 1926, from 57 to 508 members.[37] The *Gaue* Rhineland-North and Westphalia, which were to form *Gau* Ruhr in 1926, had enrolled some 1,420 members by May 1925.[38] A year later, according to a breakdown listing the individual membership strengths of 113 branches and *Stützpunkte* situated in *Gau* Ruhr, the Nazi Party had 3,750 supporters.[39] Of these, 2,303 were resident in the area previously controlled by *Gau* Rhineland-North, and of these in turn 1,875 were in the Rhenish half of the Ruhr area, with sizeable branches at Essen (508 members), Elberfeld (211), Duisburg (172), Barmen (114), and Oberhausen (104). In the Westphalian half of the Ruhr only the branches of Hattingen (with 376 members) and Bochum (213) had reached the hundred or over mark.[40] The membership growth was admittedly only impressive in contrast to the weak position of the NSDAP in the Ruhr before the mid-1920s. In comparison with the major parties established in the region, such as the SPD or the Centre Party, the NSDAP was little more than a speck on the fringe of local politics for much of the 1920s.[41] It was from 1930 onwards that the NSDAP was to become a significant political factor in the Ruhr. The membership mobilized by the Nazi Party in the Ruhr by 1926, however, does not emerge that badly in a comparison with that of the other extremist movement established in the region by 1925, the KPD.[42] It has also to be noted that the expansion of Nazism in the Ruhr did make *Gau* Ruhr a major growth area of the movement in 1925 and early 1926. By mid-1926 it contained approximately 10 per cent of the Nazi Party's national membership.[43]

The social characteristics of a significant proportion of the Nazi membership of the western Ruhr area is captured in some detail in a number of branch membership lists which have survived for 1925 and early 1926. The 874 members listed in Table 2.2 probably account for two-thirds of the Nazis in the western Ruhr by the spring of 1926, though it is impossible to be precise on this point since there is no hard information as to the total strength of the NSDAP in the region before May 1926. The information contained in the branch membership breakdowns is variable. All provide details of the name, address and occupation of the individuals listed, and ignoring the odd gap here and there, most do contain the date of birth of the members, though in the case of the Barmen branch this detail is only provided for the last third of its membership. The list for Mülheim/Ruhr and the first two lists recording 144 members enrolled in the Essen branch by August 1925 also give information on the marital status of each member. The first two Essen branch lists and the breakdown of the Hammerthal branch for December 1925 also

Table 2.2 The social and occupational structure of the membership of various NSDAP branches in the western Ruhr, 1925–6 (by %)[44]

Class	Occupational subgroup	*(1)* Essen *(1925)*	*(2)* Langerfeld *(1925)*
LOWER	1. Agricultural workers	0	0
CLASS	2. Unskilled workers	14.4	14.8
	3. Skilled (craft) workers	29.1	50.0
	4. Other skilled workers	4.0	0
	5. Domestic workers	0	0
Subtotal		47.5	64.8
Lower-	6. Master craftsmen	0.7	0
&	7. Non-academic professionals	4.7	1.8
middle-	8. White-collar employees	24.4	3.7
MIDDLE	9. Lower civil servants	8.0	5.5
CLASS	10. Merchants	6.0	13.0
	11. Farmers	0.7	0
Subtotal		44.5	24.0
Upper-	12. Managers	0	0
MIDDLE	13. Higher civil servants	0	0
CLASS &	14. University students	0	0
UPPER	15. Academic professionals	0.7	1.8
CLASS	16. Entrepreneurs	0.3	0
Subtotal		1.0	1.8
STATUS	17. Non-university students	1.3	1.8
UNCLEAR	18. Pensioners/retired	0.7	0
	19. Wives/widows	0.3	0
	20. Military personnel	0	0
	21. Illegible/no data	4.7	7.4
Subtotal		7.0	9.2
TOTAL (%)		100	100
Frequency (*N*)		299	54

Table 2.2 continued

(3) Mörs (1925)	(4) Mülheim/Ruhr (1925)	(5) Oberhausen (1925)	(6) Barmen (1926)	(7) Essen (1926)
0	0	0	0	0
12.5	13.0	10.0	5.2	25.0
16.6	41.3	16.0	37.7	25.8
0	2.2	2.0	1.9	4.0
0	0	0	0	0.8
29.1	56.5	28.0	44.8	55.6
4.2	0	2.0	0	0.8
12.5	4.3	4.0	2.6	2.4
12.5	23.9	32.0	15.6	24.2
8.3	2.2	8.0	2.6	5.6
12.5	10.9	6.0	12.3	2.4
0	0	0	0.6	0
50.0	41.3	52.0	33.7	35.4
4.2	0	2.0	0.6	0
0	0	0	0	0
4.2	0	0	0.6	0
0	0	0	0	0
0	0	0	0	0
8.4	0	2.0	1.2	0
4.2	0	2.0	0	0
0	0	2.0	0	0.8
0	2.2	8.0	4.0	3.2
0	0	0	0	0
8.3	0	6.0	16.2	4.8
12.5	2.2	18.0	20.2	8.8
100	100	100	100	100
24	46	50	154	124

Table 2.2 continued

Class	Occupational subgroup	(8) Rheinhausen (1926)	(9) Essen (1925–6)
LOWER	1. Agricultural workers	0	0
CLASS	2. Unskilled workers	7.7	17.5
	3. Skilled (craft) workers	53.8	28.1
	4. Other skilled workers	15.4	4.0
	5. Domestic workers	0	0.2
Subtotal		76.9	49.8
Lower-	6. Master craftsmen	0	0.7
&	7. Non-academic professionals	0	4.0
middle-	8. White-collar employees	0	24.3
MIDDLE	9. Lower civil servants	0	7.3
CLASS	10. Merchants	15.4	5.0
	11. Farmers	0	0.5
Subtotal		15.4	41.8
Upper-	12. Managers	0	0
MIDDLE	13. Higher civil servants	0	0
CLASS &	14. University students	0	0
UPPER	15. Academic professionals	0	0.5
CLASS	16. Entrepreneurs	0	0.2
Subtotal		0	0.7
STATUS	17. Non-university students	0	0.9
UNCLEAR	18. Pensioners/retired	0	0.7
	19. Wives/widows	0	1.2
	20. Military personnel	0	0
	21. Illegible/no data	7.7	4.7
Subtotal		7.7	7.5
TOTAL (%)		100	100
Frequency (*N*)		13	423

Table 2.2   continued

(10) Hamborn (1925–6)	(11) Hammerthal (1925–6)	(12) Mettmann (1925–6)	(13) Rheinhausen (1926–7)	(14) Western Ruhr (1925–6)	(15) Party officials (1925–6)
0	0	2.9	0	0.1	0
15.8	18.4	11.8	18.2	13.9	4.6
44.7	34.2	35.3	40.9	32.5	18.6
2.6	5.3	0	9.1	3.1	4.6
0	0	0	0	0.1	0
63.1	57.9	50.0	68.2	49.7	27.8
2.6	2.6	0	0	0.8	0
5.3	0	0	0	3.5	7.0
21.0	18.4	26.5	0	20.9	25.6
0	2.6	5.9	0	5.5	9.3
7.9	10.5	0	22.7	7.7	25.6
0	2.6	5.9	0	0.7	0
36.8	36.7	38.3	22.7	39.1	67.5
0	0	0	0	0.3	4.6
0	0	0	0	0	0
0	2.6	0	0	0.3	0
0	0	0	0	0.3	0
0	0	0	0	0.1	0
0	2.6	0	0	1.0	4.6
0	2.6	8.8	0	1.2	0
0	0	0	0	0.4	0
0	0	0	0	1.8	0
0	0	0	0	0	0
0	0	2.9	9.1	6.4	0
0	2.6	11.7	9.1	9.8	0
100	100	100	100	100	100
38	38	34	22	874	43

record how many members were unemployed.[45] A further item which could have provided some insight into the financial situation of individual branches, the monthly contributions paid by each member, is only given in the accounts attached to the early Essen membership lists and suggests that the amounts paid by individual members was quite variable. While the standard monthly due of 1 *Mark* was paid by 82 of the 144 members registered in the Essen branch by the end of August 1925, the 17 unemployed members (split virtually equally between lower-class and *Mittelstand* elements) paid nothing, 35 members paid 50 *Pfennige*, and the remaining handful (predominantly older members belonging to the *Mittelstand* in occupational and status terms) contributed from 1.50 to 5.00 *Mark*.[46]

Ignoring such descriptions as 'pensioner', 'student' or 'housewife', which occur rarely anyway, one finds around 230 job descriptions covering the 874 entries listed in Table 2.2. The most frequent entries found are for 'commercial employee' (*Handlungsgehilfe*) and 'locksmith' (*Schloßer*), which each account for 8.1 per cent of the membership. The bulk of the commercial employees were contained in the Essen branch, of which the local business manager of the *Deutschnationaler Handlungsgehilfenverband* was also a member. Some 5.9 per cent of the members described themselves as 'merchant' (*Kaufmann*), 4.9 per cent as 'worker' (*Arbeiter*), and 2.6 per cent as 'miner' (*Bergmann*). The great majority of the latter were resident in the Essen area. Lorry drivers, fitters, mechanics, crane drivers, bakers, steel workers and casual labourers also appear relatively frequently in the lists.

The data relating to occupational categories (see Table 2.2) shows that skilled craft workers formed a major element in all but two of the Nazi branches on which we have information (the exceptions being Mörs and Oberhausen), accounting for almost one-third of the recorded membership, with particularly high percentages in the Langerfeld, Hamborn and Mülheim/Ruhr branches. Unskilled workers were also of importance in the membership of the Essen, Hammerthal, Hamborn and Langerfeld branches. Significant in all branches were lower- and medium-grade white-collar employees, especially in Oberhausen, where this occupational group was by far the most important. Not surprisingly, given the age profile of the membership (see Table 2.5), master craftsmen hardly feature in the membership, while the almost totally urban nature of the membership (see Table 2.5), master craftsmen hardly feature in the membership, while the almost totally urban nature of the membership (see Table 2.6) accounts for the virtual absence of agricultural workers and farmers within the ranks of the NSDAP in the western Ruhr.

In Table 2.3 the occupational data relating to the Nazi Party in the western Ruhr has been arranged in social class terms at the branch level. It should be noted that the data does not allow for a precise comparison between the social make-up of the party branches with that of the population of the towns, given that the percentage values in columns *b* are based on census data for 1925 which relate to the working population only, whereas the percentages in columns *a* are calculated on the basis of the total membership of the branches, including those whose occupational status is not clear. The comparison at the regional level is further distorted by the fact that the western Ruhr was but part of the *Regierungsbezirk* Düsseldorf, which contained a number of predominantly agrarian counties which influence the percentage values given in column 10b. The data in Tables 2.2. and 2.3 suggest that in the 'take-off' stage of its development in the western Ruhr, the Nazi Party secured half of its membership from the lower class and just short of 40 per cent from *Mittelstand* elements, with virtually no support coming from the upper-middle class and upper class. In the bulk of the towns listed in Table 2.3 the lower-class component was high, especially in Hamborn and Langerfeld, as well as among those recruited in Rheinhausen from 1926 to 1927. With the exception of Mörs and Oberhausen, the social structure of the Nazi branches listed does not show dramatic deviations from that of the working population of the towns in which they were situated. Although the class structure of the party's membership did not match that of the social structure of the region precisely, it is clear that the NSDAP in the western Ruhr drew the major share of its membership from the lower class, and had a marked heterogeneous composition at this point in its development. It was only among the party functionaries at branch level that the *Mittelstand* loomed very large (see Table 2.2, column 15).[47] Of the eight branch leaders who can be indentified, only two pursued lower-class occupations, namely an unskilled labourer in Langerfeld and an apprenticed bricklayer in Hammerthal. One remarkable variant in the leadership structure of the branches was that provided by Mörs. Here the feuding between rival factions following its formation in 1925 was so acute that the branch was permanently threatened with

Table 2.3 The social structure of the membership of Nazi Party branches and of the working population of the towns in which they were situated in the western Ruhr, 1925–6 (by %)[48]

Class	Occupational subgroup	(1) Barmen (N: 154) a	b	(2) Essen (N: 423) a[1]	b	(3) Hamborn (N: 38) a	b	(4) Hammerthal (N: 38) a	b[2]
LOWER CLASS	Workers[5]	44.8	56.5	49.6	58.4	63.1	73.6	57.9	64.7
	Domestic Workers[6]	0	4.3	0.2	5.6	0	4.3	0	3.2
Lower-middle-MIDDLE CLASS	White-collar/civil servants[7]	20.8	22.6	35.6	25.4	26.3	14.9	21.0	12.9
	Self-employed[8]	13.5		6.2		10.5		18.3	
Upper-MIDDLE CLASS	Managers[9]	0.6		0		0		0	
	Higher civil servants[10]	0	13.8	0	8.7	0	5.4	0	9.6
UPPER CLASS	Factory/estate owners[11]	0		0.2		0		0	
STATUS NOT CLEAR	Others[12]	20.2	—	8.0	—	0	—	2.6	—
	Working family members	—	2.4	—	1.9	—	1.7	—	9.5

Notes: 1 Includes members resident in *Landkreis* Essen.
2 Is based on the working population of *Landkreis* Hattingen (Province of Westphalia) in which the Hammerthal is situated.
3 Includes the branches listed here and the new members who joined the Rheinhausen branch (*N:* 13) in 1926.
4 The percentages are based on the working population of the *Regierungsbezirk* Düsseldorf.
5 Subgroups 1–4 listed in Table 2.2.

(5) Langerfeld (Barmen) (N: 54)		(6) Mettmann (N: 34)		(7) Mörs (N: 24)		(8) Mülheim/ Ruhr (N: 46)		(9) Oberhausen (N: 50)		(10) Western Ruhr (N: 874)	
a	b	a	b	a	b	a	b	a	b	a[3]	b[4]
64.8	56.5	50.0	57.4	29.1	60.9	56.5	59.7	28.0	65.0	49.6	56.1
0	4.3	0	5.8	0	5.3	0	5.6	0	5.4	0.1	4.8
11.0	22.6	32.4	18.4	33.3	15.9	30.4	23.0	44.0	20.1	29.9	20.8
13.0		5.9		20.9		10.9		8.0		9.5	
0		0		4.2		0		2.0		0.3	
	13.8		12.7		11.4		9.3		7.5		12.7
		0		0		0		0		0	
		0		0		0		0		0.1	
11.0	—	11.7	—	12.5	—	2.2	—	18.0	—	10.1	—
	2.4		5.6		6.5		2.3		1.9		5.6

6 Subgroup 5 listed in Table 2.2.
7 Subgroups 7-9 listed in Table 2.2.
8 Subgroups 6, 10-11, and 14 listed in Table 2.2.
9 Subgroup 12 listed in Table 2.2.
10 Subgroup 13 listed in Table 2.2.
11 Subgroup 16 listed in Table 2.2.
12 Subgroups 15 and 17-20 listed in Table 2.2.

Table 2.4   Nazi membership in various Essen districts according to class
(by row %)[49]

District	Lower class	Lower- & middle-middle class	Upper-middle- & upper-class	Status unknown
Workers = 75% plus of working population in				
ALTENESSEN (*N:* 18)	66.6	22.2	0	11.1
KATERNBERG (*N:* 27)	74.1	25.9	0	0
Workers = 70–75% of working population in				
BORBECK (*N:* 21)	57.1	33.3	0	9.5
Workers = 60–70% Civil Servants & White-collar = 25–30% of working population in				
ESSEN-ALTSTADT (*N:* 258)	44.2	46.9	0.4	8.5
ESSEN-WEST (*N:* 83)	56.6	36.1	0	7.2
Workers = 40–45% Civil Servants & White-collar = 45–50% of working population in				
RELLINGHAUSEN (*N:* 8)	37.5	50.0	12.5	0

dissolution. That this did not happen was due to the work of its business manager, a woman teacher, whose *de facto* authority and leadership 'until such time that the affairs of the branch can be finally regulated', was confirmed by Goebbels in September 1925.[50]

The ability of the Nazi Party to attract support from various occupational groups, to adjust to the social geometry of the population and reflect the varied social patterns at the grassroots level within the western Ruhr is underlined if one looks at the structure of the largest branch the party was able to develop by early 1926, that of Essen.[51] Here a breakdown of support at the district level reveals that though the party was firmly rooted in only two areas, Essen-Centre (the six districts making up the *Altstadt*) and Essen-West, with a more limited presence in Altenessen, the districts which made up Borbeck, and the Katernberg district (at

Table 2.5 The age of NSDAP members by social class and by occupational subgroup in the western Ruhr[a] in 1925-6 and of the (male) working population of the Rheinprovinz, Prussia and Germany in 1925 (by %)[52]

Class	Occupational subgroup	Under 20	20-9	30-9	40-9	50-9	Over 60
LOWER	1. Agricultural workers	0	0.1	0	0	0	0
CLASS	2. Unskilled workers	3.6	9.4	1.1	1.2	0.3	0
	3. Skilled (craft) workers	9.2	18.5	1.7	1.7	0.1	0
	4. Other skilled workers	1.6	1.2	0.3	0.1	0.1	0
	5. Domestic workers	0.1	0	0	0	0	0
Subtotal		14.5	29.2	3.1	3.0	0.5	0
Lower-	6. Master craftsmen	0	0.4	0.4	0.1	0	0
&	7. Non-academic						
middle-	professionals	1.1	1.7	0.8	0.3	0.1	0
MIDDLE	8. White-collar employees	6.2	12.5	2.4	1.1	0.3	0.1
CLASS	9. Lower civil servants	0.1	3.2	1.3	1.1	0	0.1
	10. Merchants	1.1	3.0	1.3	0.3	0.7	0
	11. Farmers	0.3	0.1	0.1	0	0	0
Subtotal		8.8	20.9	6.3	2.9	1.1	0.2
Upper-	12. Managers	0	0.1	0	0	0	0
MIDDLE	13. Higher civil servants	0	0	0	0	0	0
CLASS &	14. University students	0.1	0.3	0	0	0	0
UPPER	15. Academic professionals	0	0	0.3	0.1	0	0
CLASS	16. Entrepreneurs	0	0	0	0.1	0	0
Subtotal		0.1	0.4	0.3	0.2	0	0
STATUS	17. Non-university students	0.8	0.7	0	0	0	0
UNCLEAR	18. Pensioners/retired	0	0	0.1	0.1	0.1	0
	19. Wives/widows	0	0.5	0.4	0.1	0.3	0
	20. Military personnel	0	0	0	0	0	0
	21. Illegible/no data	1.9	1.9	0.5	0.1	0.1	0
Subtotal		2.7	3.1	1.0	0.3	0.5	0
TOTAL (%)		26.1	53.6	10.7	6.4	2.1	0.2
Rheinprovinz		16.6	27.1	19.1	18.0	12.2	6.9
Prussia		16.7	26.2	19.3	17.5	12.8	7.4
Germany		16.9	25.9	19.0	17.5	13.1	7.6

Note: a Based on 741 members whose age was recorded in the membership lists.

that stage still part of *Landkreis* Essen; it became a suburb of Essen following the boundary changes of 1929), its recruitment pattern in social terms reflected the social mix of these districts (see Table 2.4). By early 1926, except for a marginal presence in Rellinghausen, the Nazis had hardly taken root in the more upper-middle-class and upper-class districts which were to give such strong support to the NSDAP in the early 1930s.[53]

Two characteristics of the Nazi membership in the western Ruhr conform with those well-established in the literature on the nature of the party as a whole: it was almost exclusively a male movement and was dominated by the younger age groups (see Table 2.5). The 34 female members account for but 4 per cent of the total membership of the western Ruhr in 1925–6, of which 91.2 per cent were recruited in the large cities. The percentage of female members recruited in the large Ruhr cities does show variations, ranging from 11 per cent of the membership in the Barmen branch, to 8 per cent in Oberhausen and only 2.1 per cent in Essen.

As in the case of the males who joined the NSDAP, the younger age groups made up the majority of the female membership, though the dominance of those under 30 was very much less marked, accounting for only 53 per cent of those whose age could be determined, as against the figure of 80 per cent for the male membership. Just over one quarter of all members were under 20 years of age,.and 79.7 per cent under 30 (see Table 2.5). The age/ class profile of the Ruhr membership suggests that lower-class elements under the age of 20 were more likely to join the Nazi Party than their lower- and middle-middle-class equivalents (the split is 62.1 and 37.3 per cent respectively), a feature which is less strong for the 20 to 29 year-old age group (59.3 : 42.6 per cent), and one which is reversed in the case of those members aged 30 and over (37.6 : 59.4 per cent). Not perhaps surprising, given the age profile, is that of those (relatively few) members whose marital status can be established, the majority were single, irrespective of their occupational status.[54]

Whether or not community size had a bearing on the class recruitment pattern of the Ruhr NSDAP is difficult to determine given that 87.3 per cent of the total membership was resident in cities with populations of 100,000 and over (see Table 2.6). The data does suggest that lower-class members were easier to recruit in smaller communities and middle-sized towns than in the big cities.

Table 2.6 The class recruitment pattern of the membership of the NSDAP (*N:* 874) in the western Ruhr according to community size (by %)

| Class | Community size | | | | |
	below 2,000	*2,000- 4,999*	*5,000- 19,999*	*20,000- 99,999*	*Over 100,000*
LOWER CLASS	53.8	—	51.0	60.0	48.8
Lower- & middle- MIDDLE CLASS	41.0	—	34.7	32.0	39.8
Upper-MIDDLE CLASS & UPPER CLASS	2.6	—	4.1	2.0	6.0
TOTAL (%)	100	—	100	100	100
Frequency (*N*)	39	—	49	50	736

III

From late 1926 the progress of Nazism in the Ruhr as a whole slowed down significantly, if indeed the party did not go into decline. The collapse of the tripartite leadership of *Gau* Ruhr in the summer of 1926, when Kaufmann was elected as *Gauleiter* (much to Goebbels' disappointment),[55] the appointment of the former leader of the Westphalian NSDAP, Pfeffer von Salomon, to head the SA, and the loss of Goebbels and his flair for propaganda following his appointment to *Gau* Berlin, left Kaufmann saddled with an area which he found increasingly difficult to control. Challenges from his subordinates, especially the assertive Terboven of the Essen branch, and major internal squabbles in 1927 and 1928, all combined to undermine Kaufmann's authority.[56] The party was in the doldrums, lacking cash and leaders of calibre, unable to attract the interest of the population at large. Police reports on some Ruhr branches for 1927 outline a picture of stagnation in many parts of *Gau* Ruhr, not least in the Ruhr area itself, where the party suffered quite significant membership reductions in a number of branches.[57] The inability of the party to build on the promising start made in 1925 to 1926, and the marginality of its electoral base, was driven home to the Nazis by the poor showing of the party in many Ruhr cities and towns in the May 1928 *Reichstag* election.[58]

Kaufmann was removed from the *Gauleiter* position in the autumn of 1928 and transferred to head *Gau* Hamburg. His

removal was accompanied by a fundamental restructuring of
Gau Ruhr, which was divided into *Gau* Westphalia, led by the
former Bochum branch leader Josef Wagner, and two independent districts, that of Essen under Terboven, and the Bergisches
Land, controlled initially by Härtel, and from 1929 by Florian.
These two districts were given *Gau* status in 1930, emerging as
Gau Essen and Düsseldorf respectively, the former containing the
bulk of the western Ruhr region. These changes took place at a
time when the onset of the depression of post-1929 rapidly
brought about a dramatic change in the fortunes of the Nazi
Party in the Ruhr, as elsewhere in Germany. One indication of
the surge towards the party is provided by the often quite
staggering membership increases recorded in a number of branches situated in the Ruhr region. By June 1930 the Essen branch
alone had a membership of 2,000, which increased to 6,600 by
December 1931.[59] Between May 1929 and March 1932 the
Duisburg-Hamborn NSDAP grew twenty-fold, the enrolled
membership rising from 250 to 5,000.[60] In the Bochum branch,
which was one of the major growth centres of the NSDAP in the
eastern Ruhr with a membership of 2,100 by July 1930, the party
officials were unable to cope with the flood of applications and
had to introduce a temporary ban on accepting new members.
This lasted from 1 July to 1 October, by which time the backlog
had been cleared.[61] In Westphalia as a whole the membership
increased from 3,500 in January 1930 to 32,186 by 31 October
1930, a large percentage of which was resident in the Ruhr, an
area in which the NSDAP had its most sizeable party branches
throughout the 1920s.[62]

Unfortunately the type of detailed evidence on the social
characteristics of the Ruhr NSDAP contained in the branch lists
which have survived for the western Ruhr in the mid-1920s is
lacking for the late 1920s and early 1930s. One set of data which
allows an insight into the social characteristics of the Nazi
Party's membership in the Ruhr region in this crucial period is
that provided by the *Partei-Statistik* for the three *Gaue* which
contained the Ruhr (see Table 2.7). The 'workers' category
formed an important section of the membership of the Nazi Party
in all three *Gaue*, especially in Westphalia-South. Given that all
three *Gaue* included predominantly agrarian areas (which were
quite extensive in the Westphalian *Gaue*), recruitment from the
lower class in the Ruhr towns must have been very strong in

Table 2.7 The occupational breakdown of the membership of the NSDAP in *Gaue* Essen, Westphalia-North and Westphalia-South as of 14 September 1930 and 30 January 1933 (by %)[63]

Category	Essen 1930	Essen 1933	Westphalia-North 1930	Westphalia-North 1933	Westphalia-South 1930	Westphalia-South 1933
Workers	33.1	39.6	32.4	37.6	35.3	43.8
White-collar employees	31.6	26.4	28.1	21.1	29.6	24.1
Self-employed	17.5	16.0	19.6	17.8	19.3	16.0
Civil servants	5.3	6.4	5.7	5.7	5.9	4.9
Farmers	3.5	3.1	6.1	7.4	2.4	3.5
Others	9.0	8.5	8.1	10.4	7.5	7.7

order to achieve the percentages recorded in the *Partei-Statistik*.

The comparatively high 'workers' percentages undoubtedly reflect the strong lower-class component contained within the membership of the NSDAP in the Ruhr, and are broadly substantiated by other evidence. It would help to explain the exceptionally strong presence of the lower class within the functionary corps of *Bezirk* Essen in late 1929.[64] According to a report on the social structure of the NSDAP drawn up towards the end of 1930 by the Düsseldorf *Regierungspräsident* (his region included *Gau* Essen), farm workers made up 5 per cent of the Nazi membership, industrial workers 14 per cent, and artisans and tradesmen 34 per cent.[65] Since the bulk of the latter were probably dependent, the data can be interpreted as showing a 40 to 50 per cent lower-class content for the party in the region as a whole. Given that the Düsseldorf administrative region contained strongly agrarian areas, it is almost certain that the percentage of the lower class within the branches situated in the western Ruhr was considerable higher. That this is highly probable is suggested by the figures produced in November 1930 by the Westphalian *Gauleiter* for what he termed the 'inner industrial area of Westphalia', which can only mean the eastern Ruhr.[66] In this 'secret' report submitted to the *Parteileitung* in Munich, Wagner stated that 57.7 per cent of the membership (the total size of which he does not give) were 'workers', divided into 26.2 per cent for miners and 31.5 for workers. What Wagner described as '*Mittelständler*' made up 19.5 per cent of the membership, while civil servants and white-collar employees accounted for 18.1, with 2 per cent drawn from the 'free professions'.

47

That the lower class made up an important component of the Westphalian NSDAP is also borne out by the class background of the recipients of the 'Golden Party Badge' in Westphalia, that is members of the party who had joined the movement between 1925 and 1928, and who were still in the party at the outset of the Third Reich. Many of the 'old fighters' who secured these badges were from towns in the the Ruhr region. Of the 672 members on whose background Kater could obtain information, 40.9 per cent were from the lower class.[67]

IV

The available evidence on the social structure of the NSDAP in the Ruhr points to a strong lower-class presence and a heterogeneous membership. It is misleading to describe the Nazi Party in the Ruhr as a 'bourgeois party', a conclusion reached by Böhnke in his study on the Nazi Party in the region,[68] and one shared by Johannes Wagner in his history of the NSDAP in Bochum.[69] Böhnke was probably unaware of the existence of the individual membership lists which have survived for the 1925–6 period, which would have acted as a corrective to his one-sided approach to the question of the social structure of the party in the Ruhr. It is unclear why Böhnke did not at least mention *Gauleiter* Wagner's breakdown for the Westphalian section of the Ruhr, given that he did consult the file containing this material.

A reluctance to consider the idea that the lower class gave the NSDAP strong support is a marked feature of Böhnke's work on the Ruhr. Although he accepts that some members of the Nazi Party came from the working class, even the industrial working class, he tends to minimize this as far as possible. The occupational and class structure of the membership of Nazi branches in the western Ruhr in 1925–6 forces one to the conclusion that the lower class played an important role in the NSDAP in this part of Germany and it is improbable that the social mix of the mid-1920s was dramatically changed subsequently, or that the Nazis were unable to sustain lower-class support. If one looks at the (admittedly) few members recruited by the Rheinhausen branch in 1926 and early 1927, the high lower-class element among the new intake is very striking (see Table 2.2, column 13). Even Böhnke points to the increased influx of workers into the Ruhr NSDAP from 1930 onwards.[70] The data provided by the *Partei-*

Statistik for the period 1925 to 1933 and the material on the social structure of the NSDAP in *Regierungsbezirk* Düsseldorf and in the eastern Ruhr region for late 1930 all point to a sizeable presence of the lower class.

There is additional inferential evidence which broadly sub-stantiates the view that the lower class was a major component in the social composition of the Nazi Party in the Ruhr. The ability of the party to make significant inroads on the lower class in the region is indicated in the detailed local study by Buchloh on the Duisburg area.[71] The little detailed analysis that we have on the electoral support secured by the Nazis in the Ruhr towns also demonstrates that the lower class was an important element in the Nazi vote.[72] Böhnke also observes that the Nazis secured an often sizeable share of the vote in predominantly industrial towns, especially by the time of the 1932 elections.[73] It is clear from the available evidence that the NSDAP in the Ruhr was heavily dependent on the lower class, both for its membership and for its electoral support. This is not to ignore or deny the fact that this class was under-represented within the party in the Ruhr in comparison with the social structure of the working population of the region. But in the Ruhr the NSDAP was clearly neither a 'bourgeois party' nor a *Mittelstandsbewegung*.

3

GAU WÜRTTEMBERG
1928–30

Although the history of the Nazi Party in southern Germany has been well-researched at the regional level, with a series of studies analysing its genesis and development in Bavaria,[1] Baden[2] and the Saarland,[3] there is as yet no detailed account of its progress in Württemberg.[4] This is surprising on a number of counts. Beyond the fact that Württemberg[5] was one of the first *Länder* in which Nazism took root outside of Bavaria, with the formation of a branch at Stuttgart as early as 8 May 1920,[6] it is the subsequent history of Nazism in the region, one of relative failure before 1933, which is at first glance puzzling. In Württemberg all the essential religious and socio-economic pre-conditions theoretically conducive to Nazi growth and success were present.[7] It was a predominantly Protestant region, with a Protestant population of 68 per cent. The 30.9 per cent Catholic part of the population was, beyond a small enclave in the north-east, heavily concentrated in the southern and south-western parts of Württemberg and in the two counties constituting the small Prussian province of Hohenzollern, in which 94.4 per cent of the population was Catholic (see map 2).[8] In terms of its economic structure,[9] agriculture was still of great importance during the Weimar period, employing 41.7 per cent of Württemberg's working population in 1925, marginally ahead of the 39.1 per cent engaged in industry and crafts, though by the time of the 1933 census this situation had been reversed, with 35.4 per cent now working in the primary, and 40.6 per cent in the secondary sector. Despite the fact that a number of important lines of communications traversed the region, such as the Paris-Vienna, Berlin-Milan, and Mannheim-Nuremberg railway lines, which made Stuttgart an important communication centre, transport and

50

trade was a less important economic sector than in many other German *Länder*, employing only 10.5 per cent of the working population in 1925 and 12.7 per cent in 1933, considerably lower than the national average of 16.5 and 18.4 per cent respectively.

In the agrarian sector small units of production predominated, with farms of 20 hectares and less accounting for 82.5 per cent of all cultivated land, while only 1.7 per cent consisted of large units of over 100 hectares.[10] Small-scale farming was thus very much the norm in Württemberg, where 91.7 per cent of all farms were owner-occupied, with tenant-farming accounting for a mere 6.8 per cent.[11] It was the north-eastern and southern parts of Württemberg which were essentially agrarian in character. Except for these areas, and the industrial region around Stuttgart, agriculture and industry lived cheek by jowl (see Map 3). Industry was widely, though not evenly, distributed.[12] The major concentration of industrial activity was to be found in the Neckar valley from Reutlingen to Neckarsulm, while in the upper reaches of the Neckar a small industrial region had developed in the counties of Balingen, Rottweil and Oberndorf. An abundance of water and the availability of cheap labour had also led to the penetration of industry into a number of small valleys elsewhere in Württemberg, so that Heidenheim in the Brenztal and Göppingen and Geislingen in the Filstal had developed into centres of flourishing industry. In general, industry was an important employer in the area between Stuttgart, Ulm, Heidenheim and Schwäbisch-Gmünd.

The chief characteristic of Württemberg's industrial structure in the 1920s was its heavy dependence on the finishing industry, a major consequence of its development pattern since the 1850s. Despite the fact that Württemberg had had a long tradition of craft-based manufacturing, its lack of natural resources led to the inability of the region to connect with, and keep pace with, the economic progress achieved in Germany as a whole from the latter half of the nineteenth century. Thus heavy industry played no role in the economy of the area. It was the textile industry, the construction of vehicles and machinery, the manufacture of electrical consumer products and of optical and scientific instruments which were of premier significance, while the clothing, wood, paper and tobacco industries were also of importance. In Württemberg some branches of specialized, labour-intensive industry were particularly prominent. Some 36.7 per cent of

Catholic		Protestant
	55–64.9%	
	65–84.9%	
	85–100%	

Map 2 The confessional structure of Württemberg-Hohenzollern.[13]

Agriculture

☐ 40.1–50%

▨ 50.1–70%

▩ 70.1–90%

Industry/Trade

☐

▨

▩

Map 3 The economic structure of Württemberg-Hohenzollern.[14]

Table 3.1 The social structure of the working population of Württemberg-Hohenzollern in 1925 (by %)[15]

	Self-employed	White-collar workers/civil servants	Workers	Working family members	Domestic workers
Württemberg	20.5	12.2	35.9	28.3	3.1
Hohenzollern	26.2	6.8	25.5	39.1	2.0
Germany	17.3	16.5	45.1	17.0	4.1

those engaged in Germany in 1925 in the manufacture of harmonicas were employed in the region, as well as 30.4 per cent of all those working in the clock industry, which was especially widespread in the Schwarzwald. Large-scale units of production were comparatively rare in Württemberg, and of the 1,351 factories employing 50 or more workers, only 26 employed a workforce of 1,000 or more. These large concerns accounted for only 20.5 per cent of the workforce in plants employing 50 or more workers.[16]

Given the continued importance of agriculture and the nature of Württemberg's industry, the social structure of the working population in the region showed some significant variations in comparison with that relating to Germany as a whole (see Table 3.1). Especially striking was the high percentage represented by working family members within the Württemberg workforce, and the comparatively low percentage made up by the workers category. It was the size of the agrarian sector in Württemberg, along with the high percentage of owner-occupiers farming small units of production with the help of their family dependents, which accounts to a considerable extent for the over-representation of the self-employed and working family members categories. But the significant under-representation of the workers category in Württemberg is strange, given that the secondary sector employed roughly the same percentage of the working population in the region as it did in Germany (39.1 and 41.4 per cent in 1925 respectively). Two main reasons are generally advanced to account for Württemberg's divergence from the national pattern.[17] The first is that the large number of small farms worked by the proprietors and their families meant that agricultural labourers were not that numerous, accounting

54

for only 4.3 per cent of the workforce in Württemberg in 1933, as against 7.8 per cent for Germany as a whole. The second reason relates to the relative insignificance of the trade and transport sector in Württemberg, with fewer workers being employed in this sector.[18]

Given such factors as the predominance of the Protestant faith in Württemberg, the importance of agriculture in its economy, the rural, small-town nature of the population, the comparatively high percentage of the self-employed, and the preponderance of trained, skilled craft workers in the working population of the region, as well as the absence of any massed concentration of unskilled labour employed in large units of production, Nazism should have flourished in Württemberg. In its infancy the development of the NSDAP did indeed show some promise,[19] undoubtedly aided by the fact that along with Bavaria, Württemberg was one of the few *Länder* in which the party could organize itself freely in the early 1920s, not being banned in the region until after the attempted Nazi Putsch in November 1923. However, from the time of its first participation in the *Reichstag* election of May 1924 until that of November 1932, the performance of the NSDAP in electoral district 31, Württemberg, was pretty dismal.[20] The Nazis were unable to secure extensive electoral backing for their ideas, and the NSDAP's share of the vote in Württemberg was consistently well below that which it secured nationally. The factors which help to explain the retardation of the NSDAP in the region are the entrenched tradition of liberal democracy in Württemberg since the late nineteenth century, the continuously functioning parliamentary system at the *Land* level throughout the Weimar era, and the greater resilience of the regional economy in face of the severe economic recession which affected Germany from 1928-9.[21] An important additional factor which also constantly undermined the NSDAP's progress in Württemberg until the early 1930s was the inability of the regional Nazi hierarchy to get its act together and provide effective leadership and drive.

I

From the time of the re-formation of the NSDAP in Württemberg in the spring of 1925 until the early 1930s the party struggled constantly, but unsuccessfully, to make a noticeable impact on the region. A major problem for the Nazi movement throughout the late 1920s were constant factional and personality conflicts within the *Gau* in general, and within its largest branch, that of Stuttgart, in particular, which neither the first *Gauleiter* Eugen Munder (who held the post from 1925 to early 1928), nor his successor Wilhelm Murr (in office from 1928 to 1945) were able to prevent.[22] A constant source of irritation for Munder was that the National Socialist Freedom Party, which had organized *völkisch* and National Socialist elements under one banner during 1924, continued to exist as a rival to the re-formed NSDAP until 1927, when its leader, Professor Christian Mergenthaler, was finally reconciled with Hitler.[23] Following his entry into the NSDAP, Mergenthaler was more often than not one of the leading players in various disputes which periodically rocked the *Gau*. It was Mergenthaler who had a hand in the events which ultimately led to Munder's resignation as *Gauleiter* in early 1928.[24] Munder lacked the will or ability to impress his authority on his subordinates. His circulars to the branches were not so much an expression of the leadership principle, but more an appeal for support and co-operation.[25] Murr found his leadership questioned virtually continuously. He had not been long in office when there were calls from the disgruntled Stuttgart branch leader for Murr's resignation due to his 'laxity' as *Gauleiter*.[26] In January 1929 further attacks were made on Murr's leadership capacity, especially his lack of 'oratorical gifts'.[27] Two months later Murr was embroiled in a conflict with the SA-*Führer* of Württemberg,[28] while quarrels within the Stuttgart SA were threatening to get out of hand.[29] A year later Murr faced even more severe problems. It appears that his personal relationship with his *Gaupropagandaleiter* had broken down at a time when Murr was being intrigued against by Dreher, the Nazi *Reichstag* deputy for Württemberg, as well as by the branch leader of Stuttgart. To compound his difficulties yet another dispute among the Stuttgart SA became so acrimonious as to occasion a split, opposition elements going on to occupy the NSDAP's party offices in the city.[30] Murr's capability as *Gauleiter* was still being questioned as late as the summer of 1930, a time when the Württemberg Nazi Party was beginning to expand in all directions.[31]

Beyond the constant squabbling within its ranks, the Württemberg NSDAP faced a number of other serious difficulties which worked against its success. One problem, which was only gradually resolved when the party began to expand rapidly in the early 1930s, was that of attracting and retaining individuals who had the capacity to organize the movement or who exhibited a talent for propaganda.[32] A particular handicap for the party was its lack of capable speakers, a problem heightened by the virtual withdrawal of the two most experienced public speakers Mergenthaler and Schlumpberger (two characters perpetually involved in various intrigues against the *Gauleitung*) from this activity in 1929.[33] Given the slow growth of the party until 1930, and the limited opportunities open to party officials to carve out a worthwhile career in a movement which was seemingly going nowhere slowly, turnover in branch funtionaries was also a noticeable feature in the 1920s. Even Stuttgart, a relatively sizeable branch, went through a succession of branch leaders between 1925 and 1930. The constant changes in the leadership gave rise to a lack of continuity, a situation which could hardly have assisted the movement.[34] Another perennial problem was the lack of cash which restricted the propaganda (and organizational) activity of the Württemberg Nazi Party until the late 1920s.[35] Even for larger branches, such as Stuttgart, the costs involved in financing the (by later standards) very modest campaign in the May 1928 *Reichstag* election had still not been fully met some six months later.[36] The poor financial position of the *Gau*, which repeatedly forced the *Gauleitung* to ask the *Reichsleitung* for support, was strongly underlined in Murr's report on the position of the party in Württemberg at the end of 1929.[37]

The organizational and financial problems of the NSDAP in Württemberg were linked to, and an expression of, the inability of the party to generate support. Matters were made worse by the fact that the existing membership more often than not failed to show much enthusiasm for the party cause,[38] or to meet its financial obligations, leading to a large number of branches facing membership arrears.[39] One possible source for generating income, namely by attracting large crowds to its public meetings, also proved problematical before 1930. Even the best attended Nazi meetings in Stuttgart in the late 1920s could only register an audience of 600-700 on the odd occasion, whereas in the run-up to the *Reichstag* election of September 1930 a total of around 12,000 people, paying entrance fees ranging from 0.50 to 1.00

Table 3.2 The recruitment pattern of the membership of *Gau* Württemberg-Hohenzollern, March 1928 to September 1930[40]

	1928			1929			1930		
	I^a	II^b	III^c	I	II	III	I	II	III
January	—	—	—	43	4.1	1.0	—	—	—
February	—	—	—	52	5.0	1.3	12^d	0.5	0.3
March	21^d	3.9	0.5	59	5.7	1.4	232	9.1	5.6
April	93	17.5	2.2	39	3.7	0.9	234	9.2	5.7
May	58	10.9	1.4	92	8.9	2.2	335	13.1	8.1
June	70	13.1	1.7	96	9.2	2.3	183	7.2	4.4
July	73	13.7	1.8	63	6.1	1.5	339	13.3	8.2
August	12	2.2	0.3	159	15.3	3.9	447	17.5	10.8
September	31	5.8	0.7	95	9.1	2.3	765	30.0	18.5
October	84	15.8	2.0	126	12.1	3.1	(826)	—	—
November	51	9.6	1.2	126	12.1	3.1	(c1050)	—	—
December	39	7.3	0.9	88	8.5	2.1	—	—	—
TOTALS	532	99.8	12.7	1,038	99.8	25.1	2,547	99.9	61.6

Notes: a Number of recruits per month.
      b Number of recruits per month expressed as percentage for the year.
      c Number of recruits per month expressed as percentage for the period March 1928 to September 1930.
      d Only partial figure for the month.

RM, came to three Nazi mass meetings in Stuttgart in August alone.[41] By the time of the September election the monotonous entry on the Württemberg NSDAP in the reports by the police in the latter half of the 1920s, to the effect that the party's membership was stagnant or at best growing only very slowly in comparison with other regions of Germany, finally ceased.[42] From the late spring of 1930 onwards the situation reports begin to note the swing towards Nazism in Württemberg, a growth in support which the police ascribed in part to the 'general political situation' and in part to 'the skilled and intensive propaganda' pushed out by the Nazis in the region.[43]

The slow growth of the Württemberg NSDAP during the 1920s, and the transformation in its fortunes from 1930, are confirmed by the data available on its recruitment pattern from March 1928 to September 1930 (see Table 3.2). Between 1928 and 1929 the growth-rate of the party doubled, though it has to be said that the average monthly enrolment figures for the *Gau* were hardly earth-shattering. In the course of 1930, however, there was a very marked acceleration in membership recruitment. In September 1930 the Württemberg NSDAP recruited more members in one month than it had in the whole of 1928, while in November the intake was slightly in excess of the total recruitment achieved in 1929. The virtually complete list of new entrants submitted by the *Gauleitung* to Munich provides a good insight into both the party's organizational development and the geographical distribution of its membership in Württemberg during this period. The sort of detail provided by the *Neuaufnahmen* is unfortunately lacking for the years 1925 to 1928, but there is some data relating to the strength of the movement by early 1928. According to figures cited by the *Gaupropagandaleiter* in a letter to Gregor Strasser dated 2 January 1929, the membership of the Württemberg NSDAP stood at 900 at the beginning of 1928 and at 1,150 a year later.[44] This very modest rise was seen by the *Gaupropagandaleiter* as marking progress! Given the known enrolment of 532 members between 27 March and 31 December 1928, at a monthly increase averaging out at around 50 new members per month, it is probable that the total number of new members for 1928 as a whole was approximately 600.[45] Some 350 members must therefore have left the party in the course of the year, a loss of 23 per cent of the total membership. The net gain per month, at around the 20 mark, demonstrates the very slow growth rate experienced by the Württemberg Nazi Party during the year. The high turnover rate continued in 1929, a year in which the party recruited a further 1,038 new members in the region. In mid-December 1929 Murr anticipated that by the end of the year there would be 1,500 paid-up Nazi members in Württemberg,[46] which would suggest that of the 1,150 in the party at the beginning of 1929, and of the 1,038 who had joined in 1929, some 600 or so had left by the end of the year, a loss of around 30 per cent. Approximately a further 2,150 were to join by 15 September 1930.[47] Of the roughly 4,000 members known to have joined the *Gau* Württemberg-Hohenzollern before 15 September 1930 (the total membership was probably around the 4,500 mark if one assumes the membership losses before 1928 were the same as from 1928), 2,751 were still in the NSDAP by the time of the national party census of 1934, suggesting a loss rate of between 30 to 40 per cent.[48]

Provinz Hohenzollern

Map 4 The administrative districts of the State of Württemberg and of the Province of Hohenzollern in 1930.

Branches

●   Enrolling in 1928

✚   Enrolling from 1929

✖   Enrolling from 1930

Map 5 The distribution of Nazi Party branches recruiting in *Gau* Württemberg-Hohenzollern, 1928–30.

The number of branches in which the membership of the Württemberg NSDAP was organized increased from 20 in 1925, to 31 in 1928 and to 147 by 1930.[49] In the *Neuaufnahmen* the members entering the party in 1928 were listed under 42 branches, to which were added a further 27 in 1929 and 47 by mid-September 1930 (see Map 5). The distribution of the branches and of the membership within Württemberg was very uneven. Most striking throughout the period before September 1930 is the very limited presence of the NSDAP in the predominantly Catholic parts of Württemberg-Hohenzollern.[50] In the four strongly Catholic counties of Schwäbisch-Gmünd, Aalen, Ellwangen and Neresheim in north-eastern Württemberg, there were but two branches recruiting in 1928, to which a third was added by September 1930! In southern and south-eastern Württemberg and in the province of Hohenzollern a similar pattern is discernible. In the fifteen predominantly Catholic counties in this area the Nazis had a mere five branches recruiting members by the end of 1928, to which four more were added in the course of 1929, and an additional six by September 1930. In contrast to the late 1920s, the Nazi Party had had much more success in penetrating the Catholic regions of Württemberg in the early 1920s. Among the 236 people who joined the NSDAP in Württemberg between 25 September and 9 November 1923, there were small groups scattered around solidly Catholic areas, with a few members recruited in the counties of Laupheim, Ellwangen, Spaichingen and Schwäbisch-Gmünd. A dozen entered the party in Leutkirch and nine in Saulgau, two counties in which the NSDAP was almost non-existent from 1928 to 1930.[51]

The other noticeable feature relating to the spatial distribution of Nazi branches and members is that they were virtually all situated in the urban centres of Württemberg. Only six of the 42 branches recruiting members in 1928 were in villages. The development of a higher Nazi profile in rural areas did not take place until 1930. This is not to suggest that the party was not recruiting at the village level in 1928 to 1929, but the numbers involved (and these usually attached themselves to nearby urban branches while a minority became *Gau* members) was small. Although 46.8 per cent of Württemberg's population was resident in communities of under 2,000 (according to the census of 1925), the Nazi Party in Württemberg-Hohenzollern recruited a mere 13.5 per cent of its membership from such communities in

1928, a percentage which rose to 21.8 in 1929 and to 35.2 in 1930. There is no doubt that the party was finding it difficult to make much headway in parts of Württemberg, including some Protestant areas. The catchment area of some branches, even as late as September 1930, was often very extensive. The most extreme example of this organizational aspect is provided by the Ulm branch, which recruited individuals resident in the counties of Heidenheim, Ulm, Blaubeuren, Ehingen and Laupheim, as well as in Bavarian Neu-Ulm and its hinterland. The often wide catchment area of individual branches led to organizational overlap in some cases, with different branches recruiting in the same county or town. For example, both the Aalen and Ulm branches recruited in the town and county of Heidenheim in the late 1920s, while in Hirsau and Hochmössingen some party members were organized in local branches, while others were attached to Calw and Oberndorf respectively. These organizational confusions were the consequence of lack of co-ordination of party activity in parts of *Gau* Württemberg-Hohenzollern in the late 1920s, and a reflection of the thinly scattered branch network. Even in the predominantly Protestant counties it is the exception rather than the rule to find more than one or two branches established by September 1930.

The number of branches in place in particular counties, itself a yardstick with which to measure the activism and organizational ability of local Nazi leaders, was of critical importance in providing the NSDAP with a high public profile, which seems to have produced electoral dividends. There are a number of examples provided by the performance of the Nazi Party in the *Reichstag* election of 1930 which suggest that a relationship existed between organizational activism and electoral success.[52] In the adjacent counties of Gerabronn, Crailsheim and Schwäbisch-Hall, the populations of which were broadly identical in terms of religion and socio-economic aspects, the number of branches in place were nine, two and two respectively. In Gerabronn the party achieved one of its better returns, 17.9 per cent, almost double the average of 9.4 per cent achieved in electoral district Württemberg-Hohenzollern, and more than double the party's performance in the counties of Crailsheim (7.4 per cent) and of Schwäbisch-Hall (5.6 per cent). The best result by far was achieved by the NSDAP in Nagold, where it polled 33 per cent. Here the Nazi branch had been rapidly expanding in all directions in the course of 1930, recruiting heavily in numerous villages in the county. The activism of the local Nazi leadership was clearly one important factor behind the 22.8 per cent share of the vote for the NSDAP in the county in September 1930.

If one uses the data provided by the membership recruitment figures for 1928 to 1930, Nagold was one area benefitting from the steadily increasing surge towards Nazism from 1930. This general trend did not benefit all branches equally, and the recruitment pattern of the NSDAP in Württemberg in the months before, and in the weeks following, the September election shows some odd variations. While the bulk of Nazi branches do reflect a spurt in their growth, which in some cases one can justifiably describe as explosive in form, quite a number continued to show the drip-feed recruitment pattern character-istic of the lean years of the 1920s. Even in quite sizeable towns, such as Friedrichshafen, Freudenstadt and Heilbronn, places in which the party had been active for years, the party could only recruit a handful of members from time to time, while the entry of one additional member into these branches is not unusual either, even during the 'surge' phase from early 1930. By September 1930 the party was still languishing, both organizatio-nally and electorally, in some parts of Württemberg.

II

The extensive data contained in the lists recording persons who joined the Nazi Party in *Gau* Württemberg-Hohenzollern from March 1928 to September 1930 allows one to reconstruct in some detail the occupational and class characteristics of those actively supporting Nazism in the region[53] (see Table 3.3, in which all branches which recruited 25 or more members by September 1930 are listed). The noticeable feature of the membership of many of the branches, especially those situated in smaller towns or villages (one should bear in mind that virtually all the branches, Stuttgart being an exception, recruited on an often county-wide basis) is their high lower-class content. In 21 of the 43 branches listed in Table 3.3 lower-class elements formed the absolute majority of the membership, while in a further six the lower-class members represented the relative majority. These branches were situated predominantly, though not exclusively, in counties in which industry and crafts combined with trade and transport employed the bulk of the working population, irrespective of whether, as in the majority of cases, the population was solidly Protestant, or, as in the case of Aalen, Rottweil and Schwäbisch-Gmünd (see Table 3.3, columns 1, 30 and 32), predominantly Catholic. A number were also to be found in 'mixed' areas where neither agriculture nor industry and trade had an outright dominance, as in Backnang, Calw, Freudenstadt, Kupferzell, Metzingen, Stammheim, Trossingen, Tuttlingen and Wangen (see Table 3.3, columns 3, 8, 11, 19, 22, 33, 35, 37 and 39). All of these were, with the exception of Wangen, in solidly Protestant parts of Württemberg. Three of the highest lower-class percentages were, however, achieved in the branches of Altensteig, Bondorf and Wildentierbach (see Table 3.3, columns 2, 7 and 41), which were situated in counties in which agriculture was the most important economic sector, and where the nucleus of the branch was either a village or small 'rural' town (*Landstadt*). Skilled (craft) workers, a significant occupational subgroup in the bulk of the Württemberg Nazi branches, formed an absolute majority of the membership in both Altensteig and Bondorf, while agricultural workers figured prominently among the lower-class members in Wildentierbach. Few branches actually recruited agricultural workers in any great number, even in strongly agrarian areas, and the relatively high percentages achieved by this subgroup in the branches of Blaufelden, Kupferzell, Lampoldshausen and Wildentierbach (see Table 3.3, columns 6, 19, 20 and 41) were atypical.

The Nazi Party in Württemberg-Hohenzollern, except in 1929, attracted slightly more new members from the lower- and middle-middle class than from the lower class (see Table 3.3, columns 44-7). The response of the various occupational subgroups which constituted the middle class, though variable from branch to branch, shows some surprising features demanding comment. Most striking, in view of the significance of agriculture in many parts of Württemberg-Hohenzollern (see Map 2), was the strong under-representation of farmers in the Nazi Party. The data on Württemberg-Hohenzollern does not show 'the dramatic increase in the proportion of farmers coming into Hitler's party in 1928', nor the significance of this subgroup among Nazi recruits at the national level in the period 1928 to 1930.[54] It is clear that the party found it very difficult to mobilize farmers even in strongly Protestant agrarian areas, as can be seen

Table 3.3 The social and occupational structure of the membership of various NSDAP branches in *Gau* Württemberg-Hohenzollern, 1928–30 (by %)[55]

Class	Occupational subgroup	(1) Aalen (1928–30)	(2) Altensteig (1928–30)
LOWER	1. Agricultural workers	0	0
CLASS	2. Unskilled workers	13.9	14.6
	3. Skilled (craft) workers	41.8	51.2
	4. Other skilled workers	0	0
	5. Domestic workers	0	2.4
Subtotal		55.7	68.2
Lower-	6. Master craftsmen	2.3	2.4
&	7. Non-academic professionals	4.6	2.4
middle-	8. White-collar employees	4.6	2.4
MIDDLE	9. Lower civil servants	2.3	0
CLASS	10. Merchants	25.6	19.5
	11. Farmers	2.3	4.9
Subtotal		41.7	31.6
Upper-	12. Managers	0	0
MIDDLE	13. Higher civil servants	0	0
CLASS &	14. University students	0	0
UPPER	15. Academic professionals	0	0
CLASS	16. Entrepreneurs	0	0
Subtotal		0	0
STATUS	17. Non-university students	0	0
UNCLEAR	18. Pensioners/retired	0	0
	19. Wives/widows	2.3	0
	20. Military personnel	0	0
	21. Illegible/no data	0	0
Subtotal		2.3	0
TOTAL (%)		100	100
Frequency (N)		43	41

Table 3.3 continued

(3) Backnang (1928-30)	(4) Balingen (1928-30)	(5) Biberach (1929-30)	(6) Blaufelden (1928-30)	(7) Bondorf (1930)	(8) Calw (1928-30)
0	0	0	28.2	6.9	0
13.2	14.7	17.1	12.8	6.9	12.2
43.4	38.2	14.3	12.8	51.7	35.1
2.4	1.5	0	0	0	5.8
0	0	0	0	0	0
59.0	54.4	31.4	53.8	65.5	47.3
1.2	2.9	2.8	0	13.8	2.7
0	0	2.8	0	0	1.3
4.8	5.9	5.7	5.1	0	5.4
9.6	11.8	2.8	15.4	0	9.4
15.7	17.6	20.0	2.6	6.9	17.6
2.4	2.9	2.8	17.9	10.3	2.7
33.7	41.1	36.9	41.0	31.0	39.1
1.2	0	0	0	0	1.3
0	0	0	0	0	0
0	0	2.8	0	3.4	0
1.2	1.5	11.4	0	0	2.7
0	1.5	2.8	0	0	2.7
2.4	3.0	17.0	0	3.4	6.7
0	0	5.7	0	0	0
1.2	0	2.8	0	0	0
1.2	0	2.8	0	0	1.3
0	0	0	0	0	0
2.4	1.5	2.8	5.1	0	5.4
4.8	1.5	14.1	5.1	0	6.7
100	100	100	100	100	100
83	68	35	39	29	74

Table 3.3   continued

Class	Occupational subgroup	(9) Ebingen (1928–30)	(10) Esslingen (1928–30)
LOWER	1. Agricultural workers	0	0
CLASS	2. Unskilled workers	7.7	12.7
	3. Skilled (craft) workers	28.8	23.9
	4. Other skilled workers	5.8	0
	5. Domestic workers	0	1.5
Subtotal		42.3	38.1
Lower-	6. Master craftsmen	7.7	4.5
&	7. Non-academic professionals	0	8.2
middle-	8. White-collar employees	11.5	11.9
MIDDLE	9. Lower civil servants	5.8	5.2
CLASS	10. Merchants	26.9	21.6
	11. Farmers	0	0
Subtotal		51.9	51.4
Upper-	12. Managers	1.9	0.7
MIDDLE	13. Higher civil servants	0	0
CLASS &	14. University students	0	0.7
UPPER	15. Academic professionals	0	2.2
CLASS	16. Entrepreneurs	0	0.7
Subtotal		1.9	4.3
STATUS	17. Non-university students	0	1.5
UNCLEAR	18. Pensioners/retired	0	0.7
	19. Wives/widows	0	0
	20. Military personnel	0	0
	21. Illegible/no data	3.8	3.7
Subtotal		3.8	5.9
TOTAL (%)		100	100
Frequency (*N*)		52	134

Table 3.3 continued

(11) Freudenstadt (1928-30)	(12) Friedrichs- hafen (1928-30)	(13) Gaildorf (1929-30)	(14) Geislingen (1928-30)	(15) Göppingen (1928-30)	(16) Heidenheim (1930)
0	0	0	4.8	0	2.7
12.5	7.1	16.2	11.2	25.6	6.7
39.6	30.0	21.6	28.9	25.6	22.7
2.1	1.4	0	1.1	0	1.3
0	0	0	1.1	0	0
54.2	38.5	37.8	47.1	51.2	33.4
2.1	1.4	8.1	5.9	0	9.3
6.2	8.6	8.1	4.3	2.3	14.7
12.5	11.4	2.7	6.9	9.3	9.3
0	8.6	5.4	3.7	0	2.7
18.7	12.8	24.3	19.2	30.2	20.0
0	2.8	5.4	4.8	4.6	1.3
39.5	45.4	54.0	44.8	46.4	57.3
2.1	0	0	1.1	0	2.7
0	0	0	0	0	0
0	0	0	0.5	0	1.3
0	4.3	0	1.1	0	1.3
2.1	0	2.7	1.1	0	1.3
4.2	4.3	2.7	3.8	0	6.6
0	2.8	0	0	0	0
0	1.4	0	1.1	0	1.3
0	1.4	0	0.5	0	0
0	0	0	0	0	0
2.1	5.7	5.4	2.7	2.3	1.3
2.1	11.3	5.4	4.3	2.3	2.6
100	100	100	100	100	100
48	70	37	187	43	75

Table 3.3 continued

Class	Occupational subgroup	*(17)* Heilbronn *(1928–30)*	*(18)* Kirchheim Teck *(1929–30)*
LOWER	1. Agricultural workers	0	0
CLASS	2. Unskilled workers	17.6	5.8
	3. Skilled (craft) workers	29.4	34.6
	4. Other skilled workers	2.5	0
	5. Domestic workers	0	0
Subtotal		49.5	40.4
Lower-	6. Master craftsmen	1.7	11.5
&	7. Non-academic professionals	3.4	5.8
middle-	8. White-collar employees	12.6	13.5
MIDDLE	9. Lower civil servants	3.4	1.9
CLASS	10. Merchants	21.8	15.4
	11. Farmers	0	3.8
Subtotal		42.9	51.9
Upper-	12. Managers	0.8	0
MIDDLE	13. Higher civil servants	0	0
CLASS &	14. University students	0	1.9
UPPER	15. Academic professionals	0	0
CLASS	16. Entrepreneurs	0	1.9
Subtotal		0.8	3.8
STATUS	17. Non-university students	0.8	0
UNCLEAR	18. Pensioners/retired	0	0
	19. Wives/widows	0.8	0
	20. Military personnel	0	0
	21. Illegible/no data	5.0	3.8
Subtotal		6.6	3.8
TOTAL (%)		100	100
Frequency (*N*)		119	52

Table 3.3 continued

(19) Kupferzell (1929-30)	(20) Lampolds- hausen (1929-30)	(21) Ludwigsburg (1928-30)	(22) Metzingen (1928-30)	(23) Mühlacker (1928-30)	(24) Nagold (1928-30)
23.8	16.0	0	0	0	0.6
9.5	12.0	14.1	15.1	7.7	8.6
23.8	28.0	30.4	42.4	15.4	45.1
0	0	1.1	0	2.6	1.2
0	0	0	0	0	1.8
57.1	56.0	45.6	57.5	25.7	56.7
7.1	0	2.2	0	10.2	6.8
4.8	8.0	5.4	0	2.6	5.5
0	8.0	8.7	9.1	15.4	3.7
2.4	0	6.5	6.1	7.7	3.7
4.8	4.0	18.5	18.2	25.6	10.5
16.6	24.0	0	0	0	5.5
35.7	44.0	41.3	33.4	61.5	35.7
0	0	2.2	0	0	1.2
0	0	0	0	0	0
2.4	0	1.1	3.0	5.1	0
2.4	0	0	0	0	0.6
0	0	0	0	5.1	1.2
4.8	0	3.3	3.0	10.2	3.0
0	0	5.4	3.0	0	1.2
0	0	0	0	2.6	0.6
0	0	1.1	0	0	0.6
0	0	0	0	0	0
2.4	0	3.3	3.0	0	1.8
2.4	0	9.8	6.0	2.6	4.2
100	100	100	100	100	100
42	25	92	33	39	162

Table 3.3 continued

Class	Occupational subgroup	(25) Neuenbürg (1928–30)	(26) Nürtingen (1929–30)
LOWER	1. Agricultural workers	0	0
CLASS	2. Unskilled workers	21.4	14.2
	3. Skilled (craft) workers	14.2	35.7
	4. Other skilled workers	0	0
	5. Domestic workers	3.6	0
Subtotal		39.2	49.9
Lower-	6. Master craftsmen	10.7	3.6
&	7. Non-academic professionals	3.6	3.6
middle-	8. White-collar employees	7.1	10.7
MIDDLE	9. Lower civil servants	14.2	3.6
CLASS	10. Merchants	14.2	17.8
	11. Farmers	0	0
Subtotal		49.8	39.3
Upper-	12. Managers	3.6	0
MIDDLE	13. Higher civil servants	0	0
CLASS &	14. University students	0	3.6
UPPER	15. Academic professionals	3.6	0
CLASS	16. Entrepreneurs	3.6	0
Subtotal		10.8	3.6
STATUS	17. Non-university students	0	7.1
UNCLEAR	18. Pensioners/retired	0	0
	19. Wives/widows	0	0
	20. Military personnel	0	0
	21. Illegible/no data	0	0
Subtotal		0	7.1
TOTAL (%)		100	100
Frequency (N)		28	28

Table 3.3   continued

(27) Owen Teck (1928-30)	(28) Pfullingen (1928-30)	(29) Ravensburg- Weingarten (1928-30)	(30) Rottweil (1929-30)	(31) Schorndorf (1928-30)	(32) Schwäbisch- Gmünd (1928-30)
0	0	1.7	0	3.0	0
5.7	9.8	14.0	13.8	6.1	12.5
14.3	26.8	28.1	34.5	36.4	37.5
0	2.8	8.8	3.4	0	0
0	1.4	0	0	0	0
20.0	40.8	52.6	51.7	45.5	50.0
17.1	1.4	7.0	13.8	3.0	2.5
0	4.2	3.5	3.4	0	10.0
5.7	21.1	5.3	0	6.1	7.5
11.4	0	5.3	3.4	3.0	10.0
20.0	23.9	8.8	10.3	39.4	17.5
8.6	1.4	8.8	6.9	0	0
62.8	52.0	38.7	37.8	51.5	47.5
0	0	1.7	0	0	0
2.8	0	0	0	0	0
0	0	0	6.9	0	0
2.8	1.4	0	3.4	0	0
0	0	3.5	0	0	0
5.6	1.4	5.2	10.3	0	0
5.7	0	0	0	0	0
0	0	1.7	0	0	0
0	0	0	0	0	0
0	0	0	0	0	0
2.8	5.6	1.7	0	3.0	2.5
8.5	5.6	3.4	0	3.0	2.5
100	100	100	100	100	100
35	71	57	29	33	40

Table 3.3 continued

Class	Occupational subgroup	(33) Stamm-heim (1930)	(34) Stuttgart (1928–30)
LOWER	1. Agricultural workers	0	0
CLASS	2. Unskilled workers	13.8	5.9
	3. Skilled (craft) workers	48.3	17.1
	4. Other skilled workers	0	0.7
	5. Domestic workers	3.4	0.6
Subtotal		65.5	24.3
Lower-	6. Master craftsmen	6.9	2.2
&	7. Non-academic professionals	0	5.9
middle-	8. White-collar employees	3.4	10.3
MIDDLE	9. Lower civil servants	0	3.5
CLASS	10. Merchants	6.9	36.2
	11. Farmers	10.3	0.9
Subtotal		27.5	59.0
Upper-	12. Managers	0	1.6
MIDDLE	13. Higher civil servants	3.4	0.3
CLASS &	14. University students	0	3.3
UPPER	15. Academic professionals	0	2.9
CLASS	16. Entrepreneurs	0	0.7
Subtotal		3.4	8.8
STATUS	17. Non-university students	0	2.0
UNCLEAR	18. Pensioners/retired	0	1.0
	19. Wives/widows	0	1.3
	20. Military personnel	0	0.1
	21. Illegible/no data	3.4	3.3
Subtotal		3.4	7.7
TOTAL (%)		100	100
Frequency (*N*)		29	688

Table 3.3 continued

(35) Trossingen	(36) Tübingen	(37) Tuttlingen	(38) Ulm	(39) Wangen	(40) Weikersheim
(1930)	(1928-30)	(1929-30)	(1928-30)	(1928-30)	(1930)
0	0.9	0	0.8	2.7	4.6
18.7	4.6	5.9	7.5	21.6	2.3
33.3	19.4	47.0	27.9	37.8	20.9
0	1.8	2.9	1.6	0	0
0	3.7	0	0.3	0	0
52.0	30.4	55.8	38.1	62.1	27.8
6.2	1.8	2.9	4.3	0	4.6
0	0	11.8	2.4	8.1	0
2.1	8.3	5.9	10.7	2.7	13.9
6.2	2.8	2.9	6.9	8.1	2.3
16.7	13.0	14.7	18.5	10.8	23.3
2.1	0.9	2.9	6.9	5.4	20.9
33.3	26.8	41.1	49.5	35.1	64.9
0	0	0	0.8	0	4.6
0	0	0	0.3	0	0
0	32.4	2.9	0	0	2.3
0	1.8	0	1.3	0	0
4.2	0	0	1.1	0	0
4.2	34.2	2.9	3.5	0	6.9
0	2.8	0	1.1	2.7	0
0	0	0	0.3	0	0
4.2	1.8	0	4.0	0	0
0	1.8	0	0	0	0
6.2	1.8	0	3.5	0	0
10.4	8.2	0	8.9	2.7	0
100	100	100	100	100	100
48	108	34	373	37	43

Table 3.3   continued

Class	Occupational subgroup	(41) Wilden-tierbach (1929–30)	(42) Winter-lingen (1928–30)
LOWER	1. Agricultural workers	29.0	0
CLASS	2. Unskilled workers	9.7	25.0
	3. Skilled (craft) workers	25.8	43.7
	4. Other skilled workers	0	0
	5. Domestic workers	0	0
Subtotal		64.5	68.7
Lower-	6. Master craftsmen	0	9.4
&	7. Non-academic professionals	0	0
middle-	8. White-collar employees	0	3.1
MIDDLE	9. Lower civil servants	0	0
CLASS	10. Merchants	0	9.4
	11. Farmers	35.5	3.1
Subtotal		35.5	25.0
Upper-	12. Managers	0	3.1
MIDDLE	13. Higher civil servants	0	0
CLASS &	14. University students	0	0
UPPER	15. Academic professionals	0	0
CLASS	16. Entrepreneurs	0	0
Subtotal		0	3.1
STATUS	17. Non-university students	0	0
UNCLEAR	18. Pensioners/retired	0	0
	19. Wives/widows	0	0
	20. Military personnel	0	0
	21. Illegible/no data	0	3.1
Subtotal		0	3.1
TOTAL (%)		100	100
Frequency (*N*)		31	32

Table 3.3   continued

(43) Zuffenhausen	(44) Gau	(45) WÜRTTEMBERG-HOHENZOLLERN	(46)	(47)
(1928-30)	(1928)	(1929)	(1930)	(1928-30)
0	0.7	1.1	2.8	2.1
5.0	12.8	11.3	9.2	10.2
40.0	28.0	31.4	27.0	28.2
0	1.7	1.6	1.2	1.4
0	0.7	0.9	0.5	0.6
45.0	43.9	46.3	40.7	42.5
5.0	3.4	2.8	4.8	4.1
2.5	5.3	3.8	3.8	4.0
12.5	10.3	8.9	7.4	8.1
2.5	6.2	6.3	4.3	5.1
22.5	21.6	17.6	20.3	19.8
0	0.9	3.7	6.8	5.3
45.0	47.7	43.1	47.4	46.4
0	0.7	0.4	1.4	1.0
0	0	0.4	0.1	0.2
0	0.6	1.3	2.4	1.9
5.0	0.6	1.2	1.9	1.6
2.5	0.7	0.7	0.8	0.8
7.5	2.6	4.0	6.6	5.5
0	1.5	1.3	1.0	1.1
0	0.4	0.4	0.5	0.5
0	0.6	1.2	1.0	1.0
0	0.2	0.1	0.03	0.1
2.5	3.0	3.5	2.6	2.9
2.5	5.7	6.5	5.1	5.6
100	100	100	100	100
40	532	1,038	2,547	4,117

in the low level of support recorded in the branches of Altensteig, Gaildorf, Kirchheim Teck and Nagold (see Table 3.3, columns 2, 13, 18 and 24), while in the rural Mühlacker branch (see Table 3.3, column 23) farmers do not figure at all. Even in those branches in which farmers were relatively heavily represented, as in Blaufelden, Kupferzell, Lampoldshausen, Weikersheim and Wildentierbach (see Table 3.3, columns 6, 19, 20, 40 and 41), and to a lesser extent Bondorf and Stammheim (see Table 3.3, columns 7 and 33), it is unlikely that many of them were 'farmers' as such. Judging from the age-groups from which the Nazi Party recruited these 'farmers', the bulk were in reality sons of farmers anticipating their inheritance! This is borne out, for example, by the age-profile of 'farmers' in the Wildentierbach branch, in which 54.5 per cent of those listed as 'farmers' were aged 20 or under, while 81.8 per cent were aged 30 or under. In the branches at Blaufelden and Kupferzell all the 'farmers' listed were aged 30 or under. Few 'genuine' independent farmers were recruited by the Nazi Party in Württemberg-Hohenzollern before 1930 (see Table 3.3, columns 44–7). Of the 217 'farmers' who entered the party by September 1930, 80.2 per cent joined in the course of 1930, the main influx taking place in the run-up to the *Reichstag* election. The comparatively early penetration of the NSDAP into the (Protestant) farming community in other regions of Germany is not mirrored in Württemberg-Hohenzollern.[56]

Another case of misrepresentation involves the 'merchant' subgroup, an important one in virtually all the branches listed in Table 3.3, and particularly so in the case of Göppingen, Schorndorf and Stuttgart (see Table 3.3, columns 15, 31 and 34). Here again one is dealing with a case of wishful thinking on the part of many commercial employees describing themselves as 'merchants'. The age-profile of the merchant subgroup (the majority of the individuals listed under the category were aged 30 or under) leads one to suspect that perhaps only a quarter of all those listed as 'merchants' were of independent status. The great majority of 'merchants' should be placed in the white-collar employees subgroup, the percentage of which is not very high in the bulk of the branches listed in Table 3.3. The distortion of the merchant and white-collar employees occupational subgroups is clearly linked, and in this instance the proportions of these two groups within the party in *Gau* Württemberg-Hohenzollern before September 1930 as given in the *Partei-Statistik* is probably a more accurate guide (see Table 3.5, column 1). Combined, these two subgroups formed the core of the middle-class representation in the NSDAP in Württemberg-Hohenzollern, and in the case of Mühlacker, Pfullingen, Schorndorf and Stuttgart accounted for between 41 and 46.5 per cent of the branch membership (see Table 3.3, columns 23, 28, 31 and 34). The 'bourgeois' nature of the Stuttgart branch, by far the largest in the *Gau*, was a feature from the time of its formation back in May 1920, its first dozen supporters giving it a strong middle-class profile, with 'merchants' alone accounting for a third of the membership.[57] It appears that the branch did not lose its middle-class nature following the re-formation of the NSDAP in Stuttgart in the spring of 1925. Goebbels' impression of the Stuttgart branch following a speech he gave there early in 1926 led him to declare that 'at present little can be achieved in Württemberg since the whole movement is bourgeois (*bürgerlich*)'.[58]

The upper-middle class and upper class as a rule did not figure prominently among the membership of *Gau* Württemberg-Hohenzollern before September 1930, though in the branches at Biberach, Mühlacker, Neuenbürg and Rottweil (see Table 3.3, columns 5, 23, 25 and 30) these elements did provide over 10 per cent of the members, while in Tübingen the relatively large number of university students who joined the branch pushed the figure to an astronomically high atypical 34.2 per cent (see Table 3.3, column 36). Upper-middle-class and upper-class types generally kept clear of the Nazi Party in Württemberg-Hohenzollern in 1928, showed limited interest in 1929, and joined in some numbers in the course of 1930, with university students expressing the strongest interest. Of the 226 individuals drawn from this stratum by September 1930, 75.2 per cent entered the party in 1930.

The main strength of the Nazi Party in *Gau* Württemberg-Hohenzollern throughout the period 1928 to 1930 lay in the urban centres of the region, with a noticeable over-representation from the small town (*Kleinstadt*) and medium-sized town sectors (for the following see Table 3.4). The data shows the inability of the Nazis to penetrate effectively into rural communities with a population of 2,000 and under, with the proportion of Nazi members recruited in such communities well below that of the total population living in such areas in Württemberg-Hohenzollern. However, the data also reveals that it was in the rural communities that the Nazi Party achieved a high degree of lower-class mobilization. Although only 28.9 per cent of the total members entering the Nazi Party in Württemberg-Hohenzollern lived in rural communities, 34.4 per cent of its lower-class support came from them, while villages and rural towns (*Landstädte*) with populations below the 5,000 mark provided the party with 49.5 per cent of its total lower-class membership. If one adds small towns (*Kleinstädte*) as well, the figure rises to 75.6 per cent. In Württemberg-Hohenzollern the Nazis found it difficult to attract lower-class members in large towns and in the city of Stuttgart where they found it much easier to mobilize middle- and upper-class support. The relative inability of the Nazi Party to make much headway in attracting lower-class recruits in the larger urban centres is undoubtedly related to the fact that the left-wing parties had a high public profile in Württemberg's major urban centres, and acted as effective blocks to a more systematic penetration into the lower class by the Nazis.[59] In the case of Stuttgart the 'bourgeois' character of the movement, commented on earlier, may have deterred workers from joining the party.[60] Workers living in a small-town or rural environment, where they were less likely to be mobilized by the left, were more open to appeals from other parties. The wide dispersal of small and medium-sized industrial concerns in the more industrialized counties of Württemberg resulted in a corrresponding dispersal of workers into the countryside, rather than their concentration in large units of production located in major centres of industrial activity. Moreover, many workers who found employment in large towns and cities were also often resident in villages, the commuter phenomenon manifesting itself particularly early and strongly in Württemberg.[61] It was from the lower class resident in rural, small-town environments that the Nazi Party secured the majority of its worker support.

III

The data on the 4,117 members enrolled by the Nazis in *Gau* Württemberg-Hohenzollern by the end of September 1930, marginally distorted by the inclusion of 63 members included in the Ulm branch, but resident in Bavarian Neu-Ulm and its hinterland, shows that the social make-up of the (predominantly male) membership of the NSDAP and that of Württemberg's

Table 3.4 Persons joining the NSDAP in *Gau* Württemberg-Hohenzollern (*N*: 4,054[a]) in the period 1928 to 1930 by place of residence (by %)[62]

		Community size				
Class	Occupational subgroup	Under 2,000	2,000-4,999	5,000-19,999	20,000-99,999	Over 100,000
LOWER	1. Agricultural workers	1.8	0.04	0.2	0.04	0
CLASS	2. Unskilled workers	3.3	1.6	2.4	2.0	1.0
	3. Skilled (craft) workers	9.0	4.4	7.8	4.1	2.6
	4. Other skilled workers	0.2	0.2	0.4	0.1	0.1
	5. Domestic workers	0.1	0.1	0.1	0.2	0.1
Subtotal		14.4	6.3	10.9	6.4	3.8
Lower-	6. Master craftsmen	1.4	0.6	1.2	0.5	0.3
&	7. Non-academic professionals	0.7	0.4	1.2	0.7	1.0
middle-	8. White-collar employees	1.4	0.7	2.4	2.0	1.8
MIDDLE	9. Lower civil servants	1.5	0.8	1.1	0.9	0.7
CLASS	10. Merchants	3.0	2.5	4.5	3.6	6.1
	11. Farmers	4.4	0.5	0.3	0.02	0.1
Subtotal		12.4	5.5	10.7	7.7	10.0
Upper-	12. Managers	0.3	0.07	0.3	0.2	0.3
MIDDLE	13. Higher civil servants	0.1	0	0.02	0.02	0.04
CLASS &	14. University students	0.3	0.1	0.3	0.8	0.4
UPPER	15. Academic professionals	0.3	0.2	0.4	0.1	0.5
CLASS	16. Entrepreneurs	0.2	0.1	0.2	0.07	0.1
Subtotal		1.2	0.5	1.2	1.2	1.3
STATUS	17. Non-university students	0.02	0.2	0.3	0.3	0.3
UNCLEAR	18. Pensioners/retired	0.04	0.04	0.1	0.04	0.2
	19. Wives/widows	0.1	0.07	0.2	0.4	0.2
	20. Military personnel	0	0	0.02	0.02	0.02
	21. Illegible/no data	0.7	0.3	0.8	0.5	0.5
Subtotal		0.9	0.6	1.4	1.3	1.2
TOTAL (%)		28.9	12.9	24.2	16.6	16.3
Württemberg (*N*: 2,580,235)		46.8	13.4	16.2	10.3	13.2
Hohenzollern (*N*: 71,480)		82.6	2.9	14.5	—	—
Germany (*N*: 62,410,619)		36.0	10.6	13.0	13.6	26.8

Note: a Excludes members resident in Bavaria recruited by *Ortsgruppe* Ulm.

male working population was not that dissimilar (see Table 3.5, columns 2–6). Within the Nazi membership the lower class was only marginally under-represented, and the lower- and middle-middle class slightly over-represented, in comparison with their respective share in the male working population. As far as specific occupational groups are concerned, farmers were clearly under-represented in the party, while the self-employed figure more prominently among the Nazi membership, primarily the consequence, as suggested earlier, of too many commercial employees assigning themselves to the (independent) merchant category. That this was undoubtedly what happened seems to be confirmed if one compares the self-employed and white-collar employees percentages in the *Partei-Statistik* with the values calculated from the *Neuaufnahmen* material (see Table 3.5, columns 1 and 5).

In contrast to the broad similarity of the social characteristics of Nazi members who joined the party between March 1928 and September 1930 and of Württemberg's male working population, are the striking differences between the *Neuaufnahmen* and *Partei-Statistik* data. Especially noticeable is the large discrepancy between the percentage values of the workers category in the two sets of data. It is unlikely that the Nazis would have understated the number of workers supporting their cause in the *Gau* when they collated the census returns on the party's membership in 1934. The conclusion one is led to is that the Nazi Party did mobilize considerable lower-class support by 1930, but found it much more difficult to retain it over time, giving rise to a significant understatement in the *Partei-Statistik* of the worker element active in the party. The implications of this understatement for the 'middle-class theory' of Nazism are profound, not only in the Württemberg case, but for the party as whole. The *Volkspartei* image which comes through so strongly in the *Neuaufnahmen* data is diluted in the *Partei-Statistik*. In *Gau* Württemberg-Hohenzollern the Nazi Party was clearly even more of a *Volkspartei* from 1928 to 1930 than the Nazis claimed on the basis of their own data.

Table 3.5 The membership of the Nazi Party in *Gau* Württemberg-Hohenzollern by operationally (horizontally) classified occupation (by %)[63]

	(1) Partei- Statistik Gau *members* *as on* *14.9.30*	(2) *1928*	(3) *Newly enrolled members*[a] *1929*	(4) *1930*	(5) *1928-30*	(6) *Male* *working* *population* *of* *Württemberg* *(1925)*
Workers	29.2	43.9[b]	46.3[b]	40.7[b]	42.5[b]	45.3
Domestic workers		0.7[c]	0.9[c]	0.5[c]	0.6[c]	0.02
White-collar employees	30.0	16.3[d]	13.1[d]	12.6[d]	13.1[d]	15.8
Civil servants	9.8	6.4[e]	6.8[e]	4.4[e]	5.4[e]	
Self-employed	19.0	26.3[f]	22.3[f]	27.8[f]	26.3[f]	12.7
Farmers	4.3	0.9[g]	3.7[g]	6.8[g]	5.3[g]	16.2
Working family members	—	—	—	—	—	9.9
Others	7.7	6.1[h]	7.7[h]	7.5[h]	7.4[h]	——
TOTAL	100	100	100	100	100	100
Frequency (N)	2,751	532	1,038	2,547	4,117	870,629

Notes: a Includes 63 members of the Ulm *Ortsgruppe* who were resident in Bavaria.
    b Subgroups 1-4 listed in Table 3.3.
    c Subgroup 5 listed in Table 3.3.
    d Subgroups 7-8 and 12 listed in Table 3.3.
    e Subgroups 9, 13 and 20 listed in Table 3.3.
    f Subgroups 6, 10 and 15-16 listed in Table 3.3.
    g Subgroup 11 listed in Table 3.3.
    h Subgroups 14, 17-19 and 21 listed in Table 3.3.

4

GAU
HESSE-NASSAU-SOUTH
1929–1931

The general history of the Nazi Party in Hesse, both at the regional[1] and at the local[2] level, has received considerable attention by historians and social scientists since the 1970s. Specialist studies have also appeared dealing with the nature of the electoral support mobilized by the Nazis in the region.[3] Not only are the broad contours of the Nazi Party's organizational development in Hesse now well-established, but much detail on the variable development pattern of the party at the local level is also available, providing often penetrating analyses at the micro level. One aspect of the development of the Nazi Party in Hesse which has generally been neglected until of late, is the evaluation of the social types drawn to actively support the party in its *Kampfzeit* phase.[4] This omission is astonishing in view of the sizeable holdings available in the Hessian archives on the rank and file membership and leadership of the NSDAP, as well as the extensive but more fragmentary material on the SA and the SS.[5] A section of the material available on the Hessian NSDAP is analysed here, namely the *Neuaufnahmen* submitted at frequent intervals by the *Gauleitung* to Munich, which recorded those individuals recruited by the Nazis in *Gau* Hesse-Nassau-South in the period 11 September 1929 to the end of 1930.[6] The same source is also used to establish the subsequent pattern of recruitment for 1931 at three-monthly intervals (based on the *Neuaufnahmen* for March, June, September and December). As in the case of *Gau* Württemberg evaluated in the previous chapter, the data covers a critical time-span in the fortunes of the Nazi Party, the phase which witnessed its transition from comparative obscurity to breakthrough and success in mobilizing mass-support, both in membership and in electoral terms.

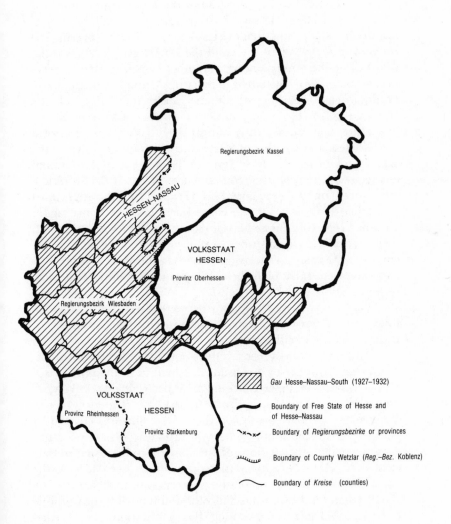

Map 6 The political and administrative areas of Hesse.

I

Gau Hesse-Nassau-South emerged as a distinct organizational entity in April 1925. The division of the Hesse region into two *Gaue*, that of Hesse-Nassau-North (covering the bulk of *Regierungsbezirk* Kassel) and that of Hesse-Nassau-South (covering the *Regierungsbezirk* Wiesbaden and the *Volksstaat* Hesse), was the result of deliberations among a number of Nazi district leaders rather than any initiative emanating from Munich party headquarters.[7] The extent of the operational zone of the *Gauleitung* of Hesse-Nassau-South (which was centred on Frankfurt) was significantly curtailed with the formation of a further Hessian *Gau*, that of Hesse-Darmstadt (which covered the area constituting the Free State of Hesse), an organizational change which was the consequence of a Hitler directive announced on 25 February 1927. From February 1927 until December 1932, when *Gau* Hesse-Darmstadt was once again absorbed into *Gau* Hesse-Nassau-South, the latter was made up of the counties constituting *Regierungsbezirk* Wiesbaden, the county of Wetzlar (an enclave which was administratively part of *Regierungsbezirk* Koblenz belonging to the Rheinprovinz until its integration into *Regierungsbezirk* Wiesbaden on 1 October 1932), and a part of *Regierungsbezirk* Kassel, comprising the town and county of Hanau, along with the counties of Gelnhausen and Schlüchtern (see Map 6).

According to the census returns of 1925, Protestants outnumbered Catholics by a considerable margin in the province of Hesse-Nassau (68.1 per cent and 28.1 per cent respectively), a dominance not so strongly reflected in *Regierungsbezirk* Wiesbaden – which constituted the bulk of the area covered by *Gau* Hesse-Nassau-South – where the ratio was 57 to 38 per cent.[8] As in so many other regions of Germany, a confessional mosaic existed in Hesse-Nassau at the county level (see Map 7), the consequence of the fusion of diverse territorial units acquired by the Prussian State over time. Thus the dominance of the Catholic faith (at 87.3 per cent) among the population of the Rheingaukreis can be traced back to it having been part of the Archbishopric of Mainz, while the strong Catholic presence (78.3 per cent) in the counties of Westerburg and Limburg, and in the Unterwesterwaldkreis, was the result of their former connection with the Archbishopric of Trier. With these exceptions, and that

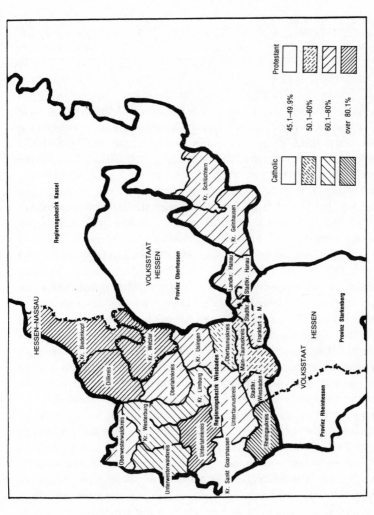

Map 7 The confessional structure of the counties (*Kreise*) comprising *Gau Hesse-Nassau-South* in 1925.
Source: Adapted from Alfred Milatz, *Wähler und Wahlen in der Weimarer Republik* (Bonn, 1965), Appendix, Map 2.

Table 4.1 The occupational breakdown of the working population of Province Hesse-Nassau in 1925 (by %)[9]

	Agriculture & forestry	Industry & crafts	Trade & transport	Other
Reg.-Bez. Wiesbaden	23.4	40.4	21.8	14.4
Province Hesse-Nassau	31.0	38.5	17.8	12.6
Germany	30.5	41.4	16.5	11.6

of the Obertaunuskreis (where Catholics – at 53 per cent – were in a slight majority) and county St Goarshausen (where the Protestant and Catholic faith was almost on par, at 49.6 and 49.1 per cent respectively), the counties contained within *Gau* Hesse-Nassau-South were, at 60 per cent or more, predominantly Protestant. The strongest concentration of Protestants (at 90 per cent of the population and over) was in the Unterlahnkreis, Dillkreis and Biedenkopf, and in the Rheinprovinz enclave of county Wetzlar (93.7 per cent[10]).

As far as the socio-economic structure of *Regierungsbezirk* Wiesbaden is concerned (see Table 4.1), it was predominantly industrial, with agriculture playing a subordinate role to industry and crafts in virtually all of its counties (see Map 8). By the time of the 1925 census 23.4 per cent of the working population was still engaged in agriculture and forestry, which was of special importance in county Westerburg (forestry was especially significant in this part of the Westerwald), and slightly less so in the counties of Usingen and Schlüchtern.the hill areas of the Taunus and the Westerwald, which were heavily wooded, forestry rather than agriculture played a more important role in the economic activity of these regions, with numerous saw and paper mills feeding the wood and paper industry of these parts of *Regierungsbezirk* Wiesbaden. In the Rhine and Main valleys, and in the Rheingaukreis in particular, there were extensive vineyards and orchards, giving rise to numerous concerns involved in the manufacture of liquors and spirits. The bulk of the farms (86.5 per cent) in Hesse-Nassau were worked by their owners, the rest rented. Small-scale family concerns predominated in the province, with the majority of the farms (68.3 per cent) under 20 hectares in size, with large farms of between 20 and

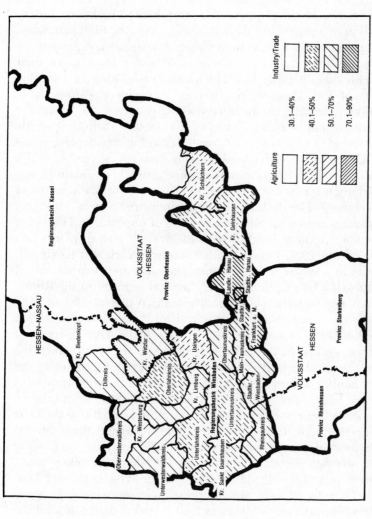

Map 8 The economic structure of the counties (*Kreise*) comprising *Gau* Hesse-Nassau-South according to the census of 1925. *Source:* Adapted from Milatz, *Wähler und Wahlen*, Appendix, Map 3.

100 hectares accounting for 31.3 per cent, and estates of over 100 hectares for a mere 3.3 per cent.[11]

It was industry and crafts which dominated the region comprised by *Gau* Hesse-Nassau-South, centred on a major industrial area stretching along the Rhine-Main valleys from Wiesbaden to the Frankfurt-Hanau region. The heavy concentration of industry in this area is reflected in the high percentage of the population of *Regierungsbezirk* Wiesbaden dependent on industry and crafts, as well as trade and transport, for their livelihood (see Table 4.1). The towns in the industrial conurbation of the Rhein-Main attracted a considerable number of workers resident in the surrounding counties, the commuter phenomenon – dating back to the 1890s – being especially prominent in the Frankfurt area.[12] Beyond its significance as one of Germany's premier banking and commercial centres, and a focal point of the communications network, Frankfurt[13] was important for its metallurgical industry and the manufacture of machinery. The clothing and paper industries were of some size, and food-processing and brewing also of importance. Following the absorption of Höchst (with its large IG-Farben plant) into the city in 1926, Frankfurt also markedly increased its significance as a centre of the German chemical and pharmaceutical industries. Other centres of the chemical industry in the Rhine-Main region were at Wiesbaden-Biebrich and at Hanau. The latter town was also the seat of a sizeable jewellery industry, as well as being of some importance as a manufacturing centre of leather goods. In the Lahn-Dill valleys, a region in which the metallurgical industry had been of significance for centuries, the availability of iron-ore and chalk had led to the development of some heavy industry centred on Wetzlar, a town closely associated with the German optical industry, the seat of the Leitz concern.[14] An important employer in many parts of the Westerwald area was the quarry and china-clay industry, while the wood-processing industry, in the shape of many small concerns, was widely scattered around the Westerwald and Taunus. Worthy of note also in providing employment in some areas, were the many spas and health resorts dotted around the region (such as Wiesbaden, Bad Schwalbach, Bad Homburg, Bad Ems, Bad Soden), which exploited the numerous natural springs which abounded in the Taunus and Lahn areas.[15]

The concentration of economic activity along the Rhine-Main

area stretching from Wiesbaden to Frankfurt strongly influenced the pattern of the population distribution in *Regierungsbezirk* Wiesbaden. The striking feature of the spatial distribution of the population in the area covered by *Gau* Hesse-Nassau-South during the Weimar period is the high percentage of the population living in the cities, the relative absence of medium-sized and small towns, and the large percentage of people living in small rural communities (see Table 4.4). In 1925 some 43.7 per cent of the population lived in the cities of Frankfurt and Wiesbaden. By 1933 some 38.7 per cent of the total population of *Regierungsbezirk* Wiesbaden lived in Frankfurt alone, a reflection not only of the economic power centred on the city, which had been attracting manpower from the agrarian regions surrounding it since the nineteenth century, but also a consequence of its successful policy of annexing surrounding towns (such as the absorption of Höchst in 1926) and villages, the chief reason for its population increase from 467,520 in 1925 to 555,857 by 1933. If one adds Wiesbaden (which also increased its size through annexation, such as the town of Biebrich in the mid-1920s), the percentage share of the population living in cities with a population of over 100,000 rises to 49.8 per cent by 1933.[16] It was inevitable that in *Regierungsbezirk* Wiesbaden the fortunes of any party were critically influenced by its performance in the cities of Frankfurt and Wiesbaden.

II

Little is known in any detail about the formative years of the development of the Nazi Party in what was later to become *Gau* Hesse-Nassau-South beyond the sketchy outline provided by Schön.[17] His account centres primarily on the emergence of Frankfurt as a 'rallying centre in Hesse for *völkisch*-nationalist groups' in the early 1920s, the specific Nazi component being submerged in the confused history of the *völkisch* movement in Hesse between 1922 and 1925. It was not until the Spring of 1925 that the NSDAP was to emerge as a distinct movement, with the formation of a small branch of 20 to 30 members in Frankfurt, and a number of even smaller branches, with usually a dozen or so members, in Wiesbaden ('officially' founded only on 30 March 1926), Bad Homburg, Dillenburg and Herborn. With the formation of *Gau* Hesse-Nassau-South in April 1925 the beginning of an organizational framework linking the newly emerging Nazi branches was established, though it was not before 1928 that significant progress was made in the development of an effective *Gau* party apparatus.[18] Although nothing is known of the exact strength of the membership of *Gau* Hesse-Nassau-South during the 1925 to 1928 period, and little about the development of branches in the region during these years, such evidence as has emerged to date suggests that in most parts of the *Gau* this was a time of very limited progress for the NSDAP. As in other regions of Germany, the combination of a lack of finance, of inadequate leadership material, and of numerous squabbles within the party, as well as conflicts between the party and its most important specialist organization the SA, when allied to the comparatively more stable economic and political situation after 1925, combined to limit the electoral appeal and membership strength of the Nazi movement.[19] By the spring of 1928 the three Hesse *Gaue* combined had only about 50 branches, the majority of which were in dire financial straits and unable to mount any effective propaganda activity.[20]

Despite the generally limited progress made by the Nazis in *Gau* Hesse-Nassau-South after 1925, the party had nevertheless established a number of centres of hyper-activity by 1928. The admittedly limited advances made by the party were registered in the *Reichstag* election of May 1928, in which the Nazis secured one of their better results in Hesse-Nassau, polling 3.6 per cent of the vote as against the national average of 2.6 per cent.[21] The NSDAP's 3.1 per cent share of the poll in *Regierungsbezirk* Wiesbaden was slightly lower than that achieved in Hesse-Nassau as a whole, but notable successes were secured in the rural county of St Goarshausen (11.2 per cent) and in the Dillkreis (6.0 per cent), as well as in the urban centres of Wiesbaden (8.7 per cent) and Frankfurt (4.4 per cent). In the small town of Braubach (county St Goarshausen) the NSDAP polled 27.6 per cent, while in Nassau (Unterlahnkreis) it achieved 18.7 per cent.[22] In a number of villages in which the NSDAP was to organize comparatively strong membership support in 1929 and 1930, such as Nastätten (county St Goarshausen), and Eibelshausen and Langenaubach near Dillenburg (Dillkreis), the party was already the strongest electoral force by May 1928.[23] However, the often high percentages secured by the NSDAP in a number of small towns and villages in *Regierungsbezirk* Wiesbaden should not deflect attention from the fact that the electoral return of the party in Frankfurt alone represented 46.6 per cent of the total vote cast for Nazism in *Regierungsbezirk* Wiesbaden, while the share of the big-city vote rises to 71.8 per cent when Wiesbaden is also added. A very similar pattern unfolded in the *Reichstag* election of September 1930, when the NSDAP acquired 61.7 per cent of its vote in *Regierungsbezirk* Wiesbaden in the two cities of Wiesbaden (17.4 per cent) and Frankfurt (44.3 per cent), and 64.4 per cent of its total vote in the urban areas of the region.[24]

The dominant role played by Frankfurt in the electoral fortunes of the Nazi Party in *Gau* Hesse-Nassau-South is also a characteristic of the recruitment pattern of the party in the region in the early 1930s. Of the 4,428 individuals who joined the Nazi Party in *Gau* Hesse-Nassau-South between 11 September 1929 (when the *Neuaufnahmen* commence) and 14 September 1930 (the day of the *Reichstag* election), 38.8 per cent were recruited in Frankfurt (this figure does not include those recruited by the Höchst branch), and of the 10,623 members analysed in Table 4.3, 39.3 per cent were resident in the city (including those recruited by the Höchst branch). The percentage figure of new city members rises to 54.4 per cent if one adds the 1,607 members who were recruited into the Nazi Party in Wiesbaden between September 1929 and December 1931. Both in electoral and membership terms, Nazism in *Gau* Hesse-Nassau-South was very much a big-city phenomenon in the period under review.

The survival of the complete *Neuaufnahmen* for *Gau* Hesse-Nassau-South from September 1929 onwards allows one to reconstruct the recruitment pattern of the party in considerable detail and to provide some insight into the geographic spread of its branches from late 1929 to the end of 1931 (see Map 9). The existence of the 33 branches noted as recruiting in the last quarter of 1929 cannot be taken as representing the sum total of branches in existence in the *Gau* at that time,[25] but does probably involve the great majority of them.[26] It was in 1930 that most of the branches grew rapidly at a time when new branches emerged in some number, so that a network of at least 170 branches is suggested by those recorded as enrolling new members during the year. Judging from the recruitment pattern of new branches which appear in the *Neuaufnahmen* in the course of 1930, the vast majority were centred on village or small-town communites, most being small affairs until the significant boost given to

93

Table 4.2 The recruitment pattern of the membership of *Gau* Hesse-Nassau-South, September 1929 to the end of 1930/1

	1929			1930			1931	
	I^a	II^b	III^c	I	II	III	I	II
January	—	—	—	348	5.9	5.2		
February	—	—	—	408	7.0	6.1		
March	—	—	—	351	6.0	5.2	440	11.2
April	—	—	—	253	4.3	3.8		
May	—	—	—	337	5.7	5.0		
June	—	—	—	238	4.1	3.6	273	6.9
July	—	—	—	692	11.8	10.3		
August	—	—	—	718	12.3	10.7		
September	235^d	28.3	3.5	305	5.2	4.6	401	10.2
October	266	32.0	4.0	1,389	23.7	20.8		
November	203	24.4	3.0	381	6.5	5.7		
December	126	15.2	1.9	435	7.4	6.5	2,824	71.7
TOTAL	830	99.9	12.4	5,855	99.9	87.5	3,938	100

Notes: a Number of recruits per month.
     b Number of recruits per month expressed as percentage for the year.
     c Number of recruits per month expressed as percentage for the period 1929–30.
     d Probably only partial figure for the month.

Nazism in the region by the feverish activism of the party in the run-up to the September election,[27] reflected in a major surge in membership recruitment in July and August and in the weeks immediately after the *Reichstag* election. The distribution of the branches within *Gau* Hesse-Nassau-South was somewhat uneven by the end of 1930, with cluster formations in some counties, the product primarily of the propaganda activity of older established branches in their surrounding hinterland. In a number of counties the Nazi Party was still virtually invisible as an organized entity, as in the predominantly Catholic Unterwesterwaldkreis, in the southern half of the Catholic county Westerburg and the northern parts of the predominantly Catholic Rheingaukreis. The religious factor probably played a role in limiting the response to Nazism in these areas, though it should be noted that there were also some strongly Protestant regions in which the party struggled to establish a branch network, such as in the north-eastern parts of the Dillkreis, the eastern half of county Biedenkopf, and much of county Usingen,

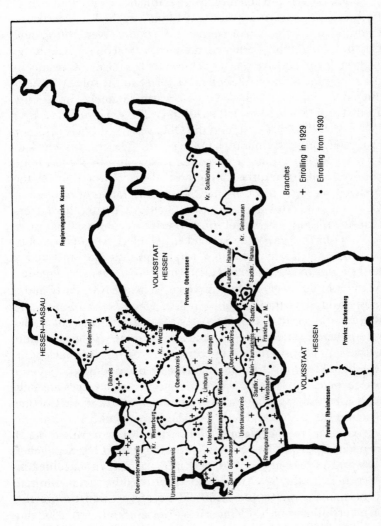

Map 9 The distribution of Nazi Party branches recruiting in *Gau* Hesse-Nassau-South, September 1929 to December 1930.

where the branch established at Rod an der Weil was the sole growth point until the spring of 1930. Moreover, the response of the more solidly Catholic areas of *Gau* Hesse-Nassau-South to Nazism was not uniformly negative, as witnessed by the number of comparatively sizeable branches established in predominantly Catholic counties, such as those at Eltville in the Rheingaukreis, Gemünden in the northern part of county Westerburg, and Camberg, Limburg and Niederselters in county Limburg. Although the NSDAP was to achieve its best electoral results in the *Reichstag* election of September 1930[28] in the solidly Protestant areas of *Gau* Hesse-Nassau-South, namely in county Biedenkopf (28.3 per cent), the Dillkreis (27.8 per cent), *Stadtkreis* Wiesbaden (27.4 per cent) and the Oberwesterwaldkreis (24.3 per cent) and county Gelnhausen (13 per cent). The reasons why – in view of their similar socio-economic structure – the Catholic county Limburg returned an almost identical low poll for the NSDAP (of 10.2 per cent) as that of the adjacent Protestant Oberlahnkreis (10.1 per cent) must obviously lie in other factors than the religious beliefs of the respective electorates. That there was not – by the time of the September 1930 election – an inevitably negative correlation between Catholicism and Nazism[29] and a positive one between Protestantism and Nazism, is also suggested by the comparatively high return secured by the Nazi Party in the most strongly Catholic county in *Gau* Hesse-Nassau-South, the Rheingaukreis, in which the party secured 18.1 per cent of the vote, whereas in county Wetzlar, almost totally Protestant and with a broadly similar socio-economic structure to that of the Rheingaukreis, it could only manage 15 per cent.

vote, whereas in county Wetzlar, almost totally Protestant and with a broadly similar socio-economic structure to that of the Rheingaukreis, it could only manage 15 per cent.

According to the *Neuaufnahmen* the Nazis recruited 4,428 members in *Gau* Hesse-Nassau-South between 11 September 1929 and 14 September 1930, over a quarter of whom joined in the run-up to the *Reichstag* election initiated by the dissolution of parliament on 16 July 1930. There are no statistics on the membership strength of *Gau* Hesse-Nassau-South by 1930, and the only available data there is, the information provided by the *Partei-Statistik,* does not permit any precise conclusions to be reached on the question.[30] In all probability the 4,428 members enrolled in *Gau* Hesse-Nassau-South between 11 September 1929 and 14 September 1930 involve a large percentage of the total number mobilized in the *Gau* since the re-emergence of the Nazi Party as a distinct organized force in the spring of 1925 and as such represents an acceptable guide to the sociology of the party in the region before September 1930. The 2,205 members who joined the NSDAP in the aftermath of the Nazi electoral breakthrough, involves what the established Nazis disparagingly labelled *Septemberlinge*, whose social background can also be identified. An insight into the membership attracted in the course of 1931 (based on a sample taken at three monthly intervals) is provided by the 3,938 members who joined by the end of 1931. The 10,623 members analysed in Table 4.3 represent a high proportion of those who had joined the Nazi Party in the *Gau* by the end of 1931.[31] The data involves by far the largest number of Nazis concentrated in one locality over a relatively short time-span identified to date, a unique source-base which allows a comparatively comprehensive evaluation of the social base of Nazism at both the regional and local level.

III

Virtually nothing is known about the sociology of the Nazi Party in its formative development phase in *Provinz* Hesse-Nassau and in *Land* Hesse in the early 1920s. In a list of members who had joined the NSDAP by August 1921 there are, among the very few members recorded as resident outside of Bavaria, entries for a bank employee and an architect living in Darmstadt, and a bank employee in Wiesbaden, who had all joined the party in 1921.[32] Listed in the most sizeable NSDAP membership fragment to survive from the pre-1923 period, in which 4,786 individuals who had joined the party between 25 September and 9 November 1923 are recorded, are 134 recruits resident in Hesse, of whom 27.5 per cent were from the lower class, 58 per cent from the lower- and middle-middle class, 7.3 per cent from the upper-middle class and upper class, with an additional 6.6 per cent made up by those whose occupational and social status is unclear.[33] Except for a small number of members recorded as living in Kassel (seven recruits) and Frankfurt am Main (nine recruits), who were enrolled in branches operating (illegally) in these cities, all others were entered as members of the Munich branch of the NSDAP. In two counties the recruitment pattern of the Nazi

97

Party suggests that these were areas of significant Nazi activity by late 1923.[34] The occupational background of the recruits enrolled in the Dillkreis shows that the lower class provided two-thirds of the 20 new recruits living in Dillenburg, Eibelshausen, Frohnhausen, Haiger, Hirzenhain, Oberscheld, and Straßebersbach. In county Friedberg, however, the social background of the 18 new members recruited in Bad Nauheim, Butzbach, Feuerbach and Friedberg, was very mixed. By far the largest concentration of new members recorded in the membership list, however, were resident in Bad Homburg (with 21 new recruits) and Marburg (with 19 new recruits), towns in which it would seem that the Nazis were particularly successful in mobilizing membership support, the majority of which, at 66.7 and 57.9 per cent respectively, coming from the middle class.

Except for a membership list of the Bad Nauheim branch submitted by *Ortsgruppenleiter* Ernstberger to Hitler at the beginning of March 1925,[35] nothing as yet has been unearthed to throw light on the social configuration of the NSDAP in Hesse in the years immediately following its re-formation in 1925. On the branches which developed in *Gau* Hesse-Nassau-South we know virtually nothing beyond the limited evidence advanced by Ulrich Mayer on Wetzlar and by Dieter Rebentisch on Frankfurt. Mayer used oral evidence in his attempt to reconstruct the social profile of the membership of the Wetzlar branch, which he characterises as 'bourgeois' before 1929, composed predominantly of young and unemployed elements, with sons of merchants and commercial employees forming the 'strongest group' within its ranks, while 'only few workers belonged to the party'. Mayer suggests that it was only from 1931 onwards that the Wetzlar branch began to recruit from all social classes, including unemployed workers.[36] Rebentisch does not attempt to define the broad social contours of the Frankfurt Nazi Party in the mid- and late 1920s, but points towards its difficulty in recruiting workers, emphasizes the early drift towards it by students (initially in Frankfurt-Bockenheim), and underlines the significant role played by civil servants in the local party cadre.[37]

The data provided by the *Neuaufnahmen*, seemingly complete from 11 September 1929 onwards, permits the detailed reconstruction of the social types attracted to Nazism in *Gau* Hesse-Nassau-South at the regional and local level given in Table 4.3, in which are listed all those branches which recruited 25 or more members by the end of 1931. One striking feature of the new recruits enrolled by the party is the remarkable consistency of the percentage share secured every year by each of the class groupings, which show only minimal fluctuations. Similar consistency is also in evidence when one looks at the recruitment pattern of the individual occupational subgroups over time (see Table 4.3, columns 61 to 66). The occupational and social types who entered the party before the electoral breakthrough of September 1930 are indistinguishable from the *Septemberlinge* joining the party in the post-election period. What the electoral success effected was a short-term massive increase in the rate of entry in October 1930 (the monthly recruitment fell dramatically by November 1930), rather than a surge of members drawn from any particular class. Another noticeable feature of the recruitment pattern of the Nazi Party in the *Gau* was the high percentage of new members mobilized in the two cities in the region. In Frankfurt alone (including Höchst, which became administratively part of the city in 1928, but continued to organize its own 'branch'), the Nazis recruited 39.5 per cent of the membership on which the present analysis is based. If one adds Wiesbaden, the percentage share of 'big city Nazis' rises to 54.9 per cent (see Table 4.4). Given the large number of Nazis recruited in Frankfurt and Wiesbaden, the occupational and social structure of these city branches played a significant role in determining the overall social configuration of the Nazi support mobilized in *Gau* Hesse-Nassau-South.

In both cities, especially in Frankfurt (though not in the Höchst branch), the lower- and middle-middle class loomed very large among the new Nazi members (see Table 4.3, columns 16, 28 and 59). A comparison of the social background of new Nazi members in Frankfurt with that of the male working population of the city[38] underlines the inability of the party to make a major impact on the lower class, despite the repeated propaganda efforts made by the Nazis in the working-class districts of the city and the anti-capitalist slant of the local Nazi press in the late 1920s.[39] The resistance to Nazism by the well-entrenched and strongly organized working-class parties in the city was one of the major factors limiting the recruitment potential within the Frankfurt working class.[40] It was only in Höchst, whose economy was dominated by the giant IG-Farben concern, that the lower class was strongly represented among the new Nazi members, blue-collar workers forming the absolute majority among those

Table 4.3 The social and occupational structure of the membership of the NSDAP in various branches in *Gau* Hesse-Nassau-South, 1929–31 (by %)

Class	Occupational subgroup	(1) Ailertchen (1930–1)	(2) Asslar (1930–1)
LOWER CLASS	1. Agricultural workers	0	0
	2. Unskilled workers	39.3	6.7
	3. Skilled (craft) workers	28.5	53.3
	4. Other skilled workers	0	3.3
	5. Domestic workers	0	0
Subtotal		67.8	63.3
Lower- & middle- MIDDLE CLASS	6. Master craftsmen	0	6.7
	7. Non-academic professionals	3.6	3.3
	8. White-collar employees	3.6	3.3
	9. Lower civil servants	0	3.3
	10. Merchants	7.1	10.0
	11. Farmers	3.6	0
Subtotal		17.6	26.6
Upper- MIDDLE CLASS & UPPER CLASS	12. Managers	3.6	3.3
	13. Higher civil servants	0	0
	14. University students	0	0
	15. Academic professionals	0	0
	16. Entrepreneurs	0	0
Subtotal		3.6	3.3
STATUS UNCLEAR	17. Non-university students	3.6	3.3
	18. Pensioners/retired	0	0
	19. Wives/widows	0	0
	20. Military personnel	0	0
	21. Illegible/no data	7.1	3.3
Subtotal		10.7	6.6
TOTAL (%)		100	100
Frequency (N)		28	30

Table 4.3   continued

(3) Bad Ems (1930–1)	(4) Bad Homburg (1929–31)	(5) Bad Schwalbach (1929–31)	(6) Bad Soden (1929–31)	(7) Biedenkopf (1930–1)	(8) Camberg (1929–31)
0	0	0	0	0	2.5
10.0	11.0	8.7	8.2	12.9	7.5
40.0	20.6	32.6	30.6	32.2	27.5
0	0.4	2.1	0	3.2	0
4.0	1.8	0	0	6.4	0
54.0	33.8	43.4	38.8	54.7	37.5
0	3.2	8.7	0	3.2	10.0
6.0	7.8	2.1	14.3	0	0
2.0	10.1	2.1	10.2	6.4	5.0
2.0	3.7	2.1	2.0	0	0
8.0	18.8	15.2	12.2	19.3	17.5
0	7.3	13.0	2.0	3.2	10.0
18.0	50.9	43.2	40.7	32.1	42.5
0	0.9	2.1	0	0	0
0	0	2.1	0	0	0
0	0.9	0	2.0	0	0
2.0	1.8	2.1	0	6.4	7.5
0	0.9	4.3	2.0	0	7.5
2.0	4.5	10.6	4.0	6.4	15.0
14.0	0.9	0	10.2	0	0
6.0	2.3	2.1	2.0	0	0
4.0	1.4	0	0	0	2.5
0	0	0	0	0	0
2.0	6.0	0	4.1	6.4	2.5
26.0	10.6	2.1	16.3	6.4	5.0
100	100	100	100	100	100
50	218	46	49	31	40

Table 4.3 continued

Class	Occupational subrgoup	*(9)* *Dillenburg* *(1929–31)*	*(10)* *Eibels-hausen* *(1929–31)*
LOWER	1. Agricultural workers	0	0
CLASS	2. Unskilled workers	19.8	12.5
	3. Skilled (craft) workers	20.8	56.2
	4. Other skilled workers	4.2	0
	5. Domestic workers	0	0
Subtotal		44.8	68.7
Lower-	6. Master craftsmen	3.1	3.1
&	7. Non-academic professionals	5.2	0
middle-	8. White-collar employees	13.5	6.2
MIDDLE	9. Lower civil servants	8.3	0
CLASS	10. Merchants	12.5	0
	11. Farmers	1.0	3.1
Subtotal		43.6	12.4
Upper-	12. Managers	0	0
MIDDLE	13. Higher civil servants	1.0	0
CLASS &	14. University students	0	0
UPPER	15. Academic professionals	2.1	0
CLASS	16. Entrepreneurs	0	0
Subtotal		3.1	0
STATUS	17. Non-university students	0	3.1
UNCLEAR	18. Pensioners/retired	1.0	0
	19. Wives/widows	3.1	6.2
	20. Military personnel	0	0
	21. Illegible/no data	4.2	9.4
Subtotal		8.3	18.7
TOTAL (%)		100	100
Frequency (*N*)		96	32

Table 4.3   continued

(11) Eichen (1930–1)	(12) Eiershausen (1928–30)	(13) Eltville (1929–30)	(14) Eppstein (1928–30)	(15) Erbach (1928–30)	(16) Frankfurt am Main (1929–31)
0	0	0	3.8	3.7	0.1
3.8	27.3	18.8	7.7	33.3	9.0
7.7	42.4	23.5	19.2	29.6	17.5
0	6.0	0	7.7	0	0.9
0	0	0	0	0	1.1
11.5	75.7	42.3	38.4	66.6	28.6
11.5	0	1.2	0	3.7	2.5
0	0	3.5	0	0	4.7
3.8	6.0	11.8	3.8	0	14.2
0	0	4.7	3.8	3.7	7.3
7.7	12.1	17.6	38.5	25.9	24.7
65.4	0	10.6	3.8	0	0.5
88.4	18.1	49.9	49.9	33.3	53.9
0	0	1.2	0	0	0.9
0	0	0	0	0	0.3
0	0	0	0	0	1.3
0	0	0	0	0	2.8
0	0	1.2	0	0	0.5
0	0	2.4	0	0	5.8
0	0	1.2	0	0	1.9
0	0	0	3.8	0	1.4
0	0	1.2	0	0	2.5
0	0	0	0	0	0
0	6.0	3.5	7.7	0	5.7
0	6.0	5.9	11.5	0	11.5
100	100	100	100	100	100
26	33	85	26	27	3,979

Table 4.3 continued

Class	Occupational subgroup	(17) Freiendiez (1929–31)	(18) Frickhofen (1930–1)
LOWER	1. Agricultural workers	0	0
CLASS	2. Unskilled workers	12.8	36.1
	3. Skilled (craft) workers	38.3	27.8
	4. Other skilled workers	4.2	0
	5. Domestic workers	0	0
Subtotal		55.3	63.9
Lower-	6. Master craftsmen	0	0
&	7. Non-academic professionals	0	0
middle-	8. White-collar employees	4.2	5.5
MIDDLE	9. Lower civil servants	12.8	0
CLASS	10. Merchants	12.8	22.2
	11. Farmers	4.2	2.8
Subtotal		34.0	30.5
Upper-	12. Managers	0	0
MIDDLE	13. Higher civil servants	0	0
CLASS &	14. University students	0	0
UPPER	15. Academic professionals	2.1	0
CLASS	16. Entrepreneurs	0	2.8
Subtotal		2.1	2.8
STATUS	17. Non-university students	0	2.8
UNCLEAR	18. Pensioners/retired	0	0
	19. Wives/widows	6.4	0
	20. Military personnel	0	0
	21. Illegible/no data	2.1	0
Subtotal		8.5	2.8
TOTAL (%)		100	100
Frequency (*N*)		47	36

Table 4.3 continued

(19) Gelnhausen (1930–1)	(20) Gemünden (1930–1)	(21) Groß-auheim (1930–1)	(22) Groß Diez (1930–1)	(23) Hachen-burg (1929–31)	(24) Haiger (1930–1)
0	0	0	7.8	0	0
5.0	9.7	8.2	13.0	11.1	6.1
25.0	66.1	18.4	32.2	25.9	45.4
0	0	0	0	0	0
0	0	2.0	0.9	0	0
30.0	75.8	28.6	53.9	37.0	51.5
5.0	3.2	0	0.9	18.5	0
7.5	1.6	10.2	1.7	0	9.1
25.0	3.2	12.2	4.3	11.1	6.1
10.0	0	12.2	0	0	0
10.0	8.1	20.4	11.3	14.8	24.2
2.5	4.8	2.0	13.9	3.7	3.0
60.0	20.9	57.0	32.1	48.1	42.4
0	0	6.1	0	0	0
0	0	0	0	0	0
0	0	0	0	0	0
2.5	0	2.0	2.6	3.7	0
0	0	0	0	7.4	0
2.5	0	8.1	2.6	11.1	0
0	0	2.0	0	0	0
0	3.2	0	0	0	0
0	0	2.0	3.5	0	3.0
0	0	0	0	0	0
7.5	0	2.0	7.8	3.7	3.0
7.5	3.2	6.0	11.3	3.7	6.0
100	100	100	100	100	100
62	62	49	115	27	33

Table 4.3 continued

Class	Occupational subgroup	(25) Hanau (1930–1)	(26) Hausen v.d. Höhe (1930–1)
LOWER	1. Agricultural workers	0.4	0
CLASS	2. Unskilled workers	10.2	16.7
	3. Skilled (craft) workers	18.4	23.3
	4. Other skilled workers	1.6	0
	5. Domestic workers	0.8	0
Subtotal		31.4	40.0
Lower-	6. Master craftsmen	2.0	3.3
&	7. Non-academic professionals	6.5	0
middle-	8. White-collar employees	14.3	0
MIDDLE	9. Lower civil servants	6.9	0
CLASS	10. Merchants	20.8	6.7
	11. Farmers	1.2	50.0
Subtotal		51.7	60.0
Upper-	12. Managers	1.6	0
MIDDLE	13. Higher civil servants	0.4	0
CLASS &	14. University students	1.2	0
UPPER	15. Academic professionals	2.8	0
CLASS	16. Entrepreneurs	0.4	0
Subtotal		6.4	0
STATUS	17. Non-university students	2.8	0
UNCLEAR	18. Pensioners/retired	1.6	0
	19. Wives/widows	0.8	0
	20. Military personnel	0	0
	21. Illegible/no data	4.9	0
Subtotal		10.1	0
TOTAL (%)		100	100
Frequency (*N*)		245	30

Table 4.3 continued

(27) Herborn (1930-1)	(28) Höchst (Frankfurt) (1929-31)	(29) Idstein (1930-1)	(30) Kaub (1929-31)	(31) Langenaubach (1930)	(32) Leun (1930-1)
0	1.8	0	1.5	2.9	0
10.2	16.7	2.1	16.2	29.4	3.3
46.1	29.6	20.8	25.0	41.2	40.0
0	4.2	0	1.5	0	0
0	0	0	0	0	0
56.3	52.3	22.9	44.2	73.5	43.3
2.6	1.8	0	4.4	2.9	0
2.6	4.6	0	4.4	0	0
5.1	8.3	66.7	17.6	0	16.7
5.1	2.3	0	1.5	0	0
17.9	15.3	0	2.9	11.8	23.3
0	0.9	2.1	14.7	5.9	10.0
33.3	33.2	68.8	45.5	20.6	50.0
0	0.5	0	2.9	0	0
0	0	0	0	0	0
0	1.4	0	0	0	0
0	2.8	0	1.5	0	0
2.6	0.9	0	0	0	0
2.6	5.6	0	4.4	0	0
0	0.9	8.3	0	0	0
0	4.2	0	0	0	3.3
0	0.9	0	1.5	0	0
0	0	0	0	0	0
7.7	2.8	0	4.4	5.9	3.3
7.7	8.8	8.3	5.9	5.9	6.6
100	100	100	100	100	100
39	216	48	68	34	30

Table 4.3   continued

Class	Occupational subgroup	(33) Limburg a.d. Lahn (1929–31)	(34) Marienberg (1930–1)
LOWER	1. Agricultural workers	1.7	0
CLASS	2. Unskilled workers	13.3	17.5
	3. Skilled (craft) workers	23.3	30.1
	4. Other skilled workers	1.7	1.6
	5. Domestic workers	0	0
Subtotal		40.0	49.2
Lower-	6. Master craftsmen	1.7	0
&	7. Non-academic professionals	0	7.9
middle-	8. White-collar employees	18.3	12.7
MIDDLE	9. Lower civil servants	3.3	1.6
CLASS	10. Merchants	23.3	14.3
	11. Farmers	0	1.6
Subtotal		46.6	38.1
Upper-	12. Managers	0	0
MIDDLE	13. Higher Civil servants	0	0
CLASS &	14. University students	0	1.6
UPPER	15. Academic professionals	1.7	4.7
CLASS	16. Entrepreneurs	0	0
Subtotal		1.7	6.3
STATUS	17. Non-university students	10.0	1.6
UNCLEAR	18. Pensioners/retired	0	4.7
	19. Wives/widows	0	0
	20. Military personnel	0	0
	21. Illegible/no data	1.7	0
Subtotal		11.7	6.3
TOTAL (%)		100	100
Frequency (*N*)		60	63

Table 4.3 continued

(35) Miehlen (1930-1)	(36) Mündersbach (1929-31)	(37) Nassau (1929-31)	(38) Nastätten (1929-31)	(39) Neuenhain (1930-1)	(40) Niedermörsbach (1929-31)
0	0	0	1.1	0	0
15.6	26.7	11.1	13.8	11.8	35.7
59.4	22.2	33.3	37.9	61.8	42.8
0	0	0	2.3	0	0
0	0	0	1.1	0	0
75.0	48.9	44.4	56.2	73.6	78.5
0	4.4	0	3.4	2.9	7.1
3.1	4.4	0	2.3	0	0
3.1	2.2	2.8	2.3	0	3.6
3.1	4.4	19.4	2.3	0	0
6.2	6.7	2.8	8.0	5.9	3.6
9.4	26.7	5.5	21.8	5.9	7.1
24.9	48.8	30.5	40.1	14.7	21.4
0	0	0	0	0	0
0	0	0	0	0	0
0	0	2.8	0	0	0
0	0	0	1.1	0	0
0	2.2	2.8	0	0	0
0	2.2	5.6	1.1	0	0
0	0	2.8	0	0	0
0	0	11.1	0	2.9	0
0	0	5.5	0	0	0
0	0	0	0	0	0
0	0	0	2.3	8.8	0
0	0	19.4	2.3	11.7	0
100	100	100	100	100	100
32	45	36	87	34	28

Table 4.3 continued

Class	Occupational subgroup	(41) Nieder-selters (1929–31)	(42) Nieder-walluf (1930–1)
LOWER	1. Agricultural workers	0	0
CLASS	2. Unskilled workers	26.3	22.2
	3. Skilled (craft) workers	40.3	22.2
	4. Other skilled workers	1.7	0
	5. Domestic workers	0	0
Subtotal		68.3	44.4
Lower-	6. Master craftsmen	1.7	3.7
&	7. Non-academic professionals	1.7	3.7
middle-	8. White-collar employees	7.0	11.1
MIDDLE	9. Lower civil servants	0	3.7
CLASS	10. Merchants	14.0	11.1
	11. Farmers	3.5	14.8
Subtotal		27.9	48.1
Upper-	12. Managers	0	0
MIDDLE	13. Higher civil servants	0	0
CLASS &	14. University students	0	0
UPPER	15. Academic professionals	1.7	0
CLASS	16. Entrepreneurs	0	0
Subtotal		1.7	0
STATUS	17. Non-university students	0	0
UNCLEAR	18. Pensioners/retired	0	3.7
	19. Wives/widows	0	0
	20. Military personnel	0	0
	21. Illegible/no data	1.7	3.7
Subtotal		1.7	7.4
TOTAL (%)		100	100
Frequency (*N*)		57	27

Table 4.3   continued

(43) Ober- lahnstein (1929–31)	(44) Ober- stedten (1930–1)	(45) Oberursel (1929–31)	(46) Rettert (1930–1)	(47) Rod. a.d. Weil (1929–31)	(48) Rüdesheim (1929–31)
0	2.9	1.5	6.7	1.7	0
15.0	17.6	6.1	30.0	8.6	14.0
16.1	41.2	25.7	16.7	43.1	8.0
0	2.9	3.0	0	1.7	0
1.1	0	0	0	0	0
32.2	64.6	36.3	53.4	55.1	22.0
0	0	4.5	3.3	0	4.0
3.2	2.9	15.1	0	0	4.0
12.9	11.8	15.1	3.3	10.3	18.0
12.9	0	0	0	1.7	4.0
18.3	0	18.2	3.3	1.7	20.0
2.1	2.9	0	36.7	19.0	0
49.4	17.6	52.9	46.6	32.7	50.0
0	0	1.5	0	0	4.0
1.1	0	0	0	0	0
0	0	1.5	0	1.7	2.0
2.1	2.9	0	0	1.7	0
0	5.9	1.5	0	0	2.0
3.2	8.8	4.5	0	3.4	8.0
0	0	1.5	0	1.7	4.0
1.1	0	1.5	0	1.7	2.0
2.1	2.9	0	0	0	0
0	0	0	0	0	0
11.8	5.9	3.0	0	5.2	14.0
15.0	8.8	6.0	0	8.6	20.0
100	100	100	100	100	100
93	34	66	30	58	50

Table 4.3 continued

Class	Occupational subgroup	*(49)* Salzburg- Waigands- hain *(1930–1)*	*(50)* Schlangen- bad *(1931)*
LOWER	1. Agricultural workers	2.2	0
CLASS	2. Unskilled workers	44.4	14.3
	3. Skilled (craft) workers	26.7	25.0
	4. Other skilled workers	0	0
	5. Domestic workers	0	0
Subtotal		73.3	39.3
Lower-	6. Master craftsmen	2.2	7.1
&	7. Non-academic professionals	0	0
middle-	8. White-collar employees	2.2	3.6
MIDDLE	9. Lower civil servants	0	10.7
CLASS	10. Merchants	2.2	10.7
	11. Farmers	17.8	0
Subtotal		24.4	32.1
Upper-	12. Managers	0	0
MIDDLE	13. Higher civil servants	0	0
CLASS &	14. University students	0	0
UPPER	15. Academic professionals	2.2	7.1
CLASS	16. Entrepreneurs	0	0
Subtotal		2.2	7.1
STATUS	17. Non-university students	0	0
UNCLEAR	18. Pensioners/retired	0	10.7
	19. Wives/widows	0	3.6
	20. Military personnel	0	0
	21. Illegible/no data	0	7.1
Subtotal		0	21.4
TOTAL (%)		100	100
Frequency (*N*)		45	28

Table 4.3   continued

(51) Schlüchtern	(52) Usingen	(53) Wachen- buchen	(54) Wächters- bach	(55) Weilburg	(56) Westerburg
(1930–1)	(1930–1)	(1930–1)	(1930–1)	(1930–1)	(1930–1)
2.2	1.7	3.0	2.7	0	0
8.7	1.7	9.1	25.3	13.8	12.3
34.8	38.6	24.2	20.0	37.9	29.8
0	0	0	1.3	0	1.7
0	0	0	6.7	3.4	0
45.7	41.0	36.3	56.0	55.1	43.8
6.5	1.7	6.1	1.3	0	12.3
4.3	3.5	6.1	8.0	13.8	3.5
10.9	3.5	0	2.7	0	12.3
0	5.3	0	2.7	0	5.3
21.7	8.8	3.0	5.3	10.3	15.8
6.5	24.6	45.4	13.3	0	0
49.8	47.4	60.6	33.3	24.1	49.2
0	1.7	0	0	0	0
0	0	3.0	0	0	0
0	0	0	0	0	0
0	1.7	0	1.3	3.4	1.7
0	0	0	0	3.4	3.5
0	3.4	3.0	1.3	6.8	5.2
0	0	0	1.3	0	0
0	0	0	1.3	0	1.7
2.2	0	0	0	6.9	0
0	0	0	0	0	0
2.2	7.0	0	6.7	6.9	0
4.4	7.0	0	9.3	13.8	1.7
100	100	100	100	100	100
46	57	33	75	29	57

Table 4.3 continued

Class	Occupational subgroup	(57) Wetzlar (1930–1)	(58) Wied (1929–31)
LOWER	1. Agricultural workers	0	0
CLASS	2. Unskilled workers	5.1	22.6
	3. Skilled (craft) workers	26.9	22.6
	4. Other skilled workers	0	0
	5. Domestic workers	0	0
Subtotal		32.0	45.2
Lower-	6. Master craftsmen	2.6	6.4
&	7. Non-academic professionals	6.4	3.2
middle-	8. White-collar employees	14.1	3.2
MIDDLE	9. Lower civil servants	6.4	6.4
CLASS	10. Merchants	12.8	9.7
	11. Farmers	1.3	9.7
Subtotal		43.6	38.6
Upper-	12. Managers	2.6	0
MIDDLE	13. Higher civil servants	1.3	3.2
CLASS &	14. University students	2.6	0
UPPER	15. Academic professionals	3.8	3.2
CLASS	16. Entrepreneurs	0	3.2
Subtotal		10.3	9.6
STATUS	17. Non-university students	2.6	0
UNCLEAR	18. Pensioners/retired	3.8	6.4
	19. Wives/widows	1.3	0
	20. Military personnel	0	0
	21. Illegible/no data	6.4	0
Subtotal		14.1	6.4
TOTAL (%)		100	100
Frequency (N)		78	31

Table 4.3 continued

| (59) Wiesbaden | (60) Wings-bach | (61) | (62) Gau | (63) | (64) HESSE-NASSAU-SOUTH | (65) | (66) |
| | | | | | (1929 to | (15.9.30 | (1929– |
(1929–31)	(1930–1)	(1929)	(1930)	(1931)	14.9.30)	to 1931)	1931)
0.4	3.4	0.2	0.6	0.9	0.6	0.8	0.7
12.3	13.8	13.5	12.6	11.9	13.2	11.9	12.4
18.7	34.5	22.2	23.9	23.7	23.1	24.1	23.7
1.0	0	1.2	1.1	0.7	1.2	0.8	1.0
1.7	0	1.4	0.7	1.2	0.8	1.0	0.9
34.1	51.7	38.5	38.9	38.4	38.9	38.6	38.7
3.6	0	2.6	2.8	2.8	2.8	2.8	2.8
5.0	3.4	3.0	4.2	4.3	3.7	4.5	4.2
13.7	0	10.1	11.3	11.6	11.4	11.2	11.3
5.3	0	8.2	4.7	4.5	6.1	4.1	4.9
17.7	6.9	20.0	18.7	15.4	18.4	17.0	17.6
3.6	37.9	3.8	5.8	7.8	5.6	6.9	6.4
48.9	48.2	47.7	47.5	46.4	48.0	46.5	47.2
1.1	0	0.8	0.7	0.9	0.8	0.8	0.8
0.5	0	0.5	0.2	0.2	0.2	0.2	0.2
0.2	0	0.2	0.8	0.5	0.9	0.5	0.7
2.4	0	1.8	1.7	2.8	1.5	2.5	2.1
0.6	0	1.1	0.5	0.8	0.6	0.6	0.6
4.8	0	4.4	3.9	5.2	4.0	4.6	4.4
1.6	0	2.1	1.4	1.5	1.4	1.6	1.5
1.9	0	1.7	1.3	1.5	1.4	1.4	1.4
3.5	0	1.9	1.9	1.8	2.0	1.8	1.9
0	0	0	0	0	0	0	0
5.0	0	3.5	4.6	5.2	4.1	5.2	4.7
12.0	0	9.2	9.2	10.0	8.9	10.0	9.5
100	100	100	100	100	100	100	100
1,607	29	830	5,855	3,938	4,428	6,195	10,623

recruited between 1929 and 1931. However, the number of workers mobilized by the party in this part of Frankfurt was comparatively small and in percentage terms did not match that represented by the worker category within Höchst's male working population.[41] It was the lower- and middle-middle class which responded most strongly to Nazism in Frankfurt, while the upper-middle class and upper class was also well-represented amongst Nazi recruits. Those describing themselves as *Kaufmann* made up a quarter of the new Nazi members alone, though it is probable that many of these were in reality commercial employees.[42] White-collar employees in commerce, banking, industry and trade, along with the self-employed, formed the core of the Frankfurt Nazi Party throughout the period 1929 to 1931. One factor which conditioned the receptivity to Nazism of these social types in Frankfurt was the rapidly deteriorating economic situation in the city. This affected the employment opportunity (or rather the lack of it!) of white-collar workers particularly severely, as is made clear in a report by the Hessian Chamber of Industry and Commerce in 1933, in which the cities of Frankfurt, Wiesbaden and Kassel were all singled out as having a very unfavourable employment situation for white-collar employees in the period 1929 to 1932.[43] For shopkeepers and independent businessmen the competition provided by Jewish-owned businesses (Jews accounted for 4.7 per cent of Frankfurt's population, by far the highest percentage in any German city) probably fed anti-Semitic attitudes which the Nazis exploited as the crisis deepened in the early 1930s.[44] Economic uncertainty combined with heightened anti-Semitism may also have motivated the sizeable number of academic professionals, particularly doctors and lawyers, to join the Frankfurt NSDAP.

In Wiesbaden the divergence between the social composition of the party's recruits and the town's male working population is less extreme than in the Frankfurt case, though workers again showed a reluctance to respond to Nazi overtures, the lower class accounting for just over one-third of the Nazi recruits between 1929 and 1931, but for almost half of the male working population in the census of 1933.[45] In Wiesbaden the Nazis were able to register early and very strong electoral support, primarily due to the radicalization of the *Mittelstand* caught up in the economic crisis from 1929 onwards, which hit the city particularly hard due to the one-dimensional nature of its economic structure.[46] It was the lower- and middle-middle class which also joined the Nazi Party in large numbers, accounting for 52.1 per cent of the Nazi recruits in the city in 1929, 48.7 per cent in 1930 and 47.3 per cent in 1931.

With the exception of the Höchst branch, the dominance of the *Mittelstand* among the recruits to the Nazi Party in Frankfurt and Wiesbaden is also a noticeable feature of the recruitment pattern of the NSDAP in the few large and medium-sized towns in *Gau* Hesse-Nassau-South which had a population of over 10,000. In Bad Homburg, Hanau and Oberursel the lower- and middle-middle-class members were in an absolute majority (see Table 4.3, columns 4, 25 and 45), while in Limburg and Wetzlar they had a relative majority (see Table 4.3, columns 33 and 57). It was the class structure of the membership of Nazi branches situated in small towns and in rural communities which were infinitely variable and without any discernible pattern relating to the confessional and socio-economic structure of the area in which they were situated. Thus while all the branches recruiting 25 or more members in the highly industrialized, predominantly Protestant county Hanau (namely those at Eichen, Großauheim and Wachenbuchen – see Table 4.3, columns 11, 21 and 53) drew the great majority of their recruits from the lower- and middle-middle class (the percentage values ranging from 57 to 88.4), all the branches in the predominantly Protestant, industrialized Dillkreis (those at Dillenburg, Eibelshausen, Eiershausen, Haiger, Herborn and Langenaubach – see Table 4.3, columns 9, 10, 12, 24, 27 and 31) attracted the majority of their support from the lower class (the percentage values ranging from 44.8 to 75.7). In the agrarian, strongly Catholic county Westerburg the lower class provided the bulk of recruits in the branches at Ailertchen, Gemünden and Salzburg-Waigandshain (at 67.8, 75.8 and 73.3 per cent respectively – see Table 4.3, columns 1, 20 and 49), whereas at Westerburg lower- and middle-class recruits were slightly more numerous than lower class joiners (at 49.2 to 43.8 per cent respectively – see Table 4.3, column 56). In the branches at Eltville, Niederwalluf and Rüdesheim (see Table 4.3, columns 13, 42 and 48) in the industrial, strongly Catholic Rheingaukreis, the lower- and middle-middle-class recruits outnumbered those from the lower class, the exception being the Erbach branch (see Table 4.3, column 15), in which middle-class elements formed one-third and lower-class recruits two-thirds of the new members. In some of the branches established in villages whose population was heavily

117

dependent on agriculture (for the following see Table 4.3, columns 20, 35, 40 and 49), such as Gemünden (in the predominantly Protestant Oberwesterwaldkreis, in which 44.4 per cent of the total population was dependent on agriculture), Miehlen (in county St Goarshausen, with its mixed Catholic–Protestant population, 63 per cent of which lived by agriculture), Niedermörsbach (in the predominantly Protestant Oberwesterwaldkreis, in which 68.8 per cent of the population was dependent on agriculture), and Salzburg-Waigandshain (in the predominantly Catholic county Westerburg, where respectively 43.8 and 79.3 per cent of the population of these two villages were dependent on agriculture for their livelihood),[47] the lower class provided around three-quarters of the branch recruits, while farmers (or farmers' sons) are a rarity among the Nazi recruits, with the partial exception of the branch at Salzburg-Waigandshain. A strong phalanx of farmers (or farmers' sons) is to be found among only a few of the rural branches, especially those established at Eichen (in the predominantly Protestant county Hanau, where 50.6 per cent of the population was dependent on agriculture) and Hausen vor der Höhe (in the strongly Protestant Untertaunuskreis, where 63 per cent of the population depended on agriculture), two villages in which farmers provided half or more of the entire branch recruitment (see Table 4.3, columns 11 and 26).

It was in the villages of *Gau* Hesse-Nassau-South that the Nazis were able to develop a large number of branches in which the lower class dominated the membership. In the 28 branches of the NSDAP (recruiting more than 25 members) situated in communities with a population of less than 2,000, the lower class provided an absolute majority in 17 (with percentage values ranging from 51.7 to 78.5), and a relative majority in a further four. In half of the 18 branches organized in small rural towns (*Landstädte*) with a population of 2,000 to 4,999, the lower class formed an absolute or relative majority. These branches were to be found in both solidly Catholic and Protestant areas, in counties which were agrarian or industrial in their economic structure. However it should be noted that despite the often high percentage of lower-class recruits in the Nazi branches situated in village communities with a population of less than 2,000 (in which they formed 53.9 per cent of the total membership) and the relatively low percentage values for the lower-class component in the party branches in the two cities of *Gau* Hesse-Nassau-South (in which workers formed only 30.7 per cent of the total membership), more workers entered the NSDAP in Frankfurt and Wiesbaden in absolute terms (see Table 4.4). Of the 4,113 lower-class recruits to Nazism, 43.8 per cent were mobilized in the cities, and 38 per cent in rural communities.

It was from the lower- and middle-middle class that the Nazis consistently secured almost half of the membership support in *Gau* Hesse-Nassau-South (see Table 4.3, columns 61 to 66). In the large towns and cities the lower- and middle-middle class provided an absolute majority of the Nazi recruits (see Table 4.4). In all of the towns and cities of the region with a population of over 10,000 by 1933 (Bad Homburg, Frankfurt, Hanau, Limburg, Oberursel, Wetzlar and Wiesbaden), this class provided the absolute or relative majority of new Nazi members (see Table 4.3, columns 4, 16, 25, 33, 45, 57 and 59). In towns and communities with a population below 10,000 the size of the lower- and middle-middle-class segment in Nazi branches was more variable, being exceptionally prominent in some, such as in the village of Eichen and the small town of Idstein (see Table 4.3, columns 11 and 29), and very marginal in others, such as in the villages of Ailertchen, Eibelshausen, Eiershausen, Neuenhain, and Oberstedten (see Table 4.3, columns 1, 10, 12, 39, and 44), as well as in the small town of Bad Ems (see Table 4.3, column 3). Neither the confessional factor nor the socio-economic structure of these towns and villages, which might have provided a common denominator to explain the marked deviation from the general trend, are constant. Except for the few branches noted previously in which farmers represented a major component among new Nazi members, white-collar employees and merchants invariably provided the bulk of the lower- and middle-middle-class recruits of the branches listed in Table 4.3. The age factor probably precluded any significant presence of master craftsmen among Nazi recruits, though in Camberg, Eichen and Hachenburg they represented an exceptional 10 per cent or more (see Table 4.3, columns 8, 11 and 23). Another occupational sub-group not much in evidence among the lower- and middle-middle-class recruits were lower- and middle-grade civil servants. Where these did provide a significant percentage of Nazi branch recruitment, as in Freiendiez, Gelnhausen, Großauheim, Nassau, Oberlahnstein and Schlangenbad (see Table 4.3, columns 17, 19, 21, 37, 43, and 50), blue- and white-collar employees of the postal and railway services usually figure prominently.

From the upper-middle class and upper class the Nazis were able

Table 4.4 Persons joining the NSDAP in *Gau* Hesse-Nassau-South (*N*: 10,570[a]) in the period September 1929 to the end of 1931 by place of residence (by %)[48]

		Community size				
Class	Occupational subgroup	Under 2,000	2,000-4,999	5,000-19,999	20,000-99,999	Over 100,000
LOWER	1. Agricultural workers	0.5	0.03	0.02	0.01	0.1
CLASS	2. Unskilled workers	4.9	1.0	0.7	0.2	5.5
	3. Skilled (craft) workers	9.0	2.7	1.6	0.3	10.0
	4. Other skilled workers	0.2	0.06	0.07	0.03	0.6
	5. Domestic workers	0.1	0.03	0.08	0.01	0.7
Subtotal		14.7	3.8	2.5	0.5	16.9
Lower-	6. Master craftsmen	0.8	0.3	0.1	0.03	1.5
&	7. Non-academic professionals	0.5	0.3	0.5	0.1	2.6
middle-	8. White-collar employees	1.5	1.1	0.8	0.3	7.7
MIDDLE	9. Lower civil servants	0.4	0.3	0.4	0.1	3.6
CLASS	10. Merchants	2.5	1.3	1.1	0.3	12.3
	11. Farmers	4.9	0.5	0.1	0.02	0.8
Subtotal		10.6	3.8	3.0	0.8	28.5
Upper-	12. Managers	0.08	0.07	0.07	0.02	0.6
MIDDLE	13. Higher civil servants	0.02	0	0.02	0.01	0.2
CLASS &	14. University students	0.03	0.04	0.04	0.02	0.5
UPPER	15. Academic professionals	0.2	0.2	0.1	0.07	1.5
CLASS	16. Entrepreneurs	0.1	0.1	0.02	0.01	0.3
Subtotal		0.4	0.4	0.2	0.1	3.1
STATUS	17. Non-university students	0.1	0.1	0.1	0.07	1.0
UNCLEAR	18. Pensioners/retired	0.3	0.1	0.1	0.03	0.9
	19. Wives/widows	0.06	0.2	0.1	0.02	1.5
	20. Military personnel	0	0	0	0	0
	21. Illegible/no data	0.9	0.4	0.4	0.1	3.0
Subtotal		1.4	0.8	0.8	0.2	6.4
TOTAL (%)		27.1	8.8	6.5	1.6	54.9
Gau Hesse-Nassau-South		38.9	8.7	7.4	2.5	42.4
Province Hesse-Nassau		44.3	10.8	8.0	5.9	30.9
Prussia		33.7	9.6	12.9	14.5	29.2
Germany		35.6	10.8	13.3	13.7	26.8

Note: a Excludes 53 members whose place of residence is unclear.

to recruit a steady trickle of support throughout the period September 1929 to 1931, with academic professionals, especially doctors, by far the most reponsive to the Nazi message. In a number of branches the 'elite' element of German society provided over 10 per cent of the Nazi recruits, as in Bad Schwalbach, Camberg, Hachenburg and Wetzlar (see Table 4.3, columns 5, 8, 23 and 57), though in absolute terms just over half of the total elite recruitment effected by the Nazi Party in *Gau* Hesse-Nassau-South (50.9 per cent) occurred in Frankfurt alone. In village communities the response of the local 'notables' was generally muted, though vets do appear with some frequency, while there is also a sprinkling of doctors, landowners with 'aristocratic' titles, as well as the occasional vicar.

IV

The 10,623 individuals enrolled by the Nazi Party in *Gau* Hesse-Nassau-South during the period September 1929 to the end of 1931 came from a broad cross-section of Hesse society. Although one is not exactly comparing like with like in Table 4.5, given that the occupational and social profile of the NSDAP membership in columns 2 to 5 relates to *all* members (including females) recruited in the *Gau* as a whole, whereas the data in column 6 relates only to the *male* working population of *Regierungsbezirk* Wiesbaden, and bearing in mind that *Gau* Hesse-Nassau-South extended beyond the area covered by *Regierungsbezirk* Wiesbaden, the differences between the percentage values in the two sets of data are not that striking. The inclusion of female recruits in the percentages relating to the Nazi Party produces only a minor distortion, given that women represented a mere 6.5 per cent of all new Nazi Party members in the period (50.8 per cent of these were mobilized in Frankfurt, and a further 23.3 per cent in Wiesbaden). Overall one is faced with an under-representation of the lower class and an over-representation of the lower- and middle-middle class in the Nazi ranks in comparison with their share in the male working population, but the extent of the under-representation of the lower class is not so great as to detract from the *Volkspartei* image of the NSDAP which emerges from the data. The imbalance between the two main class groupings is more evident when one looks solely at the *Partei-Statistik* data (see Table 4.5, column 1), in which the lower- and middle-middle-class elements do loom

Table 4.5 The membership of the Nazi Party in *Gau* Hesse-Nassau-South by operationally (horizontally) classified occupation (by %)[49]

	(1) Partei- Statistik Gau *members* as on 14.9.30	(2) 1929	(3) 1930	(4) 1929- 14.9.30	(5) 1931	(6) Male working population of Reg. Bez. Wiesbaden (1925)
		Newly enrolled members[a] in				
Workers ⎱	29.0	37.1[b]	38.2[b]	38.1[b]	37.2[b]	49.8
Domestic workers ⎰		1.4[c]	0.7[c]	0.8[c]	1.2[c]	0.01
White-collar employees	24.8	13.9[d]	16.2[d]	15.9[d]	16.8[d] ⎱	22.8
Civil servants	7.7	8.7[e]	4.9[e]	6.3[e]	4.7[e] ⎰	
Self-employed	17.4	25.5[f]	23.7[f]	23.3[f]	21.8[f] ⎱	22.0
Farmers	12.6	3.8[g]	5.8[g]	5.6[g]	7.8[g] ⎰	
Working family members	-	-	-	-	-	5.3
Others	8.4	9.4[h]	10.0[h]	9.8[h]	10.0[h]	-
TOTAL (%)	100	100	100	100	100	100
Frequency (*N*)	6,570	830	5,855	4,428	3,938	436,322

Notes: a Includes a handful of members who were resident in *Gaue* Hesse-Nassau-North and Hesse-Darmstadt.
  b Subgroups 1–4 listed in Table 4.3.
  c Subgroup 5 listed in Table 4.3.
  d Subgroups 7–8, and 12 listed in Table 4.3.
  e Subgroups 9, 13 and 20 listed in Table 4.3.
  f Subgroups 6, 10 and 15–16 listed in Table 4.3.
  g Subgroup 11 listed in Table 4.3.
  h Subgroups 14, 17–19, and 21 listed in Table 4.3.

very large. Comparing the occupational and social background of those who stayed in the party until the Nazi census of 1934 with that of the recruits attracted to the NSDAP after September 1929 suggests once more, as in the case of *Gau* Württemberg-Hohenzollern, that the lower- class members who had joined the NSDAP by 14 September 1930 were more likely to leave the party over time than members drawn from the lower- and middle-middle class. A direct comparison between columns 1 and 2 to 5 is not feasible, given that the *Partei-Statistik* data relates to the membership not only of *Gau* Hesse-Nassau-South, but also of *Gau* Hesse-Darmstadt, for by the time the census was taken the two were united once more and thus treated as a single entity in the *Partei-Statistik*.[50]

5

GAU
SOUTH-HANOVER-
BRUNSWICK
1925–33

The development of Nazism in *Gau* South-Hanover-Brunswick, which was created in 1928 and comprised the *Regierungsbezirke* Hanover and Hildesheim, as well as *Land* Brunswick (see Map 10), has been well-researched in various regional[1] and local[2] studies which have appeared since the 1960s. The region covered by *Gau* South-Hanover-Brunswick was strongly Protestant. In the province of Hanover, 83.8 per cent of the population was Protestant and 14.1 per cent Catholic. All but two of the counties of *Regierungsbezirke* Hanover and Hildesheim were over-whelmingly Protestant in their confessional structure, the exceptions being county Duderstadt (in which Catholics accounted for 91.1 per cent of the population), and county Hildesheim (in which 54.7 per cent of the population was Catholic and 44.4 per cent Protestant). In *Land* Brunswick Catholics were even more

Table 5.1 The breakdown of the working population according to economic sectors in *Gau* South-Hanover-Brunswick in 1925 and 1933 (by %)[3]

		Agriculture & forestry	Industry & crafts	Trade & transport	Other
Land	1925	27.9	43.4	17.1	11.6
Brunswick	1933	31.4	35.0	19.2	14.4
Reg.-Bez-	1925	29.4	39.4	18.9	12.3
Hanover	1933	34.9	30.4	21.4	13.2
Reg.-Bez.	1925	35.3	40.0	13.1	11.6
Hildesheim	1933	40.2	31.5	15.5	12.7
Provinz	1925	42.0	32.3	15.1	10.6
Hanover	1933	46.2	26.0	16.8	10.9

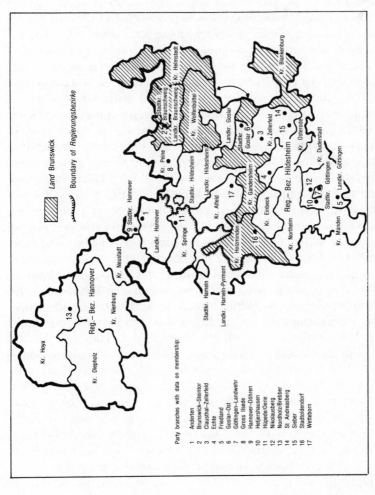

Party branches with data on membership:

1 Anderten
2 Brunswick–Steinhor
3 Clausthal–Zellerfeld
4 Echte
5 Friedland
6 Goslar–Ost
7 Göttingen–Landwehr
8 Gross Ilsede
9 Hannover–Döhren
10 Hetjershausen
11 Hüpede/Oerie
12 Nikolausberg
13 Nordholz/Brebber
14 St Andreasberg
15 Sieber
16 Stadtoldendorf
17 Wetteborn

Map 10 Gau South-Hanover-Brunswick, 1928–33.

marginal, accounting for a mere 4.9 per cent of the population, 89.8 per cent of which was Protestant.[4]

In the regions which made up *Gau* South-Hanover-Brunswick, industry and crafts combined with trade and transport employed the majority of the population in the 1920s and early 1930s (see Table 5.1).[5] The social structure of the working population of the area was broadly in line with that of Germany as a whole, though in *Land* Brunswick the 'workers' category accounted for around half of the total working population, a reflection of the highly industrialized nature of this small state (see Table 5.2). Both Hanover (where the chemical and rubber industries were important) and Brunswick (where a number of large concerns produced a variety of machinery) were centres of major manufacturing, drawing a part of their workforce from the counties adjacent to these cities. The limited amount of heavy industry in the region was centred on the iron and steel complex represented by the Ilseder Hütte in county Peine and the mining of ore in the Harz. The counties of *Land* Brunswick were the most extensively industrialized in the region, with widespread light industry, food-processing and the canning industry being of particular significance. Some brown-coal mining was also to be found in county Helmstedt. Despite the preponderance of the secondary sector as the major employer in the region comprising *Gau* South-Hanover-Brunswick, the primary sector, in which small and medium-sized owner-occupied farms predominated, was also of importance, especially in the northern part of *Regierungsbezirk* Hanover. In the counties of Diepholz, Hoya and Nienburg, agriculture dominated economic activity, with 66.1, 54.3 and 53.1 per cent respectively of the total population dependent on farming for a living. In a number of other counties the percentage of the total population working in agriculture was also still comparatively high by the time of the 1933 census, namely Neustadt (41.5), Göttingen (41.4), Einbeck (35.3), Springe (33.6), and Northeim (33.1).[6] It was in these predominantly agrarian areas that 'working family members' were primarily to be found, 90 per cent of whom were employed in agriculture in province Hanover, while in *Land* Brunswick they accounted for 80.7 per cent.[7] The continued importance of agriculture in the region is clear, though the seeming expansion of the percentage of the working population engaged in agriculture (primarily at the expense of

Table 5.2 The social structure of the working population of *Gau* South-Hanover-Brunswick in 1925 and 1933 (by %)[8]

		Self-employed	White-collar employees	Civil servants	Workers	Working family members	Domestic workers
Land	1925	16.4		16.1	51.2	11.7	4.6
Brunswick	1933[a]	15.7	12.8	4.6	48.8	13.7	4.4
Reg.-Bez.	1925	17.4		18.9	42.6	16.9	4.2
Hanover	1933[a]	16.9	14.2	5.0	41.9	18.2	3.7
Reg.-Bez.	1925	16.9		13.6	46.7	18.5	4.2
Hildesheim	1933[a]	16.6	9.7	4.5	45.3	20.1	3.8
Gau South-Hanover-Brunswick	1933	16.5	12.5	4.7	44.6	17.6	3.9
Provinz	1925	18.9		13.6	40.6	23.2	3.7
Hanover	1933[a]	18.4	9.7	4.2	40.3	23.9	3.3
Germany	1925	17.3		16.5	45.1	17.0	4.1
	1933[a]	16.4	12.5	4.6	46.3	16.4	3.8

Note: a Includes those who were unemployed in 1933, who were listed separately in the census.

industry and crafts) between the 1925 and 1933 censuses gives a misleading picture of the real structure of the regional economy in 1933, which was distorted by the mass unemployment of the early 1930s.

I

In *Gau* South-Hanover-Brunswick, a solidly Protestant part of Germany, a region in which industry was widespread but one which also contained areas in which agriculture was still the dominant economic force, the NSDAP secured some of its best electoral results throughout the Weimar period, the vote for the party in electoral district South-Hanover-Brunswick being well above the national average in all of the *Reichstag* elections from May 1924 to March 1933.[9] The receptivity of the region's population to the Nazi appeal is also reflected in the degree of penetration effected by the Nazi Party in membership terms by the time of the Nazi seizure of power. *Gau* South-Hanover-Brunswick, where the ratio of party members to the population was 1 to 18.3, was second only to Schleswig-Holstein (where the ratio was 1 to 18.1), well above the national average, which stood at 1 to 26.4.[10]

The Nazi Party took root in the southern half of the province of Hanover in the early 1920s, with the emergence of two centres of major organizational and propaganda activity, that of Hanover, where a Nazi Party branch was founded in July 1921, and that of Göttingen, where a branch was formed in February 1922.[11] It was the activities of these two branches which led to the formation of a number of additional branches and cells in province Hanover, as well as in the adjacent *Land* Brunswick. The prohibition of the NSDAP by the Prussian authorities on 17 November 1922 forced the nascent Nazi movement underground and seriously restricted the political activity of the party, though the Nazis continued to recruit and to function in various guises after the ban was imposed. In *Land* Brunswick however, which virtually split *Regierungsbezirk* Hildesheim in two (see Map 10), the authorities did not prohibit the party, and the branch formed in the city of Brunswick in February 1923 continued to enrol supporters both in the town and in the *Land* as a whole right up to the abortive Nazi putsch in Munich in November 1923.

The marginality of the NSDAP in southern Hanover and Brunswick in these early years emerges clearly when the very limited evidence which has survived on the membership strength of the party is evaluated. Thus the Hanover branch, which numbered 13 members at the time of its foundation in July 1921, grew only very slowly, increasing its membership to 25 by December 1921, a figure which rose to 104 by July 1922, to 316 by 17 November 1922,[12] and to 341 by May 1923.[13] In Göttingen the Nazis mustered 12 members at the time of the formation of the branch in February 1922, a membership which increased to 25 by November 1922, when it doubled following a mass demonstration by right-wing forces in the town in which the Nazis had participated. The Göttingen SA had 45 members at the time of its formation in November 1922, its strength growing subsequently to the point where it was able to mobilize 200 men by the time of Hitler's attempted putsch in Munich in November 1923.[14]

Given the shadowy existence led by the Nazi Party in the Hanover-Brunswick region in the early 1920s, it is surprising that a little material has survived which allows some, albeit restricted, insight into the social types drawn towards the

NSDAP in the area before November 1923. Although both the Hanover and Göttingen branches were initially led by 'workers', the lower class accounted for only 24 per cent of the membership of the Hanover branch by December 1921, whereas the lower- and middle-middle class provided 52 per cent, the upper-middle class and upper class a further 8 per cent, while 16 per cent of the occupational and social status of the membership cannot be determined.[15] Of the 12 members comprising the Göttingen branch at its formation in early February 1922, 33.3 per cent came from the lower class, another 33.3 per cent from the lower- and middle-middle class, 8.3 per cent from the upper-middle class and upper class, while the remaining 25 per cent fell into the 'status unclear' category.[16] Among the 4,786 individuals recorded as joining the NSDAP between 25 September and 9 November 1923,[17] there were 44 who were resident in the province of Hanover and 79 who were living in *Land* Brunswick. In both regions lower- and middle-middle-class types provided the bulk of new Nazi members, accounting for 59.2 per cent of the recruits in the province of Hanover and 64.5 per cent of those in *Land* Brunswick, whereas the lower class, with 18.2 and 13.9 per cent respectively, was barely visible.[18] Few of the recruits in province Hanover were actually living in *Regierungsbezirke* Hanover and Hildesheim, though there were two small clusters of Nazi recruits in Osterode (a sculptor, a farmer, a master smith, a smith, a fitter and a chimney-sweep) and in Lengede in county Peine (an electrician, a civil servant, two foremen, and a merchant), who were attached to the Brunswick city branch, as well as a handful of recruits scattered around the region who were entered as members of the Munich branch. Of the 79 members resident in *Land* Brunswick, all but twenty were living in the city of Brunswick. Of the latter some were resident in the counties of Brunswick and Gandersheim (and these were enrolled as members of the Brunswick-City Nazi Party branch), while a group of nine recruited in Holzminden (a fitter, a smith, a carpenter, a tracer, an office assistant, three merchants and a bookkeeper) were attached to the Lage branch in the adjacent small state of Lippe. To reach any definitive conclusions on the social basis of the Nazi Party in the Hanover-Brunswick region in the pre-November 1923 period is virtually impossible in view of the limited amount of data that has survived and the impossibility of calculating what proportion of the total membership it involved, since no figures on the total strength of the party in the area are available. It would seem that the members drawn towards the party before November 1923 were mainly middle-class in their occupational and social background, though there is the suggestion that some limited lower-class support was also being mobilized by the NSDAP.

The national ban on the NSDAP following the collapse of the Munich putsch threw the Nazi movement in the Hanover-Brunswick region into the same sort of confusion which characterized its development in other parts of Germany from November 1923 to the spring of 1925.[19] The struggle in the region by a section of the Nazi Party against the DVFP during the period of illegality, the refusal of part of the Nazi leadership and membership in Hanover-Brunswick to have anything to do with the NSFB, the resistance of the influential regional leader Volck to countenance the idea of giving up his anti-parliamentary stance in 1924, allied to personality conflicts and reservations about the direction taken by the party following its re-emergence in February 1925, coloured the reconstruction of the movement in 1925. At a meeting in Harburg on 22 March 1925, at which Gregor Strasser was present, a series of decisions affecting organizational questions was taken, which led to the inclusion of *Regierungsbezirk* Hanover, the northern counties of Hildesheim and the state of Brunswick in the enormous new *Gau* of Hanover-North, led by Bernhard Rust, which covered the major part of the province of Hanover. The southern counties of *Regierungsbezirk* Hildesheim (Einbeck, Northeim, Duderstadt, Göttingen and Münden) formed the small *Gau* Hanover-South, led by Ludolf Haase.[20] In the years 1925 to 1928 the mobilization of support for Nazism in both of these *Gaue* proved to be a slow affair. According to statistics produced by the Nazis in 1925 and 1926, the very large *Gau* Hanover-North mustered 793 members on 1 July 1925, a figure which had grown to 1,152 by September 1925, and to 2,408 by the beginning of November 1926.[21] Much of this growth was, however, centred on the Hanover-Brunswick region, in which five of the six largest Nazi branches – Brunswick (with 255 members), Hanover (220), Wolfenbüttel (106), Hildesheim (66) and Goslar (50) were to be found by the end of May 1926. The subsequent development pattern of the *Gau* was one of almost total stagnation, for in 1927 the party membership grew by only 164.[22] No membership figures which would allow one to measure the development of *Gau* Hanover-South are available for this period, though it does appear that by the end of 1926 its membership was in decline, and that its general development was characterized by stagnation from late 1926 and throughout 1927, in part the consequence of the withdrawal from active politics by Haase and Hermann Fobke, the two individuals primarily responsible for the relatively rapid development of Nazism in the Göttingen area in the early 1920s.[23] The total membership of the party in *Gau* Hanover-South was little more than a few hundred by the time of the organizational restructuring of the Nazi movement in the Hanover-Brunswick region in September 1928.[24] The problems facing the party in these years which limited its growth involved such aspects as the debilitating effect of continuous power struggles between rival factions which crippled the party in some localities, as for example in the city of Brunswick,[25] constant financial difficulties at the *Gau* and local level, inadequate leadership and organizational problems,[26] in short the same sort of handicaps restricting the party's growth in Germany as a whole. Added to these internal factors was, from the Nazi point of view, the unfavourable environment in which the party was attempting to win support, since the seeming economic and political stability of Weimar Germany from 1925 onwards limited the attraction of the type of radicalism on offer by the NSDAP.

Despite the limited progress made by the Nazi Party in *Gaue* Hanover-North and Hanover-South in expanding its electorate and membership in the period before 1928, the years immediately following its re-formation were nevertheless of crucial importance in retrospect. This was the period in which the party created a cadre and a network of branches which allowed it to latch onto and exploit the economic crisis which started to manifest itself in the course of 1928.[27] On the eve of the recession which was to plunge the Weimar state into the economic and political morass of the early 1930s, the Nazis effected a major organizational restructuring of the party initiated by Gregor Strasser in the form of a circular dated 15 September 1928.[28] Strasser ordered that in future all *Gau* boundaries were to correspond with those of the *Reichstag* electoral districts, an instruction which necessitated significant organizational changes in the Hanover-Brunswick region. It led to the breakup of *Gau* Hanover-North, and the amalgamation of the *Regierungsbezirk* Hanover, the northern and eastern counties of *Regierungsbezirk* Hildesheim, and the state of Brunswick with *Gau* Hanover-South in the renamed *Gau* South-Hanover-Brunswick, which equated to *Reichstag* electoral district 16. This new *Gau* had a membership of 2,268 by 31 December 1928 and 3,210 by the end of May 1929,[29] after which it grew very rapidly, with up to a thousand new recruits recorded as entering the party in some of the months towards the end of 1929.[30] In the *Partei-Statistik* the figure of 5,562 is given for members in the party by 14 September 1930, with a further 35,376 joining in the subsequent period up to 31 January 1933.[31] In the course of 1931 the Nazis began to achieve quite staggering monthly recruitment figures, with the high-point before 1933 reached in *Gau* South-Hanover-Brunswick in December 1931, when 9,250 new members were registered.[32] Reflecting the increasingly deep penetration of the party into all areas of the *Gau* is the growth in the number of party branches, which rose rapidly from 60 in January 1930 to 386 by February 1931, to 453 one year later.[33] Paralleling the organizational and membership growth of the Nazi party in the region was a more than ten-fold increase in its electoral support in the space of four years. It rose from 4.4 per cent in the *Reichstag* election of 20 May 1928, to 24.3 per cent on 14 September 1930, and to 46.1 per cent by 31 July 1932.[34]

As far as the social background of the members who joined the Nazi Party in *Gau* South-Hanover-Brunswick before 1933 is concerned, nothing is known to date beyond the data provided by the *Partei-Statistik*. This source was used by Jeremy Noakes in determining the broad social contours of the party in Lower Saxony.[35] The material presented in this essay is based on membership data relating to various Nazi branches (see Table 5.3) scattered around *Gau* South-Hanover-Brunswick (see Map 10), which allows this first detailed analysis of the social configuration of the party at the micro level. In time our knowledge of the social structure of the Nazi Party in the region will undoubtedly be further enhanced when access for research purposes to additional material – on what appears to be some very comprehensive data on particular areas – is eventually granted.[36] Although there is no way of determining how representative the data used in this chapter is, it does fortunately relate to localities in *Gau* South-Hanover-Brunswick which had quite different socio-economic structures, since the branches were situated in both rural and urban centres, in both agrarian and industrial areas. The branches evaluated below probably do represent a fair cross-section of the numerous *Ortsgruppen* established in the region by 1933.

OG Anderten

The village of Anderten (pop. 2,389 in 1933), on the southern boundary of the city of Hanover, was administratively part of the strongly industrialized county Hanover, in which agriculture was of marginal significance as an employer in the early 1930s.[37] It is likely that a considerable percentage of its population commuted to work in nearby Hanover.

Take in Table 5.3 about here

The surviving membership lists[38] indicate that this branch was formed on 1 July 1930, when 17 members were enrolled, to which two further recruits were added by the end of 1930, 12 in 1931, 18 in 1932, and 43 by 25 April 1933 (of which four joined before 31 January 1933). At the time of its formation half of its members were drawn from the lower class and half from the *Mittelstand*, a class balance which also characterized both the 1931 and 1932 recruits. In 1933 civil servants and merchants were very prominent among new members. In this predominantly male branch (only 5.4 per cent of the members were females) the lower class was an important component of the membership (see Table 5.3, column 1), though probably under-represented in comparison with the structure of the working population of the village. Barring the branch treasurer, who was a 'worker', the branch functionaries, including the head of the NSBO (a merchant), were all middle class.

OG Brunswick-Steintor

This was one of a number of branches[39] situated in the city of Brunswick (pop. 156,840), capital of the geographically fragmented state of Brunswick, one of the few small states of Germany in which the Nazis headed the regional government in the endphase of the Weimar Republic. In the 1920s and 1930s Brunswick was a significant industrial and commercial centre, with 48.6 per cent of its working population employed in industry and crafts, and 29.4 per cent in trade and transport.[40]

Table 5.3 The social and occupational structure of the membership of various NSDAP branches in *Gau* South-Hanover-Brunswick, 1925–33 (by %)

Class	Occupational subgroup	(1) Anderten (1930–3)	(2) Brunswick (OG Steintor) (1925–33)
LOWER	1. Agricultural workers	6.5	0
CLASS	2. Unskilled workers	18.4	5.8
	3. Skilled (craft) workers	17.4	10.8
	4. Other skilled workers	2.2	1.2
	5. Domestic workers	1.1	3.3
Subtotal		45.6	21.1
Lower-	6. Master craftsmen	7.6	2.6
&	7. Non-academic professionals	0	8.9
middle-	8. White-collar employees	6.5	13.8
MIDDLE	9. Lower civil servants	7.6	12.9
CLASS	10. Merchants	16.3	15.9
	11. Farmers	9.8	0.2
Subtotal		47.8	54.3
Upper-	12. Managers	1.1	0.7
MIDDLE	13. Higher civil servants	1.1	2.8
CLASS &	14. University students	0	0.7
UPPER	15. Academic professionals	0	4.4
CLASS	16. Entrepreneurs	0	1.2
Subtotal		2.2	9.8
STATUS	17. Non-university students	2.2	3.7
UNCLEAR	18. Pensioners/retired	0	1.9
	19. Wives/widows	0	5.6
	20. Military personnel	0	0
	21. Illegible/no data	2.2	6.2
Subtotal		4.4	14.7
TOTAL (%)		100	100
Frequency (*N*)		92	427

Table 5.3 continued

(3) Clausthal- Zellerfeld (1926–33)	(4) Echte (1929–33)	(5) Friedland (1932–3)	(6) Goslar (OG Ost) (1925–33)	(7) Göttingen (OG Land- wehr) (1925–33)	(8) Groß Ilsede (1930–2)
0	2.3	6.0	0.4	0.6	1.9
5.4	11.6	8.0	14.6	4.9	23.0
10.9	9.3	22.0	19.6	11.0	34.6
0.7	0	6.0	1.1	0	5.8
1.4	0	0	1.8	0	1.9
18.4	23.2	42.0	37.5	16.5	67.2
10.9	13.9	2.0	6.2	4.9	3.8
4.7	2.3	0	6.6	4.3	1.9
21.1	4.6	12.0	10.9	14.6	7.7
9.5	7.0	20.0	8.2	20.7	0
7.5	4.6	10.0	11.6	9.7	7.7
0	27.9	2.0	1.4	0	3.8
53.7	60.3	46.0	44.9	54.2	24.9
0.7	2.3	2.0	1.8	3.0	0
6.1	0	0	0.9	3.0	0
0	0	0	0	0.6	0
4.1	9.3	4.0	2.0	5.5	1.9
0.7	0	0	0.2	0	0
11.6	11.6	6.0	4.9	12.1	1.9
3.4	0	0	2.3	3.6	1.9
4.1	0	4.0	2.7	3.6	0
6.8	4.6	2.0	5.7	6.7	1.9
0	0	0	0	0.6	0
2.0	0	0	1.6	2.4	1.9
16.3	4.6	6.0	12.3	16.9	5.7
100	100	100	100	100	100
147	43	50	438	164	52

Table 5.3 continued

Class	Occupational subgroup	*(9)* *Hanover* *(OG Döhren)* *(1925-32)*	*(10)* *Hetjers-* *hausen* *(1932-3)*
LOWER	1. Agricultural workers	0.6	2.3
CLASS	2. Unskilled workers	13.7	2.3
	3. Skilled (craft) workers	15.7	34.9
	4. Other skilled workers	0.2	4.6
	5. Domestic workers	2.4	0
Subtotal		32.6	44.1
Lower-	6. Master craftsmen	3.4	0
&	7. Non-academic professionals	4.7	0
middle-	8. White-collar employees	10.1	7.0
MIDDLE	9. Lower civil servants	3.5	13.9
CLASS	10. Merchants	16.7	2.3
	11. Farmers	2.2	27.9
Subtotal		40.6	51.1
Upper-	12. Managers	1.7	0
MIDDLE	13. Higher civil servants	0.9	0
CLASS &	14. University students	0.6	0
UPPER	15. Academic professionals	1.5	0
CLASS	16. Entrepreneurs	1.1	2.3
Subtotal		5.8	2.3
STATUS	17. Non-university students	0.9	0
UNCLEAR	18. Pensioners/retired	1.5	2.3
	19. Wives/widows	7.1	0
	20. Military personnel	0	0
	21. Illegible/no data	11.4	0
Subtotal		20.9	2.3
TOTAL (%)		100	100
Frequency (*N*)		534	43

Table 5.3 continued

(11) Hüpede/ Oerie (1927-33)	(12) Nikolaus- berg (1932-33)	(13) Nordholz/ Brebber (1929-33)	(14) St Andreas- berg (1928-32)	(15) Sieber (1932-3)	(16) Stadtolden- dorf (1930-2)
26.3	5.1	28.4	0	16.7	4.1
9.4	7.7	2.0	10.8	19.0	9.3
21.6	51.3	16.7	38.5	16.7	23.7
0	2.5	0	1.5	0	0
0	0	0	7.7	0	0
57.3	66.6	47.1	58.5	52.4	37.1
2.0	2.5	0	7.7	4.8	3.1
1.3	0	0	4.6	9.5	2.1
3.4	2.5	1.0	1.5	9.5	8.2
3.4	2.5	1.0	12.3	9.5	7.2
4.7	10.3	8.8	6.1	4.8	8.2
23.6	15.4	42.1	0	0	22.7
38.4	33.2	52.9	32.2	38.1	51.5
0	0	0	0	2.3	0
0	0	0	0	0	0
0	0	0	0	0	0
0	0	0	0	0	1.0
0	0	0	0	0	0
0	0	0	0	2.3	1.0
0.7	0	0	6.1	0	1.0
1.3	0	0	3.1	2.3	0
0	0	0	0	2.3	3.1
0	0	0	0	0	0
2.0	0	0	0	2.3	6.2
4.0	0	0	9.2	6.9	10.3
100	100	100	100	100	100
148	39	102	65	42	97

Table 5.3 continued

		(17)
Class	*Occupational subgroup*	*Wetteborn (1931–2)*
LOWER	1. Agricultural workers	7.4
CLASS	2. Unskilled workers	3.7
	3. Skilled (craft) workers	7.4
	4. Other skilled workers	0
	5. Domestic workers	0
Subtotal		18.5
Lower-	6. Master craftsmen	11.1
&	7. Non-academic professionals	0
middle-	8. White-collar employees	3.7
MIDDLE	9. Lower civil servants	0
CLASS	10. Merchants	0
	11. Farmers	59.2
Subtotal		74.0
Upper-	12. Managers	0
MIDDLE	13. Higher civil servants	0
CLASS &	14. University students	0
UPPER	15. Academic professionals	0
CLASS	16. Entrepreneurs	0
Subtotal		0
STATUS	17. Non-university students	0
UNCLEAR	18. Pensioners/retired	7.4
	19. Wives/widows	0
	20. Military personnel	0
	21. Illegible/no data	0
Subtotal		7.4
TOTAL (%)		100
Frequency (*N*)		27

Notes: a Relates to the members listed in Table 5.3 whose date of entry into the NSDAP could be established.
b Relates to all members listed in Table 5.3.

Table 5.3 continued

(18)	(19)	(20)	(21)	(22)	(23)
	Nazi recruits in Gau				All members in
	SOUTH-HANOVER-BRUNSWICK[a]				Gau SOUTH-HANOVER-
		in			BRUNSWICK[b]
(1925–9)	(1930)	(1931)	(1932)	(1933)	(1925–33)
2.6	3.3	4.7	3.4	4.8	4.0
7.0	13.4	11.1	11.7	6.9	10.3
12.3	15.6	17.5	17.3	17.6	17.5
1.7	1.1	0.6	1.4	0.9	0.9
0	0.5	2.8	3.2	0.5	1.7
23.6	33.9	36.7	37.0	30.7	34.5
3.5	5.6	3.6	3.6	7.0	4.5
2.6	5.6	5.3	5.4	4.7	4.7
5.3	16.2	8.8	10.6	12.5	10.3
8.8	2.8	7.7	6.9	13.9	8.4
21.0	16.2	9.2	13.2	10.5	11.8
14.9	7.8	10.7	4.0	3.3	7.0
56.1	54.2	45.3	43.7	51.9	46.7
1.7	1.7	0.8	1.0	1.7	1.2
0	0.5	0.8	1.5	2.8	1.4
0	0.5	0.4	0.1	0	0.3
2.6	0	2.8	2.2	3.6	2.3
0.9	0	0.2	1.0	0.3	0.5
5.2	2.7	5.0	5.8	8.4	5.7
1.7	2.2	2.3	2.7	1.7	2.0
2.6	2.2	1.1	2.7	2.2	2.0
7.0	3.3	6.0	4.9	3.3	4.6
0	0	0	0	0.1	0.04
3.5	1.1	3.4	3.2	1.6	4.1
14.8	8.8	12.8	13.5	8.9	12.7
100	100	100	100	100	100
114	179	468	727	640	2,510

Dominating the industrial activity of the city was the machine-construction industry, which employed just over 8,500 workers, with the food-processing industry employing a further 7,000.[41] As a capital city, Brunswick was also a major administrative and educational centre, a role reflected in the occupational structure of its working population.[42]

The membership of the Brunswick-Steintor branch (situated in the inner city[43]) covers the period 1925 to 1 March 1933, and lists the membership alphabetically, including those who left the party for various reasons.[44] Only a fraction of the members (9.4 per cent) had joined before 14 September 1930, most of whom had entered the party between 1928 and 1930, though five could date their membership back to 1925 (including one woman, a seamstress). Three hundred and seventy three members joined between 15 September 1930 and 31 January 1933, with surprisingly few (only 11) entering the party in the month following Hitler's elevation to the chancellorship. Some 21.8 per cent of the total membership had left the branch by the time the entries ceased on 1 March 1933, the bulk of whom had moved away from the city, while a small number had either left the party voluntarily or had been excluded from it. One member's entry carries the remark 'shot', presumably a victim of the physical violence which accompanied politics in the early 1930s. The rejection of one application for party membership by an inmate of the city's prison is also noted. In one aspect the branch represents a significant deviation from the general pattern of Nazi membership in the region in that it had a comparatively high female membership which, at 21.1 per cent, was over three times higher than the average for *Gau* South-Hanover-Brunswick.[45]

The occupational and social background of the membership of the Steintor branch (see Table 5.3, column 2) was always dominated by recruits drawn from the lower- and middle-middle class, especially in the years before 14 September 1930, when it drew three-quarters of those members whose occupation can be established from this class, of which half were merchants. In the early 1930s the branch continued to recruit heavily from the lower- and middle-middle class, but the share of the merchant occupational subgroup fell as an increasing number of white-collar employees and a large number of lower- and middle-grade civil servants joined its ranks. The social basis of the branch also widened with a slight rise in support from the lower class, and a more significant level of participation by the upper-middle class and upper class, especially academic professionals and higher civil servants. Given the limited presence of the lower class within its ranks, the social profile of the Brunswick-Steintor branch bore little resemblance to the social structure of the working population of Brunswick city as a whole, though it probably reflected the social milieu to be found in the 'old city' parts of Brunswick more closely.

OG Clausthal-Zellerfeld
OG St. Andreasberg
OG Sieber

These three branches were all situated in county Zellerfeld, one of the more heavily industrialized parts of *Regierungsbezirk* Hildesheim in which, apart from a few rural communities, agriculture played only a relatively minor role in the economic life of the area, since only 12.6 per cent of the total population was still dependent on the primary sector for its livelihood by 1933.[46] Light industry was pursued in small and medium-sized concerns scattered throughout the county, with textiles and food-processing of significance, while some heavy industry could also be found, particularly in the *Kleinstadt* Clausthal-Zellerfeld (pop. 11,378), in which ore-mining was one of the most important economic sectors, its decline in the early 1930s shaking the local economy to its foundation.[47]

The sources on which the three branch membership breakdowns are based are of varied provenance. In the case of the Clausthal-Zellerfeld branch it involves a membership list of the NSDAP listing 349 members as on 15 March 1941,[48] of which only those who had joined the Nazi Party by May 1933 (when the party enforced a temporary halt to recruitment) were evaluated. Given the census date, it is obvious that the data can only provide an insight into the social background of those who had joined the branch at some time before May 1933 and had not left the party by March 1941. Although it is not made clear in the list, I suspect that it involves the membership of but one of several branches in the town, for the 147 members who had enrolled by May 1933 cannot be taken as an accurate guide to the strength of Nazism in the town before 1933, given that as early as 14 September 1930 the Nazis secured one of their best urban results

141

(34.7 per cent[49]) in *Gau* South-Hanover-Brunswick in this town. Moreover, in his account of the development of Nazism in Clausthal-Zellerfeld Sigurd Plesse notes that the strength of the party in the town had reached the 800 mark by August 1933.[50] For the reconstruction of the branch membership of the *Landstadt* St Andreasberg (pop. 3,279), two membership lists were used, one dated 1 December 1931, the other undated, but recording those entering the party up to 1 February 1932, which also provides a list of the members of the HJ and of the NSF.[51] Finally, the data on the membership of the Nazi branch in the village of Sieber (pop. 735) is taken from a party census return of February 1936, from which those members (42 out of a total membership of 49) who had joined the party by May 1933 have been evaluated.[52]

Of the three branches, the social structure of those established at St Andreasberg and Sieber (see Table 5.3, columns 14 and 15) were broadly in line with the occupational structure of the working population of county Zellerfeld, with lower-class supporters providing the majority of the membership. In St Andreasberg, a small market town in the mountainous Harz region, three of the four members who had joined the party between 1928 and 14 September 1930 were from the lower-middle class, but craft workers, especially slaughterers, formed the bulk of recruits when the branch expanded rapidly in the course of 1931. In the village of Sieber, lying some eight kilometres to the west of St Andreasberg, the primary sector dominated the local economy,[53] a feature reflected in the membership of the Nazi branch established here in March 1932, in which blue- and white-collar forestry workers were prominent. On the evidence provided by the 1941 membership list for Clausthal-Zellerfeld, the lower class appears to have been a very negligible factor in the membership of this branch (see Table 5.3, column 3) before 1933, the social configuration of which was seemingly radically different to that of the town's working population.[54] Although it is probable, in the light of other evidence, that there was a sizeable influx of middle-class elements into the branch in the early 1930s,[55] and that the middle class was undoubtedly the important component in the Nazi Party's membership in the town, it is also likely that there was a much stronger lower-class content among the membership than is suggested by the 1941 data. Certainly within the ranks of the SS following its formation in the town at the beginning of 1932, the lower class was the majority element,[56] suggesting perhaps that workers became disenchanted with the party and had left it in some numbers by the time the 1941 party membership census was undertaken.

OG Echte

Formed in 1929, this branch was centred on the small village of Echte (pop. 768) in the northern part of county Osterode in the Harz mountains. Agriculture was by far the most important economic activity in the Echte area, with 41.7 per cent of the total population dependent upon it.[57]

The membership data is taken from a list of former Nazi members belonging to the branch compiled (presumably for de-Nazification purposes) in 1945.[58] Of the 106 members recorded in the list, 43 had joined the branch by May 1933 (one member was noted as entering the party in 1922), and had not left it subsequently. The data is obviously not a complete record of the total branch membership over time, which limits its utility. What it suggests is a party branch in which the middle class always dominated the membership (see Table 5.3, column 4). The branch was formed in 1929 by a group of farmers (one of whom was still branch leader by 1945), an occupational sub-group which provided half of the 16 members recorded in the list as belonging to the branch by 1930, of whom 87.5 per cent were of lower- and middle-middle-class status. It would seem that the branch then stood still, no new members being added in the next two years, before a block of 27 further members joined in 1933, all but one on 1 May. Although a few farmers were involved in this 'surge', the occupational and social types attracted to the party on that day involved the village notables (a doctor, vet, dentist, apothecary, the manager of the savings bank, two teachers and a mill-owner), while quite a few master craftsmen also entered the party, along with a scattering of lower-class recruits, including three miners. Although the May influx broadened the social and occupational base of the branch membership, the lower- and middle-middle class retained its overall dominance.

143

OG Friedland
OG Hetjershausen
OG Nikolausberg

These small branches were all situated in county Göttingen, a strongly agrarian region in which 59.8 per cent of the working population was still employed in agriculture by the time of the 1933 census, with a further 23 per cent engaged in crafts and industry, and 11 per cent in trade and transport.[59] It was the heavy dependence on agriculture which accounted for the high percentage of the self-employed and of working family members in the occupational breakdown of the working population of the county.[60]

The three membership lists relating to these branches are survivors of what appears to have been a party membership census in county Göttingen undertaken in 1936.[61] Only those members who had joined the NSDAP by 1 May 1933 are evaluated. The branches were formed in 1932 (though Friedland had four members who could date their entry into the party before that year), and centered on what were very small village communities. Both Nikolausberg (pop. 334) and Hetjershausen (pop. 252) were on the outskirts of Göttingen, which most likely conditioned the economic activity of a part of their population since Göttingen was within easy commuting distance. There were some differences in the structure of the local economies in these three villages. In both Friedland (pop. 412) and Nikolausberg agriculture was of less significance as an employer than in Hetjershausen, where exactly half of the total population depended on it for a living.[62] The Hetjershausen branch, moreover, recruited in a number of villages in its immediate hinterland (such as Elkershausen, Gladebeck, and Volkerode) which were even more agrarian.

The nature of the catchment area of the Hetjershausen branch is reflected in the large percentage of farmers (and farmers' sons) which it attracted by 1933 (see Table 5.3, column 10), an occupational subgroup less strongly represented in the Nikolausberg branch (see Table 5.3, column 12), and virtually absent in the branch at Friedland (see Table 5.3, column 5). Skilled craft workers formed the largest occupational subgroup in all three branches, accounting for the majority of the membership in Nikolausberg by May 1933. The comparatively high percentages

144

registered by lower- and middle-grade civil servants in the Friedland and Hetjershausen branches was almost entirely due to blue- and white-collar railway staff, the bulk of whom joined in 1933.

OG Goslar-Ost

This branch was one of four in place by 1933 in the medium-sized town of Goslar (pop. 22,987). Goslar was a small industrial, commercial and administrative centre during the Weimar period, with a mixed economy in which various branches of industry were represented, with the clothing and food-processing sectors being of some significance. Industry formed the core of the local economy, employing 41.6 per cent of the working population, followed by trade and transport, which employed a further 27.3 per cent.[63] Medium-sized concerns with a workforce of between 100 to 250 were a rarity in the town, in which small-scale units of production were the norm in virtually all economic sectors, with artisanal businesses employing five or less workers predominating.[64]

A most detailed membership register has survived for OG Goslar-Ost,[65] in which 438 members (8.9 per cent of whom were female), who had joined the branch between 1925 and 1933, are listed. Beyond the entry for each member of such particulars as surname, first name, date of birth, address, date of joining the NSDAP, and membership number, the register also contains a 'remarks' column, in which additional information on members is often to be found. There are no indications as to when the register was compiled, but one suspects that this occurred some time in late 1931 or early 1932. If this suspicion is correct, the membership record provided in the register is incomplete, involving only those who were still in the party at that time. Lost therefore, obviously, would be the details of those individuals who had joined – and subsequently left – the party in Goslar-Ost before the register was drawn up. This might explain the very few members listed in the register who had joined the party between 1925 and 14 September 1930, which numbered a mere 25 (17 of whom had joined since the beginning of 1929). Of those who were noted as entering the party before 14 September 1930, 48 per cent were from the lower class (the two members recorded as joining the party in 1925 were a carpenter and a mechanic), 28 per cent from the lower- and middle-middle class, 4 per cent from the 'elite', and 20 per cent in the 'status unclear' category. The comparatively high lower-class content was reduced in the early 1930s, when merchants and white-collar workers – as well as independent master craftsmen – made up a noticeable proportion of the 202 members who joined between 15 September 1930 and 31 January 1933. This trend continued in the surge towards the party in early 1933, with 138 recruits noted as entering the party on (appropriately) April Fool's Day alone, of which quite a few were master craftsmen, merchants and lower- and middle-grade civil servants. By May 1933 the strong inflow of *Mittelstand* recruits in the early 1930s had made the lower- and middle-middle class the major component of the membership of OG Goslar-Ost (see Table 5.3, column 6). The corresponding fall in the percentage of members drawn from the lower class meant that the social structure of the Goslar-Ost branch in May 1933 no longer matched that of the towns' working population as perfectly as the pre-September 1930 membership had done.

OG Göttingen-Landwehr

In the town of Göttingen (pop. 47,149), a major stronghold of Nazism from the early 1920s,[66] the Nazi Party was well-entrenched by the late 1920s. At the time of the Nazi electoral breakthrough in the *Reichstag* election of 14 September 1930, Göttingen provided by far the highest urban poll (37.8 per cent[67]) achieved by the NSDAP in electoral district South-Hanover-Brunswick. Göttingen's socio-economic structure was conditioned by its role as a university town[68] and as an administrative centre, in which the service sector loomed large (in 1933 the service sector employed 25.4 per cent of the working population, well above the regional average). There was some industry in the town, especially the manufacture of clothing, but Göttingen could hardly be described as an industrial town. Trade and transport employed only fractionally fewer people than industry and crafts (the respective figures for 1933 are 31 and 32.4 per cent).[69]

The data on the social characteristics of OG Göttingen-Landwehr (see Table 5.3, column 7), situated in the south-east of the town (a handful of its members were resident in Geismar in county Göttingen) provides an incomplete overview of the branch membership before 1933, based as it is on a list drawn up on 31 December 1943, when the branch had 480 members. This data obviously cannot provide any information on those members who had joined and then left the branch before the 1943 census was taken. Of the 480 members listed, 164 had entered the party in the town by May 1933 (members who had joined the party elsewhere and then moved to Göttingen were excluded from the analysis), which means that one is dealing with members who had been in OG Landwehr for at least ten years, while two members had indeed been in the branch for just over twenty years (a railway official who had entered the party in 1922, and a woman – whose occupation is not given – who had joined in 1923). Of the 164 'long-established' members, 18 had been recruited before 15 September 1930, 37 had joined between 15 September 1930 and 31 January 1933, and a further 109 had entered the branch by 1 May 1933. Of the 18 members who had joined the party before 14 September 1930, 8 were recipients of the *Ehrenzeichen* of the NSDAP, denoting their early entrance into, and long membership of, the Nazi Party. Except for two females, whose status cannot be determined, the holders of the *Ehrenzeichen* all had *Mittelstand* backgrounds, half of them working in the public sector (one in the postal service, and two on the state railway). One of the local 'old guard', Elsner von Gronow, who had entered the party on 1 March 1925 while still an agricultural student, rose to some prominence within the Nazi Movement by the early 1930s, initially as the *de facto* leader of *Gau* Hanover-South following the withdrawal of Haase and Fobke from active politics in the course of 1926 and 1927,[70] and then as a 'national speaker' (*Reichsredner*) of the NSDAP on agrarian questions. Of the 12 members (whose social status could be determined) who joined OG Landwehr before 14 September 1930, 75 per cent were from the lower- and middle-middle class, a preponderance which was reduced to 59.2 per cent between 14 September 1930 and 31 January 1933, when the social base of the branch membership widened with a more noticeable influx of lower-class recruits (29.6 per cent) and a sprinkling of upper-class types (11.1 per cent). The lower-class percentage among the membership was reduced subsequently by the predominantly middle-class background of the 109 recruits who swelled the ranks of the branch in early 1933. A large number of these were civil servants and white-collar workers, while academic profes-

147

sionals also figured prominently among them. All but six of those who joined in 1933 were male, reducing the overall percentage of women among the membership from 25.4 per cent for the period up to 31 January 1933 to 11.6 per cent by May 1933. By mid-1933 the branch seems to have been made up predominantly of middle-class males, with both women and lower-class members relatively marginal among the membership. Given the overall class structure of the working population of Göttingen, it does seem that the strength of the lower class was markedly under-represented within the branch by 1933, even allowing for the probability that blue-collar workers figured more prominently in the membership turn-over than supporters drawn from the middle and upper classes.

OG Groß Ilsede

Although this branch of the Nazi Party recruited the bulk of its members in the small industrial village of Groß Ilsede (pop. 1,740), it also enrolled some 30 per cent of its members in a number of surrounding villages within a five kilometre radius, such as Klein Ilsede, Oberg, Adenstedt, Neuölsburg, and Groß and Klein Bülten. Groß Ilsede was situated in county Peine, one of the more industrialized parts of *Regierungsbezirk* Hildesheim, the economy of which was shaped to a considerable extent by the mining of ore and the metallurgical industry in general, centred on the Ilseder Hütte complex at Peine. In 1933 industry and crafts along with transport and trade employed 46.7 per cent of the working population, fractionally ahead of agriculture's 44.8 per cent.[71] In Groß Ilsede itself, however, only 7.1 of its total population was dependent on agriculture for a livelihood.[72]

Based on a number of membership lists which record the formative phase of the development of the branch,[73] the social profile of the Groß Ilsede membership was strongly lower-class (see Table 5.3, column 8). Judging from the entries of the earliest surviving membership lists, the first resident of Groß Ilsede to join the Nazi Party was an electrician (his entry date is given as 1 July 1929), but the organizational life of Nazism in the village (presumably in the form of a party cell) started on 1 May 1930, when a small group of individuals entered the party. Gradual growth, rather than any sudden spurt in membership, characterizes the subsequent development of the branch to early 1932.

Almost a quarter of all those who had joined the branch by 1932 were unskilled workers (the majority of whom were described as *Arbeiter*), while craft workers (such as butchers, bakers, carpenters, painters and bricklayers) accounted for just over one-third. The dominance of the lower class within the branch emerged gradually by 1931, and was reinforced by the nature of the membership turnover. In the first membership list of 16 February 1931, some 54.5 per cent of the 22 members recorded were lower- and middle-middle class in their status, whereas the lower class provided only 36.4 per cent of the members. However, of the six individuals who subsequently left the branch by the summer of 1931, five were from the *Mittelstand*, while the majority of new members joining the party in Groß Ilsede and its surrounds in late 1931 and early 1932 were from the lower class. Although one of the founder members of the branch was a married woman, only one further female (a servant) joined the branch by early 1932. The strong support mobilized by the party from among the male lower class in Groß Ilsede by the spring of 1932 probably gave the branch a social profile in line with the socio-economic structure of the village and its hinterland, in which industry and crafts, rather than agriculture, dominated economic activity.

OG Hanover-Döhren

By the early 1930s the Nazi Party was mobilizing considerable membership[74] and electoral[75] support in Hanover (pop. 443,920), Germany's twelfth largest city. One of the large number of Nazi Party branches active in the city by 1932 was that established in the suburb of Döhren, which lay on the southern edge of Hanover to the south of the Südstadt district, an area which included strongly bourgeois residential quarters such as Waldhausen and Waldheim.[76] The numerous small- and medium-sized firms situated in Hanover, as well as the presence of large plants employing thousands of factory workers, such as the tyre firm Continental, made Hanover a major centre of industry, with almost half (47.8 per cent) of its working population engaged in industry and crafts in 1933.[77] The industrial base of the city was a very mixed one, the most important sectors revolving around the construction of machinery, the metallurgical, rubber and chemical industries, the manufacture of textiles,

149

and the clothing industry. The city also had important trading and communication functions, an economic sector which employed a further 31.5 per cent of the workforce.

An insight into the type of individuals recruited into the Döhren branch is provided by an accounts book in which all those members paying their monthly party dues (even if for only one month) in 1931 and 1932 are recorded alphabetically.[78] The occupation of the bulk of the members is given in the book, but large gaps in the column recording the membership number of the individuals listed makes it impossible to reconstruct the recruitment pattern of the branch with any degree of certainty. It would seem from such evidence as is provided that the branch was expanding quite rapidly in 1931 and 1932, but that few of its members could trace their entry into the party back to the late 1920s, though a small group of members (judging from their low party membership numbers) had been recruited as far back as 1925. By 1932 the Döhren branch (see Table 5.3, column 9) had a heterogeneous social base, with the unskilled and skilled blue-collar workers', white-collar employees' and merchants' occupational subgroups providing the majority of the members. As in many other Nazi party branches in urban centres of some size, women formed a not insignificant 12.4 per cent of the Döhren branch membership. Given the absence of any specific data on the social configuration of the population of the Döhren district, it is impossible to make any judgement on how representative this Nazi branch was of the social milieu from which it recruited. In comparison with the social structure of the working population of Hanover as a whole, the sociology of the membership of the Döhren branch reflects a noticeable under-representation of workers and civil servants, and to a lesser degree, of white-collar employees.

OG Hüpede/Oerie

The comparatively early establishment of a Nazi presence in the north-east of county Springe, centred on the villages of Hüpede (pop. 389) – in which the NSDAP began to recruit from February 1927 – and Oerie (pop. 185), probably owes much to its close proximity to Sarstedt in adjacent county Hildesheim, a *Landstadt* where the Nazis had been active before 1923, and where the party established a strong presence from 1925 onwards.[79] The villages of Hüpede and Oerie, as well as that of Gerstorf (pop. 864), in which 40.5 per cent of the branch membership had been recruited by 1933, were located in a predominantly agricultural area. In Gerstorf 54.4 per cent of the total population was dependent on agriculture for its livelihood, in Oerie the percentage was 57.3, while in Hüpede it reached 65.9.[80]

The membership of the branch is recorded in detail in a membership book[81] (which also doubled up as an accounts book recording the payment of membership dues) which was started in early 1931, and in which are entered such details as the name, occupation, age, place of residence, date of entry into the NSDAP and party number of each member. Further information is provided on a number of members in a 'comment' column, in which the reason as to why they resigned their membership or why they were expelled from the party is given. The book allows an accurate reconstruction of membership movement between 1931 and 1933 (the 11 members recruited after 1933 are excluded from the analysis), but not for the years 1927 to 1930, given that only those members who had joined by the end of 1930, and were still in the branch when the membership book was compiled, are recorded. Between 7 February 1927 and 14 September 1930, the branch recruited at least 23 members, of whom 52.2 per cent were lower- and middle-middle class (virtually all farmers), and 43.5 per cent lower class (primarily agricultural workers). Between 15 September 1930 and 31 January 1933 a further 78 recruits joined the branch, the bulk of whom (62.8 per cent) were from the lower class, thus altering the overall social balance between the two class groupings represented in the branch in favour of the lower class (of the 101 individuals listed as joining before 31 January 1933, 58.4 per cent came from the lower class).

The social profile of this totally male branch (see Table 5.3, column 11) reflects the agrarian nature of the communities in which it recruited. Agricultural labourers formed the largest occupational group, and it is highly likely that their actual number was greater still, given that among the many who are simply described as 'worker' in the membership, some were almost certainly agricultural labourers. Farmers, particularly strongly in evidence among the early membership, formed the second largest occupational subgroup. Given that a few of these were under twenty years of age when they joined the party, while almost all were under thirty, one is essentially dealing with farmers' sons. Among the skilled craft workers, trades typical of village life (smith, wheelwright, carpenter) are much in evidence, and a number of occupations listed among the white-collar employees' and merchants' occupational subgroups (such as horse-dealer, agricultural supervisor) also show a connection with the farming world. Overall the membership of the branch, at least from the beginning of 1931, was remarkably stable, with only seven members leaving the party between the end of 1931 and 1933 (all but one in 1932), four of whom were excluded (three for 'lack of interest', and one for not paying his membership dues), while only three voluntarily left the party. The degree to which Nazism had penetrated into the male population of Oerie is quite astonishing, given that 31.9 per cent of all males in the village had been members of the party by the end of 1933. Bearing in mind the likelihood of a sizeable number of males in the village who were under 18 years old, and thus too young to become party members, and the relatively few Nazi members aged above the 35-year mark, it is likely that virtually all males between the ages of 18 and 35 were in the party by 1933. In Hüpede the degree of Nazi penetration into the male population, at 27.2 per cent, was only marginally smaller.

OG Nordholz/Brebber

This branch was situated in the southern part of the predominantly agrarian county Hoya,[82] in which the Nazi Party secured 44.4 per cent of the vote – its second highest electoral return at the county level – in the *Reichstag* election of 14 September 1930.[83] The population of the many villages in which the branch recruited, including Brebber (pop. 357), Graue (pop. 472), Helzendorf (pop. 220), Nordholz (pop. 224), Warpe (pop. 240), and Windhorst (pop. 219), was almost totally dependent on agriculture (the degree of dependence ranged from 75.9 per cent in Nordholz to 90.9 per cent in Windhorst).[84] The county was part of Jan Blankemeyer's sphere of propaganda activity in the late 1920s (he lived in the county for some time). Blankemeyer, who harangued his peasant audiences in Low German, was one of the NSDAP's most effective 'wandering speakers' in Lower Saxony in the 1920s, instrumental in carrying the Nazi message to many a village in Oldenburg and the north-western parts of the province of Hanover.[85]

An insight into the social background of the totally male membership of the branch is provided by a membership-cum-accounts book covering the years 1931 to 1934.[86] Judging from the entries for the pre-1931 period, the branch was formed by a dozen individuals, two of whom had joined the party in 1929, on 1 January 1930. Farmers and their sons, along with agricultural workers, dominated recruitment into the branch throughout the period 1930 to 1933 (see Table 5.3, column 13). Just over a quarter (27.4 per cent) of the recorded membership had left the party by the time the last entry was made on 15 October 1933, the bulk of whom left the party voluntarily (rather than being excluded) in the course of 1932.

OG Stadtoldendorf

This branch, situated in county Holzminden, recruited not only in the *Landstadt* of Stadtoldendorf (pop. 4,064) in the early 1930s, but in a number of surrounding villages, especially Linnenkamp (pop. 302) and Emmerborn (pop. 60) to the south-east of the town, and Golmbach (pop. 824) lying to the north-west. Excluding the town of Holzminden, a minor manufacturing centre, the county of Holzminden had a mixed economy in which agriculture employed 49.3 per cent of the working population, while industry and crafts (35.5 per cent) combined with trade and transport (8.4 per cent) employed a further 43.9 per cent.[87] Stadtoldendorf itself did not, however, have a mixed economy. It fulfilled a trading and service function for the agrarian hinterland which surrounded it, with few of its citizens being engaged in agriculture as such.[88]

Some insight into the social background of the members recruited in the Stadtoldendorf area is provided by two membership lists plus additional fragmentary evidence on membership matters contained in the correspondence between the branch and *Gau* headquarters in Hanover covering 1931 and early 1932.[89] Going on the party numbers held by the members of the Stadtoldendorf branch, it appears to have been founded in late 1930.[90] The nucleus of the branch, 61 members resident in Stadtoldendorf, is recorded in a list which, though not dated, was probably made at the beginning of 1932. Since only the names and addresses of the members are noted in the list, the occupational status of 57 of the 61 members was discovered by using an address book of the town.[91] A second list sent to *Gau* headquarters on 24 August 1931 lists 34 members recruited in the villages surrounding the town, in which their occupational status is given. Information on a few other members who joined the party in late 1931 is contained in correspondence between the branch and the *Gaukassenwart* in Hanover.

The mix of the two quite distinct recruitment areas of the Stadtoldendorf branch (small-town and rural) is reflected in the high percentage of farmers among the branch membership (see Table 5.3, column 16). In Stadtoldendorf members drawn from the lower- and middle-middle class were only marginally more numerous than those with a lower-class background (accounting respectively for 46.0 and 39.7 per cent of the membership resident in the town). Of the members recruited in Stadtoldendorf's agrarian hinterland, 52.9 per cent were farmers. In the countryside the lower class made up 38.2 per cent of the membership, the lower- and middle-middle class 61.8 per cent. Whereas agricultural labourers are prominent among those workers recruited in the villages surrounding Stadtoldendorf, craft workers of various description, along with a handful of factory workers, constituted the lower-class content of the branch membership resident in the town itself. The sole representative of the 'elite' recruited by the party in the area by early 1932, a doctor, was resident in Stadtoldendorf, as were the three female members mobilized by the Nazi Party in the area.

OG Wetteborn

The small branch of Wetteborn (pop. 237) in county Alfeld[92] was probably typical of the many village branches founded by the Nazis in *Gau* South-Hanover-Brunswick in the early 1930s. In its membership structure (see Table 5.3, column 17) it resembled something akin to a farmers' club. The branch was formed on 1 September 1931, when twelve farmers, one master smith and a painter joined the party.[93] Farmers and agricultural labourers figured prominently in the limited further recruitment of the branch by 1 March 1932. Not surprisingly, the branch membership was totally male, predominantly young, and led by a farmer. The majority of those listed as 'farmer' were fairly young (one indeed was only aged sixteen, below the age requirement for Nazi membership) and thus were probably sons of farmers. Significantly, within six months of its formation, the Wetteborn branch had already mobilized 25 per cent of the total male population of the village, probably involving most of the males in Wetteborn who were in their twenties and early thirties.

III

The analysis of the social and occupational profiles of the membership of those branches of the NSDAP in *Gau* South-Hanover-Brunswick on which there is detailed information shows how variable these could be. The class and occupational mix of individual branches was often quite distinct, generally reflecting the diverse socio-economic milieux of the localities in which they operated. The ability of the Nazis to mobilize support from different occupational and class elements – and their combination at branch level was infinitely variable in pattern – is demonstrated clearly in the case of *Gau* South-Hanover-Brunswick, where the party's claim to be a *Volkspartei* has validity. In the early 1930s the social base of Nazism in the Hanover-Brunswick region broadened significantly with the rise in support from both the lower class and the upper-middle- and upper class, with a corresponding fall in the share of the lower- and middle-middle class among the membership (see Table 5.3, columns 19–21). Admittedly, the rush into the party in 1933 by *Mittelstand* and 'elite' elements, especially civil servants of all grades, depressed the percentage of the lower class within the ranks of the party.

To describe the Nazi Party in *Gau* South-Hanover-Brunswick as a 'peoples' party' is not to ignore the far from perfect match between the occupational structure of the Nazi membership in the *Gau* and the occupational and social structure of the working population of the region. Clearly the lower class (see Table 5.2) was inadequately represented within the ranks of the party membership in *Gau* South-Hanover-Brunswick (see Table 5.3, columns 18–23), whereas the middle class always loomed large. However, the differences in social terms between the party and the working population in the *Gau* do not appear to have been as wide as suggested by the *Partei-Statistik*, in which the Nazis claimed that 28 per cent of *Gau* South-Hanover-Brunswick's membership was made up by workers in the period 1925 to 31 January 1933.[94] While it is true that the lower class is a marginal factor in a number of the branches analysed above, especially those of Brunswick-Steintor, Clausthal-Zellerfeld, Echte, Göttingen-Landwehr, and Wetteborn (see Table 5.3, columns 2–4, 7, and 17), in eight of the seventeen branches evaluated the lower class provides over 40 per cent of the support, a fact which makes it problematical to apply the middle-class thesis. In such branches as those established at Groß Ilsede or at Nikolausberg (see Table 5.3, columns 8 and 12), where the lower class made up over two-thirds of the membership, the *Mittelstandsbewegung* hypothesis is obviously not tenable.

The breakdown of the membership of the Nazi Party in *Gau* South-Hanover-Brunswick according to community size (see Table 5.4) shows that it was in the rural communities and small *Landstädte* that the Nazis found it comparatively easier to recruit the lower class than in the larger urban centres. Almost 50 per cent of all Nazis mobilized in communities with a population of under 5,000 came from the lower class, a figure which falls quite dramatically to 16.7 per cent of the membership recruited in small towns, while in medium-sized towns and cities the respective percentages are 31.8 and 27.5. Although in numeric terms the total of lower-class members recruited in village communities with a population of less than 2,000 was on par with the number enrolled in the cities, just over half (52.4 per cent) of all lower-class members were mobilized in medium-sized towns and cities. The skilled craft workers subgroup provided about half of the lower-class membership in every community-size category.

The overall recruitment pattern of the lower- and middle-middle class was fairly consistent – ranging between 41.2 and 51.7 per cent – across all community sizes. Ignoring the expected strong presence of farmers among this class grouping in the Nazi membership resident in communities with a population of under 2,000, community size appears to have had some bearing on the response rate of some occupational subgroups. Master craftsmen were recruited in some numbers in medium-sized towns and cities, but were a marginal factor in the party as a whole in communities with a population of under 20,000. Master craftsmen resident in villages and small towns figure much more prominently among new Nazi members after January 1933, though the potential for successful Nazi recruitment from this subgroup was already being demonstrated in some villages and small towns in the early 1930s, especially in the branches of

Table 5.4 Persons joining the NSDAP (*N:* 2,490[a]) in *Gau* South-Hanover-Brunswick by place of residence, 1925–33 (by %)[95]

		Community size				
Class	Occupational subgroup	Under 2,000	2,000–4,999	5,000–19,999	20,000–99,999	Over 100,000
LOWER	1. Agricultural workers	3.6	0.3	0	0.1	0.1
CLASS	2. Unskilled workers	2.0	1.4	0.3	2.8	3.9
	3. Skilled (craft) workers	5.5	1.9	0.6	4.2	5.2
	4. Other skilled workers	0.4	0.1	0.04	0.2	0.2
	5. Domestic workers	0.04	0.2	0.1	0.3	1.1
Subtotal		11.5	3.9	1.0	7.6	10.5
Lower-	6. Master craftsmen	0.7	0.5	0.6	1.4	1.2
&	7. Non-academic professionals	0.3	0.2	0.3	1.4	2.5
middle-	8. White-collar employees	1.1	0.6	1.2	2.8	4.5
MIDDLE	9. Lower civil servants	1.2	0.8	0.6	2.7	3.0
CLASS	10. Merchants	1.4	0.7	0.4	2.7	6.3
	11. Farmers	6.0	0.5	0	0.2	0.5
Subtotal		10.7	3.3	3.1	11.2	18.0
Upper-	12. Managers	0.1	0.04	0.04	0.5	0.5
MIDDLE	13. Higher civil servants	0	0	0.7	0.7	0.7
CLASS &	14. University students	0	0	0	0.04	0.2
UPPER	15. Academic professionals	0.3	0.04	0.2	0.7	1.1
CLASS	16. Entrepreneurs	0.04	0	0.04	0.04	0.4
Subtotal		0.4	0.1	1.0	2.0	2.9
STATUS	17. Non-university students	0.1	0.2	0.2	0.6	0.8
UNCLEAR	18. Pensioners/retired	0.3	0.1	0.2	0.7	0.6
	19. Wives/widows	0.2	0.1	0.4	1.4	2.5
	20. Military personnel	0	0	0	0.04	0
	21. Illegible/no data	0.3	0.3	0.1	0.4	2.9
Subtotal		0.9	0.7	0.9	3.1	6.8
TOTAL (%)		23.5	8.0	6.0	23.9	38.2
Land Brunswick (*N:* 501,875)		45.7	7.5	17.5	–	29.3
Reg.-Bez. Hanover (*N:* 823,006)		33.9	8.6	2.7	3.1	51.7
Reg.-Bez. Hildesheim (*N:* 594,104)		51.3	12.6	15.7	20.4	–

Note: a Based on those members in Table 5.3 whose place of residence could be established.

Clausthal-Zellerfeld, Echte and Wetteborn (see Table 5.3, columns 3, 4 and 17), in which master craftsmen provided over ten per cent of the membership. The lower- and middle-grade civil servants' sub-group demonstrates an almost identical recruitment pattern to that of the master craftsmen. Recruited in some numbers in the larger towns and cities in the region before 1933 (they are especially noticeable in OG Brunswick-Steintor and OG Göttingen-Landwehr), they rushed into the party branches based in village and small-town communities (such as Friedland and Hetjershausen in county Göttingen) only in early 1933. The tendency to gravitate towards the party of those described as 'merchants' is also most strongly pronounced in the cities, where this occupational subgroup provided 35 per cent of the lower- and middle-middle- class membership, whereas this percentage drops markedly in smaller towns. The recruitment of all occupational subgroups constituting the upper-middle class and upper class increases progressively with community size, with 'elite' elements belonging to the Nazi Party a comparative rarity in small towns and rural communities before 1933.

Community size also conditioned one other aspect of the social characteristics of the Nazi Party, namely that of female membership. In communities with a population of under 5,000 women members were a great rarity, especially at the village level, where they constituted a mere 1.5 per cent of the membership recruited by 1933. In the small and medium-sized towns females were more in evidence among the membership of the party, making up 7.5 per cent of the total membership. It was in the cities, however, that females provided stronger support for the Nazi Party, accounting for 16.3 per cent of all members. Overall females account for 9.9 per cent of the membership analysed in Table 5.3, of which two-thirds joined in 1931 and 1932. Females did not participate to any great extent in the stampede into the Nazi Party which took place in 1933, constituting a mere 5.3 per cent of all those members who can be identified as entering the NSDAP in 1933.

6

THE SA

Of the numerous specialist organizations which emerged within the Nazi Movement during the *Kampfzeit*, by far the most important in furthering the development of the NSDAP into a mass movement was the *Sturmabteilung* (or Storm Section).[1] Founded as early as 1921 in the form of a paramilitary force designed to protect the nascent Nazi Party, and utilized by Hitler to pursue his putschist ambitions, which proved such a dismal failure in November 1923, the SA re-emerged following the re-formation of the Nazi Party in February 1925 to become the 'militant and terroristic arm of the party in its political struggle for power'[2] designed, in the words of one of its lesser functionaries, 'to destroy the Marxist terror ... (and) to conquer the streets and thus prepare the ground for the conquest of the people'.[3] The violence and brutality employed by the SA to further the political objectives of the Nazi Movement are portrayed graphically in the literature on the organization.[4] For the growth of Nazism in an organizational form, especially in the more industrialized, urbanized regions of Germany, the presence of effective strong-arm squads was often a basic necessity, a prerequisite for the party's public appearance.[5] The protective and propagandistic tasks facing the SA inevitably involved the organization in numerous clashes and street brawls, primarily with the left, which were increasingly initiated by the SA in its desire to attract attention, emphasize its radicalism, and intimidate its political opponents.

Before 1930 the SA suffered from the slow growth which affected the Nazi Movement in general. By August 1929 its total strength was perhaps around the 30,000 mark, which doubled within the year to reach 60,000 by November 1930, expanding to 77,000 by January 1931.[6] The explosive phase of its membership growth occurred in 1931 and 1932, years which saw the emergence of the SA as a mass movement, paralleling the rapid, relatively massive growth of the NSDAP itself. By January 1932 the membership of the SA had risen to 290,000, to increase to 471,000 by August of the same year (this figure includes *circa* 26,000 members in the Motor SA), after which it declined to around the 450,000 mark by January 1933 as its progress was halted due to the setback in the fortunes of the NSDAP in the *Reichstag* election of November 1932.[7] Given that the SA probably suffered an even higher turnover rate in its membership than that experienced by the NSDAP (which was around the 40 per cent mark between 1930 and 1933), the actual number of men enrolling in the SA was much higher than the above figures indicate.[8] It is obvious that the SA mobilized a considerable number of individuals to support the Nazi cause before 1933. What is uncertain is how many of the SA members were also prepared to also join the NSDAP. Although Pfeffer von Salomon, in one of his numerous SA regulations in June 1927, ordered all SA members to join the Nazi Party as well,[9] it seems that many of the SA rank and file never actually complied with the order. Conan Fischer has pointed out that out of 604 SA members in Hamburg and Munich in 1932, only 56 per cent were actually in the party, and suggests 'that before January 1933 only about a half of the stormtroopers belonged to the party'.[10] Mathilde Jamin has questioned the representative nature of Fischer's sources and casts doubt on the validity of his conclusion. Jamin argues that for all we know those involved in the lists used by Fischer might all have joined the NSDAP subsequently, and also points to the often quite lengthy delays among even the higher SA leaders before these became NSDAP members as well.[11] This is still an unresolved issue, though an important one given the implication it has for the structure of the NSDAP. The problem is that only an analysis of a representative number of SA members will prove conclusively how many SA members were also, ultimately, Nazi Party members. An analysis of those membership lists included in Table 6.1 which indicate whether or not an SA member had also joined the party, provides variable results, in the majority of instances producing percentage values of party membership well below that suggested by Conan Fischer. Thus of the 130 members listed alphabetically in personal files covering the letters A to E belonging to the SA

Brigade 55 Württemberg-North, all of whom were resident in county Waiblingen and who had joined the SA between 1930 and 1934 (with amendments still being made to their files in 1935), only 39.2 per cent were also members of the party by 1935.[12] In the personal files of *Sturmbann* II/251, which was centred on Adelebsen in county Northeim in the province of Hanover, out of the 44 members recorded who had joined the SA between 1929 and 1934, only 36.4 per cent were also party members, one of whom had finally joined the NSDAP in 1937, some four years after his entry into the SA.[13] Of 47 members of SA *Brigade* 153 resident in Mannheim, all but three of whom had joined the SA in 1933 and 1934, a mere 12.8 per cent were recorded as being NSDAP members.[14] It is only in the *Stammrolle* of SA *Sturmbann* III/*Reserve* 63 based in Frankfurt-am-Main, which was still being amended by 1937, that the number of SA members (all but three of the 144 listed had joined the SA between 1930 and 1933) who were also members of the NSDAP was relatively high, standing at 58.8 per cent.[15] The problem, of course, with such evidence, beyond the fact that one cannot claim that it is representative, is that we do not know how conscientious the SA leaders involved in compiling the data and signing the individual files were in recording whether or not the SA member was also a Nazi Party member. It may well be that Conan Fischer's estimate that half of the SA joined the party is too high, or it might be that those who joined the SA in the late 1920s[16] and early 1930s were more likely to have joined the party than those who flooded into the SA in early 1933, who would have been faced with the bar on further recruitment to the NSDAP imposed by the Nazis in May of that year. It is also highly likely that there was a difference between the rank and file SA members and the lower- to middle-ranking SA leaders in the matter of whether or not they were also Nazi Party members. For example, all four leaders of *Sturmbann* II/251 (who secured the lower-level ranks of *Schar-*, *Trupp-* and *Sturmführer*), who had all joined the SA before 1933, were also members of the NSDAP. Of the nine SA leaders noted in SA *Sturmbann* III/*Reserve* 63 (from *Scharführer* to *Sturmhauptführer*, the latter reaching this rank in 1935), all but two were also in the party. That Nazi Party membership was very much the norm among the higher-ranking SA leaders is evident from data advanced by Mathilde Jamin.[17]

Irrespective of the percentage of SA members who also joined the NSDAP, it is clear that the SA, given its numeric strength by 1933, was an important part of the Nazi Movement as a whole. The nature of the social structure of the organization has an important bearing on the question of the sociology of the NSDAP itself, even if only half of the SA membership – or even less – actually joined the party before the Nazi *Machtergreifung*.

I

It is only from the 1970s onwards that scholars have given serious attention to the social composition of the SA. The empirical evidence available to date is contradictory, while the conclusions reached among those involved in the debate is far from unanimous.[18] The first meaningful analysis of the social characteristics of the SA was undertaken by Eric Reiche in his study on the SA in Nuremberg in 1972.[19] Using various sources, Reiche identified the age, occupation and place of birth of 358 Nuremberg SA members (including both the rank and file and the leadership corps) who joined the organization between 1922 and 1934. On the basis of this data Reiche concluded that the SA had a broad class base in occupational and social terms, in which the *Mittelstand* marginally outnumbered the lower class during the Weimar period, with working-class members accounting for 43 per cent of the members identified by Reiche as being in the SA between 1922 and 1923, 45.7 per cent of those in the organization between 1925 and 1929, and 41.2 per cent of the 1930 to 1932 membership.[20] On the basis of his evidence Reiche refrained from reaching any sweeping conclusions about the sociology of the SA as a whole. A few years later, in his first re-working of the autobiographical accounts of early Nazis compiled by Theodore Abel in 1934, Peter Merkl also pointed to the broad social base of the SA and SS rank and file and leaders contained in the Abel material, allocating 42 per cent of these to the 'blue-collar workers' category.[21]

A quite different social profile was advanced by Michael Kater. On the basis of raw data supplied to him by Conan Fischer relating to SA members living in rural Bavaria, Munich and Frankfurt-am-Main, including also some SA activists who had been involved in street brawls, Kater argued that the SA was essentially a petit-bourgeois phenomenon, elements of the *Mittelstand* making up about 70 to 80 per cent of its membership.[22] Kater reached this conclusion primarily because he was still subscribing to an occupational and class model which he had first adopted in his important article on the social dimensions of the early NSDAP, in which he had placed skilled (craft) workers and apprentices into the lower-middle class.[23]

Conan Fischer, in his evaluation of the same data, in which he employed a more realistic occupational and class model in which skilled workers were assigned to the lower class, arrived at radically different results to those of Kater.[24] On the basis of his analysis Fischer reached the conclusion 'that the SA was not a predominantly lower-middle-class body'.[25] According to Fischer 'workers' accounted for 63.4 per cent of his 'sample' of 1,184 SA rank and file members who were in the SA in the period 1929 to 30 January 1933, while for a larger 'sample' of 3,812 members who were in the SA in the period 31 January 1933 to 30 June 1934 the figure was even higher, at 69.9 per cent.[26] Basically Fischer reached conclusions which turned the social profile of the SA as suggested by Kater on its head. In Fischer's view the SA was 'an activist movement which won sizeable numbers of workers for the National Socialist cause'.[27] At around the same time as the appearance of Fischer's essay, Lawrence Stokes published, as part of his analysis of the social structure of the NSDAP in Eutin, a breakdown of the occupational background of 54 SA members who had joined the organization up to 1929. Stokes pointed to the 'proletarian' nature of the Eutin SA, and that 'in all likelihood, hardly more than half a dozen Eutin SA members enjoyed a middle-class existence'.[28]

It was Fischer's essay which sparked off a lively debate involving not, as one might expect, Michael Kater, but two historians then working on different aspects of the SA's structure and development, Mathilde Jamin[29] and Richard Bessel.[30] The resulting exchange in the pages of *Social History* revolved primarily around methodological questions involved in quantitative history, though some new evidence was advanced by Bessel and Jamin, which in part contradicted Fischer's results and in part also substantiated his line of argument and pointed to the probability of marked regional variations in the social structure of the SA.[31] Of the two sets of new data presented, one was broadly in line with the heavy urban-biased data which Fischer had analysed, that is a computation of 1,824 membership cards relating to the Berlin SA as of February 1931 which showed that 54 per cent of its members were unskilled or skilled workers.[32] This data was juxtaposed with a summary of the social characteristics of the SA membership (total strength of 2,144) in *Regierungsbezirk* Allenstein in East Prussia compiled by the police in June 1931, in which the lower class was hardly visible. In this very rural part of East Prussia farmers, young farmers and agricultural supervisors alone accounted for 44.9 per cent of the SA's membership, with artisans and artisans' apprentices providing a further 33.3 per cent. The 'proletariat', in the shape of agricultural workers, made up a mere 7.7 per cent of the Allenstein SA.

In the early 1980s Fischer, Bessel and Jamin all published the results of their research on the SA, studies which have enhanced our knowledge of that organization both in a quantitative and qualitative sense. Conan Fischer, taking on board aspects of the criticism levelled against him on methodological grounds, produced a more finely differentiated picture of data already published by him by placing the various SA formations he had previously aggregated into a global 'sample' in their local context.[33] His conclusion as to the social basis of the SA remained identical to that advanced by him in the late 1970s, namely that in the last years of the Weimar era 'the SA's ordinary membership was largely working class' and that the working-class character of the SA was even further enhanced after the Nazi seizure of power.[34]

In the section of his book which deals with the social background of the SA in Eastern Germany, Richard Bessel illustrated, by reference to a series of statistical tables summarizing the occupational groups represented in the SA in the province of East Prussia, which had been compiled by the police authorities in *Regierungsbezirke* Königsberg (two lists, collated in October 1930 and June 1931, involving 917 and 4,450 men respectively) and Allenstein (one list for June 1931 involving 2,144 men), that in these less urbanized and predominantly agrarian regions, the working-class presence in the SA was not significant.[35] In the police summaries of the occupational groups constituting the SA's membership, agrarian and industrial workers combined made up only 11.7 per cent of the SA in *Regierungsbezirk* Königsberg by June 1931, while in *Regierungsbezirk* Allenstein agricultural workers accounted for only 7.7 per cent of all members. The percentage values for lower-class members do rise quite significantly, however, if one includes the artisan and artisans' apprentices occupational groups in the 'working class'.[36]

A unanimous view was established in the early 1980s on one aspect of the debate concerning the social profile of the SA: the acceptance of a sharp contrast between the social make-up of its rank and file and of its leadership cadre. As far as the higher echelons (those who reached the rank of *Standartenführer* or SA colonel and above) of the SA are concerned, the meticulously researched, sophisticated quantitative analysis produced by Mathilde Jamin – a model of its kind – demonstrated that from mid-1925 up to the Nazi *Machtergreifung* (and beyond), the lower class was markedly under-represented in the higher ranks of the SA leadership corps. In the years 1925 to 1929 only 11.1 per cent of the higher SA leaders came from the lower class as against 62.6 per cent drawn from the *Mittelstand*; between 1930 and 1933 the respective figures were 12.1 per cent and 66.2 per cent.[37] It was only at the lower levels of the SA leadership, primarily at the *Scharführer* level (SA sergeant, the lowest non-commissioned rank), who were generally recruited from the rank and file membership, that the social distance which existed between the ordinary SA trooper and the middle- and higher-ranking SA-leaders was hardly in evidence.[38]

Following the veritable rash of publications on the SA which appeared in the early 1980s, which left the question of the social characteristics of the rank and file SA an issue of contention between rival schools of thought, there was an hiatus before new evidence on this issue was advanced. Beyond attempting to summarize the bulk of the available data produced by 1987 on the membership and leadership of the SA,[39] I was able to offer new material on the structure of the Munich SA in the pre-1923 period,[40] as well as the results of an investigation into the social background of 1,539 members of the Bavarian SA at the time of the temporary prohibition of the organization in April 1932.[41] The often extensive detail on these members, which usually went beyond the invariable listing of name, age, place of birth and occupation to record such matters as religion, marital status, family background and even, in some instances, the financial situation of the individual concerned, were put together by the Bavarian police authorities following house-searches of SA members resident in hundreds of small towns and villages scattered throughout Bavaria. The data, which in all probability represents a broad cross-section of the small-town, rural Bavarian SA membership, produced a consistent pattern in all parts of Bavaria. In all of the regions of the *Land* the lower class provided the majority of the SA members, ranging from 49.2 per cent in the Palatinate to 66.6 per cent in Upper Bavaria, averaging out at 61.1 per cent for Bavaria as a whole. The structure of the predominantly rural Bavarian SA in the spring of 1932 is in marked contrast to that of the SA in rural East Prussia. Farmers and sons of farmers do not figure prominently in Bavaria in comparison with the SA data on *Regierungsbezirke* Königsberg and Allenstein, accounting for a mere 7.3 per cent in Bavaria as a whole, ranging from the very marginal 2.3 per cent in Lower Bavaria to 19.8 per cent in the Palatinate.[42] In the small-town, rural Bavarian SA, unskilled (including a small percentage of agricultural labourers) and skilled workers were the prominent occupational subgroups. In broad terms the data on the Bavarian SA membership captured in the police files of early 1932 supports Fischer's contention that one is dealing with an organization in which the lower class was the major social group.

Ultimately the validity of Fischer's argument, and the suspicion that the social profile of the SA in Eastern Germany as portrayed by Bessel may be atypical, can be settled on the basis of a series of empirically-based case studies resting on material drawn from all parts of Germany which can do justice to the marked regional variations in the religious composition and socio-economic structure of German society. The material which follows is viewed as providing further data which will contribute to a more rounded, comprehensive picture of the sociology of the SA.

II

The data on the social characteristics of the SA presented in Table 6.1 is based on a variety of sources relating to SA units in the *Länder* of Baden, Hesse-Nassau and Württemberg, and the Prussian provinces of Hanover and Westphalia.[43] Involved are units of the 'ordinary' SA, of SA probationers and SA reservists, as well as SA Motor and SA Rider corps, the members of which are recorded in the form of membership lists, muster rolls or personal files.[44] Although one cannot claim that the sources provide a representative sample on which to base an evaluation of the social profile of the SA as a whole, the various lists do involve a useful mix of stormtroopers active in both rural and urban environments, in agrarian and industrial areas in predominantly Catholic or Protestant regions of Germany. The material evaluated here, however, does have a strong rural slant, with a marked under-representation of SA members resident in big cities with a population of 100,000 or over (see Table 6.3). SA men from rural communities with a population of under 2,000 account for 32.8 per cent of those analysed here who were in the SA before 30 January 1933, and 42.7 per cent of those joining the SA after 30 January 1933. If one adds those SA men living in *Landstädte* with populations of between 2,000 and 4,999, the percentages rise to 68.8 and 52.0 respectively, resulting in an over-representation of SA members from rural and small-town communities, which is especially marked in the pre-1933 period.

The data relating to the SA in Baden (see Table 6.1, columns 1, 5 and 8), and some additional material on the SA in county Donaueschingen which has not been tabulated, shows some significant variations in the social and occupational background of the stormtroopers involved. In *Sturm* 1/112 in Eberbach, a strongly Protestant *Kleinstadt* (population of around 7,500 in 1933) situated in the Neckar valley in county Heidelberg[45] in north-western Baden, and among the SA probationers recruited in a number of villages to the north and east of Eberbach, the lower class provided the bulk of the members. Despite the importance of agriculture in the area, independent farmers were probably not represented in the SA recruited in the area at all since those listing themselves as such (all of whom were under thirty years of age) were most likely farmers' sons. These 'assisting family members' provided half of the small number of SA recruits drawn from the lower- and middle-middle class, which made up just over a quarter of the total SA membership. In county Villingen[46] in south-eastern Baden, with a not dissimilar socio-economic structure to Heidelberg, but which had a predominantly Catholic population, the social characteristics of the SA[47] at first glance suggest that there were significant differences to that of the SA in Eberbach and district, with a relatively limited participation of lower-class elements, though the large number of SA men whose job description is not provided by the police probably distorts the overall social profile.

167

Table 6.1 The social and occupational structure of the SA in various towns and districts of Germany, 1929–34 (by %)[43]

Class		Occupational subgroup	*(1)* Eberbach (Baden) SA Sturm 1/112 SA Anwärter (1933)	*(2)* Frankfurt (Hesse-Nassau) SA Sturm III/R.63 (Stammrolle)
LOWER	1.	Agricultural workers	0	0
CLASS	2.	Unskilled workers	18.9	19.4
	3.	Skilled (craft) workers	43.2	26.4
	4.	Other skilled workers	0	0.7
	5.	Domestic workers	0	0
Subtotal			62.1	46.5
Lower-	6.	Master craftsmen	2.7	1.4
&	7.	Non-academic professionals	0	2.8
middle-	8.	White-collar employees	8.1	14.5
MIDDLE	9.	Lower civil servants	0	14.5
CLASS	10.	Merchants	2.7	14.5
	11.	Farmers	13.5	0
Subtotal			27.0	47.7
Upper-	12.	Managers	0	0
MIDDLE	13.	Higher civil servants	0	1.4
CLASS &	14.	University students	2.7	0
UPPER	15.	Academic professionals	8.1	2.1
CLASS	16.	Entrepreneurs	0	0
Subtotal			10.8	3.5
STATUS	17.	Non-university students	0	0.7
UNCLEAR	18.	Pensioners/retired	0	0.7
	19.	Illegible/no data	0	0.7
Subtotal			0	2.1
TOTAL (%)			100	100
Frequency (N)			37	144

Table 6.1 continued

(3) *Groß Ilsede* (Provinz *Hanover*) SA *(late 1932)*	(4) *Northeim* *County* (Provinz *Hanover*) SA Sturm II/251 *(1929–33)*	(5) *North-West* *Baden* *(Mannheim)* SA Brigade 153 (Stammrolle)	(6) (7) *Paderborn* (Provinz *Westphalia*) *Members* *Leaders* SA Sturm 2/158 (Stammrolle)	
0	11.4	0	0	0
40.0	38.6	7.0	7.4	12.5
45.0	38.6	22.8	36.8	12.5
0	0	1.7	1.2	0
0	0	0	0	0
85.0	88.6	31.5	45.4	25.0
0	0	0	0	0
0	0	0	0	6.2
5.0	0	8.8	10.4	25.0
0	0	8.8	6.7	25.0
0	0	5.3	5.5	0
5.0	9.1	0	0	0
10.0	9.1	22.9	22.6	56.2
0	0	0	0	0
0	0	0	0.6	0
0	2.2	26.3	0	0
5.0	0	8.8	9.2	6.2
0	0	0	0	0
5.0	2.2	35.1	9.8	6.2
0	0	10.5	17.2	6.2
0	0	0	0	0
0	0	0	4.9	6.2
0	0	10.5	22.1	12.4
100	100	100	100	100
20	44	57	163	16

Table 6.1 continued

Class	Occupational subgroup	(8) Villingen County (Baden) Members (1932)	(9) Leaders
LOWER	1. Agricultural workers	0	0
CLASS	2. Unskilled workers	18.9	0
	3. Skilled (craft) workers	16.2	23.1
	4. Other skilled workers	0	0
	5. Domestic workers	0	0
Subtotal		35.1	23.1
Lower-	6. Master craftsmen	2.7	0
&	7. Non-academic professionals	2.7	0
middle-	8. White-collar employees	10.8	23.1
MIDDLE	9. Lower civil servants	0	7.7
CLASS	10. Merchants	24.3	23.1
	11. Farmers	0	7.7
Subtotal		40.5	61.6
Upper-	12. Managers	0	0
MIDDLE	13. Higher civil servants	0	0
CLASS &	14. University students	0	0
UPPER	15. Academic professionals	0	15.3
CLASS	16. Entrepreneurs	0	0
Subtotal		0	15.3
STATUS	17. Non-university students	0	0
UNCLEAR	18. Pensioners/retired	0	0
	19. Illegible/no data	24.3	0
Subtotal		24.3	0
TOTAL (%)		100	100
Frequency (*N*)		37	13

Table 6.1 continued

(10) Waiblingen County (Württemberg) SA Brigade 55 (Personalakten)	(11) Wetzlar County (Hesse-Nassau) SA Sturm 23/ R.224 (1932–4)	(12) Witzenhausen County (Hesse-Nassau) Members (Various SA units) (Mannschaftslisten)	(13) Leaders 	(14) Germany Leaders (1930–4)
1.5	0	3.1	0	1.3
9.2	25.6	18.9	20.6	15.8
37.7	19.8	46.7	44.1	28.9
1.5	3.5	0.3	5.9	2.6
0	0	0	0	0
49.9	48.9	69.0	70.6	48.6
6.9	0	2.7	2.9	2.6
0.8	1.2	0.3	0	2.6
4.6	5.8	2.7	2.9	11.8
7.7	12.8	3.1	2.9	10.5
6.9	4.6	15.1	8.8	7.9
13.1	23.2	4.5	5.9	6.6
40.0	47.6	28.4	23.4	42.0
0.8	0	0	0	0
0.8	0	0.7	0	0
2.3	0	0	0	0
2.3	1.2	0.7	2.9	5.3
1.5	2.3	0.3	2.9	1.3
7.7	3.5	1.7	5.8	6.6
1.5	0	0.7	0	1.3
0	0	0	0	0
0.8	0	0	0	1.3
2.3	0	0.7	0	2.6
100	100	100	100	100
130	86	291	34	76

However if one includes those individuals suspected as being in the SA,[48] the percentage for the lower class increases quite dramatically to 59.8, with a small reduction to 37.9 per cent for members from the lower- and middle-middle class, giving values which are virtually identical with those of the SA in Eberbach and its hinterland. The bulk of individuals (37 out of 52) from the lower class suspected of being SA members were skilled workers, primarily clockmakers and mechanics, while among the unskilled workers a large percentage were described by the police as 'factory workers'. There is record of only one member drawn from the farming community, the leader of SA *Trupp* Blücher 34/113, a farmer resident in the village of Weiler. Farmers and sons of farmers were more in evidence among the SA in the adjacent county of Donaueschingen (an agrarian, Catholic region to the south of Villingen), making up 16 per cent of the 50-strong SA *Sturm* 82/6 in June 1931.[49] In this SA unit the largest single 'classification' group, the unemployed, made up 24 per cent of the membership, followed by factory workers with 22 per cent, farmers and artisans with 16 per cent each, independents with 12 per cent, and white-collar employees with 10 per cent. In the Eisenbach SA at the time of its formation in July 1931, two-thirds of its nine members were skilled workers, two were from the *Mittelstand* and one from the upper-middle class.[50] Radically different to the social structure of the Baden SA in its rural, small-town environment, was the composition of those members of SA *Brigade* 153/*Standarte* 110 (Heidelberg) recorded in the surviving muster rolls as having joined the SA between 1927 and 1934 in Mannheim. Baden's largest city, Mannheim was not only a major industrial centre, with important metal, chemical and textile plants, but also had important administrative, trading and communication functions. The 'dual' nature of its economic structure was reflected in the social make-up of its male working population, in which blue-collar workers accounted for 54.4 per cent, white-collar workers and civil servants for 30.7 per cent, and independents for 14 per cent.[51] The social structure of the Mannheim SA recorded in the muster rolls bore little resemblance to that of the male workforce. The student category was the single most important subgroup, followed by skilled workers, the two combined accounting for almost 50 per cent of the total membership.[52] The lower class was heavily under-represented within the Mannheim SA, in which white-collar workers and civil servants were also under-represented, though to a much smaller extent.

The stormtroopers (including a small number of probationers and members of the reserve SA) who had joined units of SA *Brigade* 55 Württemberg-North between 1930 and early 1934, were resident in numerous villages and small towns in the counties of Waiblingen and Schorndorf (see Table 6.1, column 10).[53] These two Protestant counties had a mixed economy in which both agriculture and industry were of almost equal importance. In county Waiblingen 42.3 per cent of the working population was employed in agriculture and 38.5 per cent in industry and crafts, while in county Schorndorf the percentages were 48.7 and 36.8 respectively.[54] In the larger towns of the area, such as Fellbach, Waiblingen, Winnenden and Schorndorf, between 85 and 95 per cent of the population worked in the secondary and tertiary sectors.[55] The social structure of the SA was quite distinct from that of the working population of the two counties. Whereas half of the members of the SA were drawn from the lower class, almost half of the working population was made up by independent farmers and assisting family members, categories which are very heavily under-represented in the SA, though (sons of) farmers did provide some limited support for the organization. The marked under-representation of the farming community in the SA was balanced by a heavy over-representation of lower- and middle-middle-class elements drawn from the industrial and service sectors and a slight over-representation of workers, who made up half of the SA membership, but only 38 per cent and 38.8 per cent of the working population of county Waiblingen and county Schorndorf respectively.[56]

The data available on the SA in the Prussian province of Hesse-Nassau relates to a unit of the reserve SA situated in the city of Frankfurt, and to various rural units in the counties of Wetzlar[57] and Witzenhausen (see Table 6.1, columns 2, 11 and 12). The muster roll of SA-*Sturmbann* III/Reserve 63 records members who had virtually all joined the SA between 1930 and 1933, though there are a few members who had entered the organization before 1930, including a locksmith who had joined the SA as far back as 1 January 1923 and who had risen to the rank of *Sturmhauptführer* by 1935. Unlike the active SA, the reserve SA in general had a more aged membership,[58] a feature reflected in *Sturmbann* III/R.63, in which the majority of members were thirty or over, with quite a number in their fifties and a few in their sixties. The age factor is also reflected in the marital status of the members of the unit, 70.8 per cent of whom were married. The membership of the *Sturmbann* was made up almost equally by lower-class and *Mittelstand* elements, with skilled (craft) workers representing the largest single occupational subgroup. The lower class was, however, slightly under-represented in the *Sturmbann* in comparison with the social make-up of the male working population of Frankfurt,[59] and in this respect this particular section of the reserve SA in the city was different in comparison with another Frankfurt reserve SA unit, *Regiment R*.97, in which the lower class made up 68.9 per cent of the membership.[60] In terms of the balance between lower-class and *Mittelstand* members which existed in *Sturmbann* III/*R*.63, it had more in common with the units which formed part of SA *Sturm* 23/*R*.224 in the Wetzlar region, though there were marked differences in the occupational subgroups represented within them. The units of *Sturm* 23/*R*.224 on which there is data, *Trupp* Hochelheim and *Trupp* Niederwetz, recruited in numerous villages to the south and south-east of Wetzlar, the great majority of the members entering the SA in the course of 1932 and 1933. An almost totally Protestant area, 55.9 per cent of the working population of county Wetzlar (excluding *Stadtkreis* Wetzlar) was still engaged in agriculture, while industry and crafts employed 32.9 per cent.[61] In the villages in which the SA recruits were resident, agriculture (with the odd exception such as Nauborn) was the major employer by far, especially in the small villages of Oberkleen, Niederkleen, Espa, Niederwetz and Groß Rechtenbach, where between 60 to 75 per cent of the total population depended on agriculture for a living.[62] It is in these villages that the relatively large contingent of farmers and farmers' sons was recruited, making up almost a quarter of the membership and virtually half of the lower- and middle-middle-class membership. Also strongly represented were lower-grade 'civil servants', blue-collar railway workers (especially signalling staff and line workers) providing the majority of this occupational subgroup. Among the lower-class unskilled workers, especially miners and foundry workers, outnumbered skilled (craft) workers, a reversal of the usual pattern to be found in many SA formations. Distinctly different in social terms to the SA units of Frankfurt and county Wetzlar were those formations operating in the Protestant county Witzenhausen in northern Hesse-Nassau, which were strongly lower class in their social structure. Unlike most of northern Hesse, which was very agrarian, Witzenhausen was relatively industrialized, with industry and trade employing 45 per cent of the working population, and agriculture 47.4 per cent.[63] It was in agriculture that the high percentage of independents and assisting family members among the working population, accounting for 17.2 and 29.1 per cent respectively, were employed. White-collar employees and civil servants made up but 8.9 per cent of the workforce, and workers 42.8 per cent. Around half of the members of the various SA units in county Witzenhausen were resident in Großalmerode, and a further 10 per cent in Witzenhausen and Hessisch Lichtenau, small urban centres where industry and trade dominated the labour market. The three active SA units belonging to *Sturm* 41/ 83 in Großalmerode were strongly lower class in composition, with 74.7 per cent of their membership drawn from this class. In the reserve SA of *Sturm* 41/83, the percentage drawn from the lower class was only 47.4, with master craftsmen, shopkeepers and lower-grade civil servants (especially from the postal service) strongly represented in the 52.6 per cent of the lower- and middle-middle-class membership. Yet even in those units recruited in a number of villages in which agriculture was by far the major employer, the lower class provided the bulk of the SA, such as in Ziegenhagen (75 per cent), Rittergut Hübenthal (85.7 per cent, all agricultural workers), Gertenbach (84.6 per cent) and Ermschwerd (76.9 per cent). In the two units of *Motorsturm* V/ 83, recruited in and around Großalmerode and Witzenhausen, the lower class (at 56.7 per cent) was less strongly in evidence, with middle- and upper-class types, who probably provided the transport available to these units, forming an important membership component.

All but a handful of the stormtroopers recorded in the muster roll of SA *Sturm* 2/158 in Paderborn (see Table 6.1, column 6) joined the unit after Hitler became chancellor on 30 January 1933. Situated in a strongly Catholic region of eastern Westphalia, an area in which the Nazi Party had made virtually no impact by 1933,[64] the medium-sized town of Paderborn (it had a population of 37,000 in 1933) was primarily a centre of administration, trade and communication, these three branches of economic activity alone employing half of the working population.

Light industry played only a limited role in the economic life of the town, though the clothing industry had some significance as an employer. Workers made up 46.1 per cent of the male working population, while civil servants accounted for 21.7 per cent, and white-collar employees and independents for 15.2 per cent.[65] Those who rushed to join the SA in Paderborn in 1933 (only five members on the muster roll had joined before the end of January 1933, and only eleven are recorded as joining between January and March 1934 when the entries cease) were predominantly young and single (only three of the 134 whose marital status is noted were married). The percentage share of lower-class members in the Paderborn SA was on a par with the social structure of the male working population, but the lower- and middle-middle class (especially civil servants) was heavily under-represented, though the large number of non-university students recorded in the muster roll were almost certainly from *Mittelstand* families. There appears to have been a veritable stampede into the SA of young barristers or law graduates, thirteen members being described as *Referendar*.

The sources on the SA in Groß Ilsede and on county Northeim (see Table 6.1, columns 3 and 4) in the province of Hanover relate to SA units operating in rural, Protestant areas, with distinctly different socio-economic frameworks. Groß Ilsede, near Peine, was essentially a large industrial village, with only 7.1 per cent of its working population dependent on agriculture.[66] In Groß Ilsede the SA membership involves only those who were noted as belonging to the organization in a list of NSDAP branch members drawn up in late 1932, and thus probably represents but a fraction of the total strength of the local SA. While the NSDAP branch membership in Groß Ilsede was dominated by the lower class,[67] the SA was, barring three of its members, totally lower-class in its social composition. An even higher percentage of lower-class support was registered among the membership of *Sturmbann* II/251 recruited in the villages of Adelebsen, Allershausen, Barterode, Eberhausen and Güntersen in county Northeim, an agrarian region in which 57.4 per cent of the working population (excluding *Stadtkreis* Northeim) was engaged in agriculture.[68] Although two individuals could trace their SA membership back to 1929, all but eight joined the SA between 1 May 1933 and 16 January 1934. Among the SA men resident in the village of Güntersen (in which just over a half of the

Sturmbann was recruited), quarry workers predominated, while agricultural workers were strongly in evidence among the small number recruited in Eberhausen, and 'workers' among those living in Adelebsen. The handful entered as 'farmers' in the personal files were clearly farmers' sons.[69]

The leaders of the various SA units evaluated here (see Table 6.1, columns 7, 9, 13 and 14) involved, with a very few exceptions, those from the lower, non-commissioned ranks of *Truppführer* and below. Unlike the middle- and higher-ranking leaders, the lower-level SA leaders generally rose from the ranks and were more representative of the social milieu represented in the rank and file active SA. However, even at this level, the chances of an SA man with a lower-class background rising to a leadership position were very much smaller than his lower- and middle-middle-class 'comrade'. The *Mittelstand* type, more willing to undertake bureaucratic functions requiring a degree of organizational and administrative skill,[70] was over-represented even among the lower-level SA leadership corps. The evidence advanced in column 14, albeit distorted by the unusual leadership pattern existing in the SA units of county Witzenhausen, would suggest that the lower-level leadership formed a social bridge between the SA men and the SA leaders at the middle and higher levels of the SA hierarchy. They were in general less lower-class than the ordinary SA man and less bourgeois than the upper echelons of the SA leadership.[71]

III

Despite some marked divergences in the social characteristics of the various SA formations evaluated in Table 6.1, their membership overall was based solidly on lower-class support, both before and after Hitler's acquisition of the chancellorship (see Table 6.2, columns 5 and 6). The possibility hinted at by Fischer[72] that there might even have been a slight increase in working-class representation within the SA after 30 January 1933 is not reflected in the data on those recruits whose date of entry into the SA could be determined. Even allowing for the rural bias contained in the data, there is a suggestion that the SA found it much easier to recruit from the lower class in rural and small-town environments rather than in large towns and cities both before and after 30 January 1933, and less difficult to acquire upper-middle- and

Table 6.2 The social and occupational background of SA recruits, 1931–4 (by %)[a]

Class	Occupational subgroup	(1) 1931	(2) Joined SA in 1932	(3) 1933	(4) 1934	(5) In SA before 31.1 1933	(6) from 31.1 1933
LOWER CLASS	1. Agricultural workers	5.2	2.4	1.5	0	2.9	1.4
	2. Unskilled workers	12.1	16.1	16.8	22.2	16.6	16.8
	3. Skilled (craft) workers	50.0	40.3	35.7	25.0	41.4	35.4
	4. Other skilled workers	0	0	0.9	5.5	0	1.5
	5. Domestic workers	0	0	0	0	0	0
Subtotal		67.3	58.8	54.9	52.7	60.9	55.1
Lower- & middle- MIDDLE CLASS	6. Master craftsmen	1.7	6.4	1.5	1.4	4.4	1.5
	7. Non-academic professionals	0	0	0.7	1.4	0.5	0.8
	8. White-collar employees	6.9	8.9	6.0	11.1	7.3	6.5
	9. Lower civil servants	3.4	4.0	7.4	6.9	3.9	7.4
	10. Merchants	15.5	12.9	8.0	6.9	15.1	7.8
	11. Farmers	1.7	4.8	6.5	8.3	4.4	6.4
Subtotal		29.2	37.0	30.1	36.0	35.6	30.4
Upper- MIDDLE CLASS & UPPER CLASS	12. Managers	0	0	0.1	0	0	0.1
	13. Higher civil servants	0	0	0.6	0	0	0.5
	14. University students	1.7	0.8	2.7	2.8	1.0	2.7
	15. Academic professionals	0	1.6	4.1	2.8	1.0	4.0
	16. Entrepreneurs	0	0.8	0.6	0	0.5	0.5
Subtotal		1.7	3.2	8.1	5.6	2.5	7.8
STATUS UNCLEAR	17. Non-university students	1.7	0.8	5.1	4.2	1.0	5.0
	18. Pensioners/retired	0	0	0.1	0	0	0.1
	19. Illegible/no data	0	0	1.4	1.4	0	1.4
Subtotal		1.7	0.8	6.6	5.6	1.0	6.5
TOTAL (%)		100	100	100	100	100	100
Frequency (N)		58	124	661	72	205	732

Note: a Based on those members tabulated in Table 6.1 whose date of entry into the SA could be determined.

Table 6.3 The class background of SA members[a] according to community size (by %)

		Community size		
	Under 2,000	2,000– 4,999	5,000– 19,999	20,000– 99,999	Over 100,000
To 30.1.1933					
LOWER CLASS	22.3	22.3	4.9	1.0	8.5
Lower- & middle- MIDDLE CLASS	9.8	10.5	5.9	0.6	8.5
Upper-MIDDLE CLASS & UPPER CLASS	0.6	0.6	0.6	0	0.6
STATUS UNCLEAR	0	2.6	0.3	0	0
TOTAL (%)	32.7	36.0	11.7	1.6	17.6
Frequency (N)	100	110	36	5	54
After 30.1.1933					
LOWER CLASS	28.4	5.6	1.8	10.2	7.9
Lower- & middle- MIDDLE CLASS	12.5	2.8	2.3	6.0	7.7
Upper-MIDDLE CLASS & UPPER CLASS	1.2	0.8	1.2	2.3	2.4
STATUS UNCLEAR	0.5	0	0.1	4.9	1.1
TOTAL (%)	42.6	9.2	5.4	23.4	19.1
Frequency (N)	314	68	40	172	141
GERMANY – 1933 (N: 65,218,416)	32.9	10.8	13.8	13.6	31.6

Note: a Based on membership data used in Table 6.1.

upper-class support in the larger urban centres, especially after 30 January 1933 (see Table 6.3).

The picture which emerges from the data of the social types active in the SA supports Fischer's contention that the SA rank and file was predominantly lower-class. There are, however, problems common to both Fischer's data and that evaluated here, which must caution one from making absolute judgements on the social characteristics of the SA in Germany as a whole. Although neither Fischer's data nor that in Tables 6.1 to 6.3 can be regarded as statistically representative, the cumulative weight of evidence points in but one direction, namely that *at least* in western and southern Germany the SA was primarily a working-class organization.[73] It strikes me as improbable that the SA in northern and eastern Germany was so drastically different in its social composition to that of western and southern Germany as to alter the social profile of the SA as a whole. The limited hard evidence on the SA in Berlin (for February 1931) and the little evidence there is on northern parts of Germany in the shape of the Eutin SA would suggest otherwise. There were undoubtedly marked variations in the social make-up of the SA even within the same region, and the regional divergence from the *general* norm to be found in the SA in some eastern parts of Germany is quite compatible with the argument that the SA was essentially a lower-class organization as a whole.

7

THE SS

Along with the SA, from which it was to recruit many of its members before 1933, the SS was one of the oldest Nazi specialist organizations by the time of the Nazi seizure of power.[1] The SS emerged in 1925 when Hitler ordered the creation of a *Stabswache* (Staff Guard) to act as his personal bodyguard and to protect the party leadership in general, a task assigned by him to Julius Schreck in April 1925. The Staff Guard recruited by Schreck, which made its first public appearance in Munich on 16 April 1925 at the funeral of Ernst Pöhner, was essentially the successor of the *Stosstrupp Hitler* which had existed briefly in 1923,[2] a formation in which Schreck and many members of the new *Stabswache* had formerly been active, and one from which the new Staff Guard also copied its death's head insignia. It was this Munich organization which was re-christened *Schutzstaffel*, a term also applied to similar formations which gradually emerged in various other localities in Germany by the autumn of 1925. Conceived very much as an 'elite' organization within the Nazi Movement, Schreck and his successor Josef Berchtold, who took over the SS on 15 April 1926, recruited the more active and reliable party members (initially only those between 23 and 35 years of age), who were charged with the protection of the movement and its meetings, as well as with furthering the propaganda activities of the party. These tasks were virtually identical with those of the SA, to which the fledgeling organization was subordinated following the appointment of Franz Pfeffer von Salomon as 'Supreme SA Leader' on 1 November 1926. For much of the late 1920s the SS grew only very slowly in the shadow of the SA. There is some uncertainty as to the actual size of the SS in the years immediately following its formation. It

181

is estimated that the organization had enrolled around 800 men by the end of 1925, its total strength rising to about 1,000 by the end of 1928, reaching the 2,000-mark by the end of 1929 and a strength of 2,727 by the end of 1930.[3] According to statistics furnished by the Nazis themselves (and these included a small number of Austrian SS members), it was only in the course of 1931 – two years after the appointment of Heinrich Himmler as *Reichsführer-SS* – that the SS began to grow in size, a beneficiary of the general expansion of the Nazi Movement in the early 1930s, with a strength of 14,964 by the end of 1931, rising to 52,048 by the end of 1932. A membership spurt in 1933 following Hitler's elevation to the chancellorship took its total strength to 209,014 by 31 December.[4] The significance of the SS also grew after 1929 as the organization developed its 'police' role within the Nazi Movement, spying on the NSDAP – as well as the SA – to root out anti-Hitler factions. Its role in the suppression of the Stennes affair of 1931 especially enhanced its position in the eyes of the party leadership.

Despite the fact that both before and after 1933 the SS was numerically relatively small in comparison with the NSDAP or with the SA, the establishment of the social profile of the membership of the SS provides an important insight not only into the sociology of Nazism as a whole, but of the social composition of the NSDAP itself, especially in its critical pre-January 1933 phase, during which membership of the party was compulsory for SS members.

I

Although the literature on the SS is now voluminous, with specialist works examining various facets of its history and sordid activities, very little light has been shed as yet on the social background of those who joined the organization, especially in the period before the Nazi seizure of power. Early attempts to grapple with the problem of the sociology of the SS undoubtedly suffered from a lack of source material and could do little more than provide impressionistic overviews.[5] In his review of the existing literature on the SS in 1962, Robert Koehl could offer little on the social background of the members of the SS, beyond noting that 'before 1933 came "bruisers" and misfits, the unemployed and unemployable, fragments of the old German elite and some of the Nazi party and SA who aspired to be a new elite within the Hitler movement'.[6] In his account of the history of the SS published in 1967, Heinz Höhne, in line with the then generally accepted view of the sociology of the NSDAP, came to the conclusion that the 'founders of the SS had come from lower-middle-class suburbia', while from 1929 'men from another level of society were flooding into the SS – the lost souls of the middle and upper-middle classes'.[7] No empirical evidence was advanced to substantiate this assertion, which makes it surprising that Michael Kater, in his article examining the social contours of the SA and SS published in 1975, cited Höhne to support his view that 'in the first four years after the formation of the NSDAP, the SS did not differentiate itself in its sociology from the SA (or from the NSDAP), that is, it was similarly lower-middle-class in character'.[8] Kater did, however, advance some fragmentary evidence to show that in the early 1930s the SS began to secure more support from the upper-middle class and upper class, especially from 'aristocratic' types, who became quite prominent among the SS leadership.[9] In the same article Kater also evaluated data relating to the rank and file membership of the General (*Allgemeine*) SS compiled by the SS authorities in December 1937, on the basis of which Kater reached the conclusion that 'around 70 per cent of all members were drawn from the lower-middle-class, while the share of the upper-middle-class was around 11 per cent, ... (whereas) the share of the working class (was) limited'. Kater pointed to the strong presence within the SS of academics, most noticeably doctors and jurists, as well as 'aristocrats', especially within its leadership corps.[10] The prominence of 'elite' sectors of society among the SS leadership corps was subsequently substantiated by Gunnar Boehnert in his research on the sociography of the SS officer corps.[11] On the basis of a statistically representative sample involving 5,250 case histories drawn from the 61,340 personnel files on SS officers held in the Berlin Document Center, Boehnert established the social profile of the SS leadership corps covering the period 1925 to 1939, highlighting not only the overwhelmingly middle-class nature of the SS-*Führer*,[12] but the quite dramatic surge of academic types into the SS hierarchy after the Nazi seizure of power.[13] The social background of those represented in the higher reaches of the SS hierarchy has continued to be the subject of research in the past decade, and a number of further studies have thrown additional light on the nature of the SS officer corps.[14]

In stark contrast to the considerable attention given by historians and social scientists to the sociology of the SS leadership, very little has appeared on the question of the social background of the rank and file membership of the SS. In my essay on the sociology of Nazism I did include a little data relating to SS formations recruited in Munich (based on various membership lists covering the years 1929 to 1932) and Ludwigshafen (based on a list compiled by the police in April 1932).[15] In his recent book on the HJ and the SS, Gerhard Rempel uses the statistical material contained in the *Statistisches Jahrbuch der Schutzstaffel der NSDAP* for 1937, data which was first utilized by Kater in his rough guide to the sociology of the General-SS. According to Rempel's calculations, 53.01 per cent of the 155,957 SS members (of the General-SS, the SD, the *Totenkopfverbände*) analysed was recruited from the lower-middle class, 28.39 per cent from the lower class, and 18.6 per cent from the elite.[16]

Whereas much is now known – on the basis of empirical evidence – about the social types which made up the hierarchy of the SS, virtually nothing of a specific nature has been published as yet on the social characteristics of the membership recruited by the SS during the Weimar period, while our insight into its structure after 1933 is essentially restricted to the data provided by the *Statistisches Jahrbuch der Schutzstaffel der NSDAP* for 1937. The analysis which follows represents the first attempt (in the sense of it being based on detailed empirical evidence) to come to grips with the question of the sociology of the rank and file SS members and the lower-ranking leadership of this Nazi specialist organization in its formative phase of development to the mid-1930s.

II

Membership lists and muster rolls of various SS units, as well as personal files on individual SS members, form the empirical evidence on which Table 7.1 is based. The data on the Bavarian SS, involving primarily membership lists compiled by the police authorities of Munich and the Palatinate, is relatively limited in the detail provided on individual members, restricted as most of it is to the name, occupation and place of residence of the SS members recorded. Limited also in terms of data provided is the list of SS men and probationers put together by the *Truppführer* of SS-*Sturm* 4/II/12 in Clausthal-Zellerfeld in March 1932, though it is noted whether or not the individual members were unemployed. The bulk of the data on the SS members analysed in Table 7.1, however, is derived from muster rolls and personal files and is much more extensive, almost invariably involving such details as occupational status (in a few files any difference between the 'learned or trained' and 'actual' occupation pursued by individual members is noted), date of birth, place of residence, marital status, confession, as well as the date of entry into the NSDAP and of the SS, while in one file the income level of some members is also given. The bulk of the *Stammrollen* and *Stammkarten* were started in 1933 or early 1934, with amendments being made to individual files subsequently, allowing an insight into the career (promotion, dismissal, transfer and so on) of many members up to the late 1930s. I was not able to secure access to some material relating to the membership of the SS in a few of the archives which I have visited in the past five years or so (the files I requested could not be found), which would have further extended the spatial distribution of the SS membership examined here. As it is, the data presented does represent a useful mix of urban- and rural-based formations of the General-SS (including specialist sub-organizations, the Motorized-SS and the Pioneer-SS) active in North, Central and South Germany. Availability and access, rather than any attempt at 'systematic sampling', conditioned the gathering of the data, which cannot be taken as representative of the SS as a whole. Involved are SS formations formed in the *Länder* of Bavaria, Bremen, Hesse, and Oldenburg, as well as SS units situated in the provinces of Hanover, Hesse-Nassau and the Rheinprovinz of *Land* Prussia.

The data on the SS in Bavaria relates to members who were resident almost exclusively in big cities and who had joined (but had not necessarily remained in) the SS before December 1932. In the case of the Munich SS (see Table 7.1, column 9), one is dealing with established members and recruits covering the period December 1929 to December 1932 who, with the exception of the SS members belonging to *Ortsgruppe* Schwabing by the end of 1929, are noted in a series of police reports covering the from early 1930 to the end of 1932. The fragmentary nature of the material allows some insight into the social types who joined the

Table 7.1 The social and occupational structure of the SS in various regions and towns of Germany, *1929-33/8* (by %)[17]

Class	Occupational subgroup	(1) Brake (Olden-burg) Sturm 3/I/24 Stamm-rolle (1930-4)	(2) Bremen (Land Bremen) Stürme 1/II/24 3/II/24 S.Z./II/24 Stamm-rolle (1929-34)
LOWER CLASS	1. Agricultural workers	4.8	0.3
	2. Unskilled workers	11.2	22.1
	3. Skilled (craft) workers	26.2	34.5
	4. Other skilled workers	1.0	3.0
	5. Domestic workers	0	0
Subtotal		43.1	59.9
Lower- & Middle- MIDDLE CLASS	6. Master craftsmen	1.9	0.3
	7. Non-academic professionals	0	3.3
	8. White-collar employees	12.6	26.8
	9. Lower civil servants	3.4	2.5
	10. Merchants	6.8	1.6
	11. Farmers	27.2	1.1
Subtotal		51.9	35.5
Upper- MIDDLE CLASS & UPPER CLASS	12. Managers	0	0.3
	13. Higher civil servants	0.5	0
	14. University students	0	0.3
	15. Academic professionals	2.4	0.8
	16. Entrepreneurs	0.5	0.5
Subtotal		3.4	1.9
STATUS UNCLEAR	17. Non-university students	1.0	1.4
	18. Military personnel	0	0
	19. Illegible/no data	0.5	1.1
Subtotal		1.5	2.5
TOTAL (%)		100	100
Frequency (*N*)		206	362

Table 7.1 continued

(3) Burgbrohl (Rheinprovinz) Sturm 1/II/M/XI	(4) Clausthal-Zellerfeld (Provinz Hanover) Sturm 4/II/12	(5) Dillkreis (Provinz Hesse-Nassau) Standarte 8/35 M./II/2	(6) Frankfurt (Provinz Hesse-Nassau) Sturm P./II/2	(7) Großenmeer (Oldenburg) Sturm 2/I/24	(8) Ludwigshafen (Palatinate)
Stammrolle (1930–3)	(20.3.1932)	Stammkarten (1931–6)	Stammrolle (1932–4)	(1930–4)	(1932)
0	2.4	0	0	19.2	0
24.4	19.0	35.3	14.0	11.5	2.8
37.8	33.3	23.5	24.3	23.1	25.7
8.9	4.8	0	7.1	0	5.7
0	0	0	0.3	0	0
71.1	59.9	58.8	45.7	53.8	34.1
0	9.5	0	1.7	2.6	8.6
4.4	0	5.9	4.3	5.1	31.4
2.2	11.9	11.8	11.4	1.3	5.7
6.7	7.1	17.6	5.1	3.8	8.6
15.5	9.5	0	20.8	7.7	11.4
0	0	0	0	23.1	0
28.8	38.0	35.3	43.3	43.6	65.7
0	0	5.9	1.4	0	0
0	0	0	0.8	0	0
0	0	0	2.3	1.3	0
0	2.4	0	2.3	1.3	0
0	0	0	0.8	0	0
0	2.4	5.9	7.6	2.6	0
0	0	0	2.6	0	0
0	0	0	0.3	0	0
0	0	0	0.3	0	0
0	0	0	3.2	0	0
100	100	100	100	100	100
45	42	17	350	78	35

Table 7.1 continued

Class	Occupational subgroup	(9) Munich (Bavaria) (various units) (1929–32)	(10) Palatinate (Bavaria) Motorstürme I & II/10 (1932)
LOWER CLASS	1. Agricultural workers	0	0
	2. Unskilled workers	20.2	15.7
	3. Skilled (craft workers)	19.0	31.4
	4. Other skilled workers	2.5	3.9
	5. Domestic workers	0	0
Subtotal		41.7	51.0
Lower- & middle- MIDDLE CLASS	6. Master craftsmen	2.5	7.8
	7. Non-academic professionals	5.1	5.9
	8. White-collar employees	21.5	15.7
	9. Lower civil servants	0.6	0
	10. Merchants	9.5	9.8
	11. Farmers	0	5.9
Subtotal		39.2	45.1
Upper- MIDDLE CLASS & UPPER CLASS	12. Managers	0	0
	13. Higher civil servants	0	0
	14. University students	5.7	0
	15. Academic professionals	0.6	0
	16. Entrepreneurs	1.3	0
Subtotal		7.6	0
STATUS UNCLEAR	17. Non-university students	4.4	0
	18. Military personnel	0	0
	19. Illegible/no data	7.0	3.9
Subtotal		11.4	3.9
TOTAL (%)		100	100
Frequency (N)		158	51

Notes: a Includes SS members and leaders, both established members and recruits.
  b Relates to SS members who joined in 1933.
  c Excludes those recruits whose date of entry is given as '1933'. It is assumed that these joined after 31.1.1933.

Table 7.1 continued

(11) Palatinate (Bavaria) Standarte 10	(12) Rhein-hessen/ Starken-burg (Land Hesse) Standarte 33	(13) Trier (Rhein-provinz) Motorsturm 3/II/M/XI	(14) Wiesbaden (Hesse-Nassau) Motorsturm M./I/2	(15) Total SS[a] Germany	(16) Total SS[b] Germany
(Führer) (1932)	Stammrolle (1931–8)	Stammrolle (1931–4)	Stammrolle (1930–3)	to 30.1.33[c]	30.1.33– 31.12.33
0	2.5	1.6	0	1.8	2.2
10.6	17.3	23.4	29.2	16.5	19.9
20.0	30.8	20.3	25.0	21.8	28.8
2.3	7.4	6.2	4.2	3.8	4.4
0	0	0	0	0	0.1
32.9	58.0	51.5	58.4	43.9	55.4
8.2	0	0	4.2	2.8	1.2
3.5	2.5	1.6	2.1	5.6	2.9
10.6	13.5	7.8	8.3	15.1	15.6
12.9	2.5	7.8	2.1	4.8	3.8
21.2	11.1	18.7	16.7	11.9	10.6
2.3	2.5	4.7	2.1	7.7	3.6
58.7	32.1	40.6	35.5	47.9	37.7
0	0	1.6	0	0.2	0.9
1.2	0	0	0	0	0.4
0	0	0	2.1	2.2	1.0
4.7	0	0	0	0.8	1.7
0	0	0	0	0.8	0.2
5.9	0	1.6	2.1	4.0	4.2
0	7.4	4.7	0	1.4	1.7
0	0	0	0	0.2	0.7
2.3	2.5	1.6	2.1	2.4	0
2.3	9.9	6.3	2.1	4.0	2.4
100	100	100	100	100	100
85	81	64	48	496	802

SS in Munich, even though the data (Frequency N: 158) obviously involves only a fraction of the total SS membership recruited in the city before January 1933.[18] In comparison with the social structure of the male working population of Munich, that of the membership of the SS reflected an under-representation of the lower class (49.3 and 41.7 per cent respectively), a marked over-representation of white-collar workers (26.6 and 14.3 per cent respectively), and a massive under-representation of civil servants (0.6 and 13.8 per cent respectively).[19] The significant student presence within the ranks of the Munich SS (university and non-university students made up 10.1 per cent of the total membership), as well as the lack of data on seven per cent of the SS membership does produce some distortions in the comparison between the social structure of the city's male working population and the SS membership. Surprisingly, though the Munich SS was less proletarian in its social structure than that of the Munich SA, the lower class furnished a higher percentage of the leadership of the SS than of the SA in the city.[20] As far as the predominantly middle-class Schwabing district of the city is concerned, for which it is possible to compare the social background of the membership of the SS with that of the NSDAP as well as the SA (as at the end of 1929), the noticeable features are that the SS recruited fractionally more support from the lower class than the SA, and that the social composition of the SS and SA reflected considerable affinity, in marked contrast to the overall social make-up of the Schwabing branch of the NSDAP, in which the lower class figured only marginally.[21]

The data on the SS in the Rhenish Palatinate (see Table 7.1, columns 8, 10 and 11) relates predominantly to members resident in the major urban centres of the province.[22] Around half of the membership lived in the city of Ludwigshafen and the sizeable *Mittelstädte* of Kaiserslautern and Pirmasens, while only a handful of members were resident in rural communities. The strong urban bias of the data on the SS in the Palatinate raises the question of how representative the material is of the SS in the region as a whole, a problem further compounded by the fact that one is dealing almost exclusively with the motorized wing and with the leadership corps of the SS in the province, rather than with elements of the 'ordinary' SS as such. In the two *Motorstürme* of *Standarte* 10 the lower class provided the bare majority of the membership,[23] with lorry-drivers and mechanics being especially prominent, while dependent white-collar employees and independent elements from the middle class made up the rest of the members in almost equal proportion. The high percentage of lower-class members is not sustained in either the leadership corps nor in the membership of the SS in Ludwigshafen. The predominance of the lower- and middle-middle-class types in the leadership corps is not that surprising. As in the case of the SA, the leadership of the SS and especially its higher ranking officials was also recruited primarily from the *Mittelstand*. Not one of the higher ranking leaders of the SS in the Palatinate (*Sturmbannführer* and above) came from the lower class, though there were two workers among the six *Sturmführer* (the lowest 'middle' rank). The social composition of the lower-ranking SS leadership at the *Sturm* level does, however, show some striking variations. For example, in *Sturm* 3/I/10 in the Landau region, not one of the *Trupp-* and *Scharführer* came from the lower class, whereas in Pirmasens, an industrialized town in which workers represented 63.8 per cent of the male work force,[24] unskilled and skilled workers accounted for 75 per cent of the SS leaders of *Sturm* 1/I/10. The different composition of the lower leadership levels of the SS in the Palatinate may well reflect similar differences in the occupational and class configuration of the membership of the various *Stürme* operating in the province. Unfortunately the only insight into the make-up of the rank and file SS in one particular locality, that of Ludwigshafen, does not lend itself to testing this hypothesis. It is highly unrepresentative, given that it basically lists only a handful of the local leaders and a few ordinary members along with what seems to be the entire membership of the SS *Musikzug* in the city (21 of the 35 individuals are identified as belonging to it), with those members described by the police as 'musicians' alone accounting for almost one-third of the membership listed.

The data on the SS in Bremen[25] (see Table 7.1, column 2), given its size and the fact that it is based on members organized in three different 'units', can be taken as fairly representative of the social structure of the SS in the city, despite the inclusion of 111 members who were resident in nearby Delmenhorst in *Land* Oldenburg.[26] Although the bulk of the SS members joined the organization in the course of 1933 and 1934, some 42 of the 252 SS members living in Bremen had joined the organization before 30 January 1933, of whom a handful could trace their membership back to before 1931,[27] a few of these having joined the Nazi Party in the 1920s. One member, a petrol attendant (his 'trained' occupation was that of 'machine operator'), had become a member of the Nazi Party in 1922 and had been active in the SA since 1926, transferring to the SS in 1931.

The significance of Bremen as one of Germany's important ports and a major trading centre is reflected in the fact that 42.6 per cent of the city's working population depended on the trade and transport sector for their employment, while industry and crafts employed a further 37 per cent, primarily in the construction industry, in the manufacture of machinery and in the various food-processing industries to be found in the city.[28] Workers, who accounted for 52.6 per cent of the male working population in 1933, were slightly over-represented in the ranks of the Bremen SS, which had a noticeable lower-class profile by 1934 (if one excludes those members resident in Delmenhorst, 58.7 of the Bremen members were from the lower class). Over-represented also were dependent white-collar employees (among whom commercial employees were particularly strongly in evidence), who accounted for some 22 per cent of the city's male working population, but provided 29.3 per cent of the SS membership. The independent, self-employed on the other hand, who represented 15.9 per cent of the male workforce, were a very marginal factor within the ranks of the Bremen SS, a feature which should not surprise one given the upper age limit of 35 years laid down in the recruitment policy of the organization in 1925, which was reduced to 30 years by Himmler in 1933, even if this limit was not always enforced.[29]

The bulk of the membership listed in the *Stammrollen* of SS-*Standarte* 33 (see Table 7.1, column 12) lived in the provinces of Rheinhessen and Starkenburg in *Land* Hesse. The muster rolls also include a small number of SS members resident in the Bavarian Palatinate, a handful of whom lived in county Frankenthal (which belonged to the catchment area of *Standarte* 33), while four members lived in the counties of Grünstadt and Kirchheimbolanden (which belonged to the region covered by *Standarte* 10). Although the SS members were widely dispersed across the two provinces, with recruits drawn from both the Catholic and Protestant communities, from rural and urban areas, from agrarian and industrial regions, the membership cannot, in all probability, be taken as wholly representative of the SS in the region. One feature limiting the representative nature of the data is the uneven spread of the recorded membership. The files contain only two members who lived in the city of Mainz, while the major urban centres of Darmstadt and Offenbach do not figure at all. There are, moreover, two membership clusters centred on the town of Worms and on county Lampertheim, which alone account for 46.9 per cent of the members recorded. One other feature of the material is that it relates almost totally to individuals who joined the SS from the end of January 1933 onwards, for only five members had joined the organization (one in 1931, four in January 1933) before Hitler became chancellor. Bearing these aspects in mind, the striking feature of SS-*Standarte* 33 is the total absence of any sign of an upper-middle-class and upper-class presence within its ranks, which is surprising given that 54.3 per cent of the recorded members had applied to join the SS during the period 1935 to 1938, a period in which the Nazi regime was rapidly consolidating its position, a time during which sections of the elite jumped on the Nazi bandwagon in some numbers.[30] The lower class, on the other hand, exhibited no such inhibition in joining SS *Standarte* 33, and was strongly over-represented within its ranks, with skilled workers especially in evidence.[31] Among the lower- and middle-middle-class elements attracted to the SS in the region there were few drawn from the sizeable farming community.[32] The independent, self-employed members of the *Mittelstand*, especially master craftsmen and peasant farmers, as well as civil servants, appear to have remained aloof from the SS in the region, in which only the dependent, white-collar employees were active in numbers commensurate with the percentage of this group in the working population.[33]

The data available on the SS in *Land* Oldenburg relates to the small port of Brake and its agrarian hinterland (see Table 7.1, column 1), the agrarian region stretching from Elsfleth to Jade in county Wesermarsch (see Table 7.1, column 7), and 111 members resident in the medium-sized town of Delmenhorst included in SS-*Sturm* 3/II/24 centred on Bremen. The social structure of the SS in these areas was generally very much in accord with the different social milieux in which it operated. Thus in the town of Brake, in which trade and industry were the dominant sectors of economic activity, with the lower class accounting for 47.7 per cent of the working population,[34] 48.9 per cent of the SS members resident in the town were workers, with white-collar workers, merchants, lower-grade civil servants and academic professionals making up the rest of the membership. In the villages around Brake, such as Ovelgönne, Strückhausen, Neustadt, Schwei, and above all the Nazi stronghold of Golzwarden,[35] rural communities in which agriculture employed the majority of the population, skilled craft workers and white-collar employees were of less significance among the SS membership. It was farmers' sons who joined the SS in large numbers, while agricultural workers also formed an important membership element. A large number of *Landwirte* in their teens and early twenties, and a strong contingent of agricultural workers, were also represented in SS-*Sturm* 2/I/24, whose membership was resident in innumerable villages stretching from Jade to Elsfleth to the west and south of Brake. The small number of white-collar employees, lower-grade civil servants and independent tradesmen, and the one academic professional in the SS in the region, resided in either of the small towns of Elsfleth and Jade. The unskilled and skilled workers, some of whom pursued artisanal crafts (village smiths, dairy workers) connected with agriculture, were fairly evenly scattered in the small-town and rural communities of the area. The long organizational history to which the Nazi Movement could look back upon in this part of county Wesermarsch is reflected not only in the large number of SS members who could date their Nazi Party membership back to 1928, and 1926 in one instance, but also in the fact that 41 per cent of the SS members recorded in the muster rolls of *Sturm* 3/I/24 by the time entries ceased in November 1934, had joined the SS before 30 January 1933. In the Brake region and in Delmenhorst the overwhelming majority of those who joined the SS did so after Hitler became chancellor, and of those who joined before 1933, only a handful had been in the party before 1930. In the industrial town of Delmenhorst in south-eastern Oldenburg, in which the manufacture of textiles and leather goods along with the provision of commercial and trading services dominated the local employment market, 64 per cent of the SS membership was recruited from the lower class, with unskilled and skilled workers being represented in almost equal proportions. Although the lower class was even more in evidence within the ranks of the SS in Delmenhorst than in nearby Bremen (organizationally the Delmenhorst members belonged to the Bremen based *Sturm* 3/II/24), it was still slightly under-represented in comparison with the social structure of the male working population of the town, in which workers accounted for 68 per cent.[36] Only the white-collar employees, who accounted for 13.1 per cent of the male working population, were strongly over-represented in the ranks of the SS, providing 20.7 per cent of its members.

An insight into the social background of the SS in the town of Clausthal-Zellerfeld in the province of Hanover (see Table 7.1, column 4) is provided by a list drawn up by the local SS leader in March 1932. All but five of the 42 individuals listed were SS-probationers, and 78.6 per cent of the total membership, including the five fully-fledged SS members, were unemployed.[37] The social profile of the SS, dominated by members drawn from the lower class, with skilled craft workers alone providing a third of the total membership, presented a stark contrast to that of the NSDAP in the town, in which the lower class was marginalized by the strong support provided by the lower- and middle-middle class, which made up over half of the party's membership.[38] It was the social composition of the SS, rather than that of the NSDAP, which was in tune with the social structure of the male working population of the town, 63.1 per cent of which was made up by the category 'workers'.[39]

The data on the structure of the SS in the cities of Frankfurt and Wiesbaden (see Table 7.1, columns 6 and 14) in the province of Hesse-Nassau does not relate to the General-SS as such, but to more specialized sub-sections within the organization, an SS *Motorsturm* and an SS *Pioniersturm* in the case of Frankfurt, and an SS *Motorsturm* in the case of Wiesbaden. Only 60 of the 350 members in the SS in Frankfurt were in the organization by 30 January 1933 and most of these had joined in the course of 1932. Only one SS member, a merchant, had been in the SS before 1930. The bulk of the SS members recorded in the *Stammrollen* had joined in the course of 1933–4. The SS recruited its members almost equally from the lower class and from the lower- and middle-middle class, giving it a social profile very much in line with that of the city's male working population.[40] The strong presence of the lower class within the Frankfurt SS, however, was primarily the result of a marked surge in recruitment from this social grouping after the Nazi seizure of power, for before 30 January 1933, the lower class provided only 38.3 per cent of the SS membership, as against 58.3 per cent recruited from the lower-

and middle-middle class. Virtually all the upper-middle-class and upper-class elements who joined the SS did so after Hitler became chancellor. Given the specialized function of the SS units under review, it is not surprising that within the membership recruited from the lower-class transport workers, (car) mechanics, (lorry) drivers, various skilled metal workers, and electricians are fairly numerous, while engineers and technicians, along with merchants (many of these were probably commercial employees judging from their age profile), figure prominently among those drawn from the lower- and middle-middle class. The majority of the SS membership of *Motorsturm* M./I/2 based in Wiesbaden[41] came from the lower class (with lorry drivers, mechanics and fitters present in some number), which was noticeably over-represented within the ranks of the organization in comparison with its strength in the male working population of the city.[42] Only 23 per cent of the members had joined the SS before 30 January 1933, the rest having been enrolled by the end of September 1933. Some of the SS members could look back to a party membership stretching back to the latter half of the 1920s, such as a mechanic who had joined the NSDAP in 1926, and a cooper and a fitter who became active Nazis in 1928. As in the case of the Frankfurt SS, there was a marked increase in support secured from the lower class after the Nazi seizure of power, with workers accounting for 45.4 per cent of the membership before 30 January 1933, and 62.1 per cent of those enrolled subsequently.

The social profile of the SS recruited in the villages and small towns of the Dillkreis (see Table 7.1, column 5) also shows a strong lower-class presence within its ranks. Just over 41 per cent of the membership recruited in this rural backwater had joined between 1931 and 30 January 1933, drawn almost equally from the lower class and the lower- and middle-middle class. Later recruits came predominantly from the lower class, which accounted for 70 per cent of those entering the SS in the area between 31 January 1933 and November 1936. Widely scattered in the villages of the county (some 70 per cent of the SS members were resident in communities with a population of under 2,000), in which 45 per cent of the gainfully employed depended on agriculture, the sociology of the SS membership bore little resemblance to that of the working population. Totally absent from the ranks of the SS were the self-employed, independent *Mittelständler* (primarily farmers), who made up 16.1 per cent of the working population (45.6 per cent if one includes assisting family members), while civil servants were – in comparison with their share in the working population – over-represented in the SS by a factor of four, and white-collar employees by a factor of two. Significantly over-represented also was the lower class, which accounted for 40.7 per cent of the working population.[43]

The catchment areas of the two SS *Motorstürme* of Burgbrohl and of Trier (see Table 7.1, columns 3 and 13) in the Rhein-provinz were relatively extensive and covered predominantly Catholic areas in the Rhein and Mosel valleys which belonged to *Gau* Koblenz-Trier, a region in which the Nazi Party had great difficulty in securing support before 1932/3.[44] The comparatively late development of Nazism – and the even later appearance of the SS – in the region, is reflected in the few members belonging to the SS units under review here by the end of January 1933, namely 10 out of 45 in the case of *Motorsturm* 1/II/M/XI (Burgbrohl), and a mere 7 out of 64 in the case of *Motorsturm* 3/II/M/XI (Trier). *Motorsturm* 1/II/M/XI covered the counties of Ahrweiler, Altenkirchen, Mayen and Neuwied, which lie on both banks of the Rhine to the north of Koblenz. A third of the total membership was resident in the medium-sized towns of Mayen and Neuwied, and the remainder was scattered around the small towns and villages of the area. Although agriculture was the most important economic sector in the counties, especially in Ahrweiler and Mayen, there were also some centres of industrial activity, especially the towns of Mayen, Neuwied, and Andernach, while industry and trade employed the majority of the working population in county Neuwied. In contrast to the social make-up of the branches of the NSDAP in these counties, in which diverse occupational groups – including farmers and agricultural labourers – were represented in variable combinations by 1931,[45] the SS recruited very heavily from the lower class. Skilled workers alone made up virtually fifty per cent of the membership of the Motorized-SS in the region, both before and after 30 January 1933, while only limited support was generated among white-collar employees, and none at all from the numerically large farming community. In *Motorsturm* 3/II/M/XI, which recruited a third of its membership in Trier, and the rest in the counties of Bernkastel, Daun, Merzig-Wadern, Prüm, Saarburg, Trier and Wittlich in *Regierungsbezirk* Trier, three-quarters of the handful of members who had joined the SS in the region before 30 January 1933 were also from the lower class. While almost half of the members who subsequently joined the SS by June 1934 (the pages presumably listing further entries are cut-off in the muster roll at this point) were also from the lower class, a significant influx of lower- and middle-middle-class elements occurred in the course of 1933 and the first half of 1934. The lower class was strongly over-represented within the ranks of the SS in the Trier region, in which the lower class formed but 25.7 per cent of the working population in 1933.[46] Overall the SS units centred on Burgbrohl and Trier (whose catchment areas covered roughly two-thirds of *Gau* Koblenz-Trier) were based on strong lower-class support, giving them a social composition markedly different to that of the NSDAP in the *Gau*, in which the *Mittelstand* provided 56.0 per cent and the lower class 38.4 per cent of the membership.[47]

III

Given that the SS recruited members from the SA in some numbers in the late 1920s and early 1930s,[48] the sizeable lower-class presence within its ranks, in view of the social make-up of the SA, can almost be expected. Indeed, if one examines the social structure of the membership of the NSDAP, the SA and the SS, and compares the percentage share of particular occupational subgroups active within them, there is a greater parallel to be found between the sociological profiles of the SS and the SA than between the SS and the Nazi Party. Given the age factor conditioning the recruitment of both the SA and the SS, the independent, self-employed *Mittelständler* are not well-represented, for the many in their twenties masquerading as 'merchants' and as 'farmers' in occupational subgroups 10 and 11 could in reality have only involved dependent commercial employees and sons of farmers. The age factor also ruled out, as it did in the SA, any significant presence of master-craftsmen within the ranks of the SS. In the Nazi Party these elements were much more strongly represented. One other interesting feature of the SS is that although it projected itself as an elite organization within the Nazi Party, the social elite of German society, which joined the NSDAP in some numbers before 1933, does not appear to have rushed to enrol in the SS before 1934.

Community size does not seem to have been a significant factor

Table 7.2   Persons joining the SS (*N*: 1,622[a]) by place of residence, 1929–38
(by %)

		Community size				
Class	Occupational subgroup	Under 2,000	2,000- 4,999	5,000- 19,999	20,000- 99,999	Over 100,000
LOWER	1. Agricultural workers	1.3	0.2	0.2	0	0
CLASS	2. Unskilled workers	2.9	0.5	1.7	3.8	8.5
	3. Skilled (craft) workers	3.4	1.9	3.8	3.5	14.6
	4. Other skilled workers	0.2	0.3	0.6	0.4	2.5
	5. Domestic workers	0	0	0	0	0.1
Subtotal		7.8	2.9	6.3	7.7	25.7
Lower-	6. Master craftsmen	0.2	0.1	0.6	0.3	1.0
&	7. Non-academic professionals	0.1	0.2	0.1	0.3	3.2
middle-	8. White-collar employees	0.7	0.5	1.5	2.5	9.9
MIDDLE	9. Lower civil servants	0.8	0.3	0.9	0.3	1.8
CLASS	10. Merchants	1.2	0.5	1.3	1.4	6.6
	11. Farmers	3.6	1.3	0.4	0.1	0.2
Subtotal		6.6	2.9	4.8	4.9	22.7
Upper-	12. Managers	0.1	0	0	0	0.4
MIDDLE	13. Higher civil servants	0	0	0.1	0.1	0.2
CLASS &	14. University students	0.1	0	0	0	1.2
UPPER	15. Academic professionals	0.1	0.1	0.4	0.3	0.6
CLASS	16. Entrepreneurs	0	0	0.1	0.1	0.3
Subtotal		0.3	0.1	0.6	0.5	2.7
STATUS	17. Non-university students	0.1	0.2	0.2	0.5	1.0
UNCLEAR	20. Military personnel	0	0	0	0	0.1
	21. Illegible/no data	0.1	0	0.1	0.1	1.1
Subtotal		0.2	0.2	0.3	0.6	2.2
TOTAL (%)		14.9	6.1	12.0	13.7	53.3
Germany (*N*: 62,410,619)		36.0	10.6	13.0	13.6	26.8

Note: a Based on data in Table 7.1, columns 1–14.

determining the social configuration of the membership pattern of the SS except in one obvious, expected way, namely that it recruited the bulk of the agricultural workers, farmers and farmers' sons to be found within its ranks in communities with a population of less than 4,000 (see Table 7.2). Although half of the membership analysed in table 7.2 was resident in the cities of Bremen, Frankfurt, Ludwigshafen and Munich, the pattern of class recruitment in the cities was virtually identical to that achieved at every level of community size. Thus the share of lower-class support fluctuated only marginally within the range of 48.1 per cent in communities with a population of over 100,000 and 52.9 per cent in communities with a population under 2,000. Leaving aside the presence of agricultural workers and farmers among SS members resident in communities with populations of less than 4,000, the response of the various occupational subgroups comprising both the lower class and the lower- and middle-middle class was remarkably even from the small town through to the big city.

Given the stipulation that only those aged between twenty-three and thirty-five (reduced to thirty for SS probationers by 1933) could become SS men, it comes as no surprise that the great majority of SS men evaluated in Table 7.1 were in their twenties and early thirties. The lower and upper age limits were not, however, always rigidly enforced, either before or after 1933. A small number of 18 and 19 year-old individuals are recorded as becoming SS probationers – and even SS men – in the records on which Table 7.1 is based. It would seem from the available evidence that the upper age limit was more often ignored when it involved those joining the 'specialist' sections of the SS. Quite a number of SS men in their late thirties and in their forties, and even a handful in their fifties, can be found among the SS-Pioneer and SS-Motor units, where the specialist skills offered by technicians or mechanics, or the supply of a lorry or car from a merchant or entrepreneur, probably opened the door to member-ship.[49] The age factor played no role when Himmler determined to recruit the German elite into the higher leadership echelons of his 'elite' organization following the Nazi *Machtergreifung*.[50]

On the basis of the data presented in Table 7.1 – bearing in mind the question of its representative nature – a number of tentative conclusions can be reached about the sociology of the SS. It would seem that the SS was in some respects different to both the Nazi Party and the SA in terms of the social character-istics of its membership and lower leadership before the Nazi *Machtergreifung*. In broad terms its sociological structure represented a sort of half-way house between the NSDAP and the SA in the sense that it was not as dependent on lower- and middle-middle-class support as was the former,[51] nor did it recruit the large lower-class element present in the latter.[52] Before

200

1933 the two major social classes were almost equally represented within the ranks of the SS (see Table 7.1, column 15). In the course of 1933 (see Table 7.1, column 16) the SS moved closer to the SA in its sociological profile, with a marked influx of lower-class elements leading to a significant reduction in the percentage share of the lower- and middle-middle class within its ranks. Like the NSDAP, the SS was a polymorphic organization in social terms, able to recruit in rural and urban environments, in solidly Protestant and predominantly Catholic districts, transcending both the class barriers and the confessional divide present in German society in the early 1930s.

CONCLUSION

The analyses of the social contours of the Nazi Party membership at the regional level presented in this study demonstrate the ability of the Nazis to mobilize support from various occupational groups and from all social strata from the mid-1920s onwards. The degree of support derived from the various classes represented in the Nazi Party in the regions evaluated was not constant, while the diversity of the occupational and class configuration of the numerous Nazi branches analysed in chapters two to five is often quite striking even within the same region. The ability of the Nazi Movement to reflect in broad terms the social geometry of the population of the regions in which it was recruiting is a feature of its development in the late 1920s and early 1930s. This is not to ignore the fact that the NSDAP in the Western Ruhr in 1925 and 1926, or in Württemberg or Hesse-Nassau in the late 1920s and early 1930s, or in South-Hanover-Brunswick in the period 1925 to 1933, mirrored the social structure of the (male) working populations of these regions imperfectly.

Obviously the Nazi Party was not, as a section of its party title proclaimed, a 'socialist . . . workers' party in any of the regions examined in this study, not even in the Ruhr region, where the number of party members mobilized from the lower class was comparatively high in the mid-1920s among the admittedly low degree of overall support mobilized by the NSDAP at that time, and where it probably sustained a high level of lower-class support throughout the period before 1933. To suggest, however, that the high incidence of lower-class support for Nazism in the Ruhr may simply be explained as the consequence of the social structure of the region in which 'fascism's normal social con-

202

stituency (was) greatly underrepresented',[1] is not a tenable argument. Such an approach assumes that the 'normal constituency' of the NSDAP was middle-class, and if this was indeed so, it raises the question of why the Nazis secured significant support in areas predominantly lower-class in their social composition. It does not help either in explaining why many Nazi Party branches in various other regions of Germany examined in this study were overwhelmingly based on lower-class recruits. Arguing on the basis of the empirical evidence advanced here that the Nazis were able to secure a considerable number of members drawn from the lower class does not ignore the fact that the NSDAP was differently constituted in sociological terms in comparison with the KPD, the only true working-class party active in the Weimar era, or the SPD, still strongly anchored in the lower class, even though it was in the process of losing its mono-class structure.[2] It is highly improbable that any KPD branches, or even any SPD branches, would have had a rank and file membership in which the lower class did not provide the absolute majority of support, with *Mittelstand* elements generally representing a marginal factor. In the case of the Nazi Party the social structure of its branches, as demonstrated in all regions examined here, does not conform to any class pattern. Although many Nazi branches, especially the larger branches, were based on a strong core of support drawn from the lower- and middle-middle class, a considerable number were overwhelmingly lower-class in their social structure. The Nazi Party recruited from the lower class to a considerable extent, though nowhere near as exclusively from this social stratum as the KPD or SPD.

That a section of the lower class supported Nazism should not be surprising, even if it is an idea which is anathema to socialist or marxist historians who, understandably, do not wish to see the lower class tainted by any association with such a nauseating creed as National Socialism. One is not talking about the odd token lower-class supporter, the equivalent of the relatively few *Mittelstand* and upper-class types, and even the odd 'aristocrat', to be found in the SPD or perhaps also the KPD, but a sizeable section of the working class. It must be borne in mind that only about 1.3 million workers were members of socialist and marxist parties for much of the 1920s and early 1930s,[3] and that at most only approximately half of the 22 to 25 million workers and their adult dependants gave their electoral support to socialist and marxist parties in the late 1920s and early 1930s,[4] with the combined vote for the SPD and KPD rising from 12,417,772, secured in the May *Reichstag* election of 1928, to the highpoint of 13,329,420 obtained in that of July 1932.[5] Bearing in mind the not insignificant support also given by Catholic workers to the Centre Party, and the sprinkling of membership support given by the lower class to what were basically bourgeois parties, such as the DDP, DVP and DNVP, there existed a considerable pool of workers who were not politically engaged elsewhere. It is from this reservoir that the Nazis attracted its sizeable lower-class membership and electoral following, as well as from workers formerly mobilized by non-socialist parties. It is highly unlikely that the Nazis secured much support from those lower-class individuals who were active in the various parties and trades unions constituting the working-class movement in the Weimar era, though some marginal cross-over cannot be ruled out.[6] It would be foolish to suggest, of course, that the bulk of the lower class was ever attracted to Nazism to the point of joining the Nazi Party, either before or after the collapse of the Weimar Republic, but what is clear is that along with the KPD, SPD, and the Centre Party, the Nazi Party was increasingly important in politicizing and organizing the lower class in the latter part of the 1920s and early 1930s.[7] All these parties recruited from the lower class, but with variable success. In all of these parties such diverse representatives of the lower class as agricultural workers, unskilled and semi-skilled workers in industry and crafts, and trade and transport, were represented, though factory workers or the unskilled proletariat employed in large units of production were more likely to find their way into the KPD or SPD than the NSDAP. Unskilled and semi-skilled agricultural and forestry workers, miners, unskilled factory workers, lorry drivers, mechanics, textile workers, dock workers, skilled craft workers of various description, and domestic workers – to name but a few 'categories' of workers which constituted the lower class in the 1920s and 1930s – were all likely to rub shoulders with members of their own class in the branches of the KPD, SPD, Centre Party or Nazi Party, though they were undoubtedly less likely to come into contact with various *Mittelstand* and 'elite' types in the KPD or SPD than the Nazi Party or Centre Party. Like the KPD, but unlike the SPD and probably also the Centre Party, it was primarily the younger age-groups of the lower class which were pulled into the Nazi orbit, a feature in evidence in the case of the Western Ruhr Nazi Party membership in 1925 to 1926 and in the overall age profile of the SS and the strongly lower-class SA, and suggested by the age-structure of the Nazi Party membership as a whole.[8] One other aspect of the lower-class support secured by the Nazis in the studies presented here is that the propensity of workers to join the movement was much greater among those who lived in rural or small-town communities. Although in absolute numeric terms workers resident in cities and larger towns constituted the largest part of lower-class support within the Nazi Party and the SA, the response rate in percentage terms of those workers living in smaller communities was noticeably higher. Community size does not appear, however, to have affected the response rate of the lower class in the case of the SS, in which the lower class represented roughly half of the membership of those units evaluated in chapter seven, irrespective of whether these were based in predominantly rural or small-town communities, or larger towns and cities.

In three of the four regional case studies on the NSDAP evaluated in this study, the lower- and middle-middle class constituted the relative majority of the membership. In the sizeable party branches situated in the cities of Stuttgart, Frankfurt and Brunswick, this social stratum formed the absolute majority of members, and in the case of Wiesbaden almost half of the membership. The invariable dominance of the *Mittelstand* element in city branches is not, however, a feature of branches situated in medium-sized or smaller towns, nor in the branches established in rural areas. Although the age profile of the Nazi Party membership in *Gaue* Württemberg-Hohenzollern and Hesse-Nassau-South could not be established, the evidence available on the Ruhr NSDAP and on *Gau* South-Hanover-Brunswick, suggests that the bulk of the lower- and middle-middle-class elements active in the party came from dependent white-collar employees rather than from the independent *Mittelstand*. The often high percentage of those classified as 'merchants' in individual branches evaluated in this study, especially in such large city branches as Frankfurt, Wiesbaden, and Stuttgart, involved primarily dependent commercial employees rather than independent merchants or shopkeepers (the latter almost invariably made their independent position clear). The bulk of NSDAP, SA and SS members masquerading as

205

'merchants' were much too young to have secured an independent economic position. The age factor also ruled out any significant support for the NSDAP from among the independent (master) craftsmen resident in either urban or rural communities. Under-represented within the Nazi Movement in the regions investigated in this study, as well as within the membership of the SA and the SS, were independent farmers, the core of the rural *Mittelstand*. It is probable that the great majority of those described as 'farmers' who were active in the Nazi Movement before 1933 were in their twenties and early thirties, which suggests that one is dealing with sons of farmers, rather than with farmers as such. This would explain the under-representation of farmers reflected in the *Partei-Statistik*, and the decision to encourage farmers to join the party, which conditioned the recruitment policy of the NSDAP from 1935.[9]

Although calculations and estimates of the size of the German elite (upper-middle class and upper class) during the Weimar era vary,[10] empirical evidence on the social structure of the Nazi Party at the macro level,[11] and the data contained in the various case studies evaluated in this study, point to a significant over-representation of this social stratum within the Nazi Party before 1933, an over-representation less marked in the case of the SA and the SS. Academic professionals, and to a lesser extent university students, formed the core of the elite supporting Nazism, particularly in Nazi branches situated in larger towns and cities. The enrolment pattern of the elite joining the Nazi Party in *Gaue* Hesse-Nassau-South and South-Hanover-Brunswick, as well as the recruitment pattern of the SS, suggests that a correlation exists between the rate of response by the elite and the community size factor, with strong support mobilized in cities and large towns, and negligible enrolment in rural and small-town environments. This relationship was not, however, a universal one, given the pattern of elite recruitment in the Nazi Party in *Gau* Württemberg-Hohenzollern and that of the SA units analysed in chapter six.

The presence of a sizeable working-class following in the NSDAP and SS, and especially the dominance of this social stratum within the SA and the HJ, as well as the strong contingent of support drawn from the elite element of German society by the Nazi Party, and to a lesser degree the SS, argues against the validity of the middle-class thesis of Nazism, and suggests that it would be unwise to continue to adhere to this interpretational hypothesis. To describe the Nazi Movement as a 'preeminently lower-middle-class phenomenon'[12] or to characterize the NSDAP as 'a predominantly lower-middle-class affair'[13] is misleading. The perpetuation of the middle-class thesis of Nazism in the light of the empirical evidence now available on the rank and file membership of the party, the SA and the SS, as well as the more limited data on the HJ,[14] both at the macro and micro level, is untenable. It is clear that in the period following the re-formation of the Nazi Party in 1925 and its *Machtergreifung* eight years later the Nazi Movement as a whole, that is the NSDAP along with a number of its more important auxiliary organizations, mobilized a following which was remarkably heterogeneous in social terms. Moreover, the polymorphic nature of the Nazi Movement is reinforced by the considerable research which has been undertaken on the electoral basis of Nazism[15] in the last decade, which also undermines the validity of the middle-class thesis of the Nazi electorate first suggested in the 1930s, a view popularized by many scholars in the post-1945 period.[16]

The Nazi Party was, as the Nazis themselves asserted in the 1920s and 1930s, a *Volkspartei*, a mass movement in which all classes were represented. This is not to ignore the fact that the sociological structure of the NSDAP, the SA and the SS mirrored the social composition of German society imperfectly, either at the macro or micro level. The lower- and middle-middle class and elite were over-represented and the lower class under-represented within the NSDAP and the SS before 1933. In the case of the SA the lower class was over-represented within its ranks, though the match between its social composition and that of the adult male population on which it was exclusively based was much closer. The characterization of the Nazi Movement as a *Volkspartei* does need to be qualified, however. It was a predominantly male affair on the one hand,[17] and primarily a movement of the younger age groups of German society on the other.[18] In these aspects of its membership structure the Nazi Movement did not represent the totality of German society before 1933.

Establishing an accurate picture of the social basis of the Nazi Movement is obviously not an esoteric exercise but of fundamental importance in any attempt to understand the Nazi phenomenon. It is only by identifying as precisely as is possible those *who* were Nazis that one can give a meaningful and convincing answer to the question of *why* they were Nazis. It is this latter question which has exercised the imagination of numerous scholars since the appearance of Nazism in the 1920s, based on answers to the former question which were basically informed – at least until the 1970s – by a mixture of observation, educated conjecture, intuition, assumption, assertion and guesswork, and little, if any, concrete data. The entrenchment of the middle-class thesis of Nazism early on in the debate on Nazism which evolved from the late 1920s, and its acceptance by Marxist and non-Marxist scholars alike as *the* diagnosis to subscribe to, has conditioned much of what has been written about the phenomenon in the pre- and post-war periods. Much intellectual capital is now invested in very sophisticated explanatory models of Nazism which are, ultimately, predicated on the erroneous notion that one is dealing in essence with a middle-class, or lower-middle-class, affair. Even scholars who have done so much to provide new *empirical* evidence on the sociology of Nazism which undermines the *Mittelstandsbewegung* approach, and here Michael Kater's important pioneering work springs especially to mind, continue to advocate the old orthodoxy.

The case studies presented in this volume provide additional perspectives on the debate concerning the social make-up of the Nazi Movement. Obviously not all of the questions surrounding the sociology of Nazism are answered in the present work. There is need for further detailed analysis of the social base of the NSDAP at the regional and local level to provide a more comprehensive geographic coverage than that which is provided here. Access to material on the social structure of the Nazi Party in Thuringia or Saxony, for example, which may be deposited in the archives of the German Democratic Republic, would be particularly useful, given that we know virtually nothing specific about the social contours of the Nazi Party in the central-eastern parts of Weimar Germany, except the information contained in the *Partei-Statistik*.[19] The question of the social types who entered and left the Nazi Party before 1933, which is touched on and partially dealt with in chapters three and four, needs much more work,[20] while further evidence on the social background of those who entered the SS before 1933 is also required.

The empirical evidence on which the present work is based cannot be accommodated within the framework of the middle-class theory of Nazism. The case studies underline the ability of the Nazi Movement to effectively transcend the class divide. The Nazi Movement was indeed, as the Nazis themselves claimed, a *Volksbewegung* in social terms. It was the unfortunate ability of the Nazi Party, despite its contradictory and cretinous ideology, to secure mass support drawn from *all* social groupings in the late 1920s and early 1930s, both in membership and electoral terms, which gave it its strength. The reasons behind the turn to Nazism by wide sections of German society, by people from all walks of life, by Catholics and Protestants, by those resident in rural and urban areas, will undoubtedly continue to be an important object of analysis, but must be based on as accurate an evaluation of the class base of the phenomenon investigated as is possible. Acceptance of the fact that irrational political behaviour is not the prerogative of any particular class, but of sections of all class groupings, is an essential step to the ultimate understanding of the very complex social response on which Nazism was based.

NOTES

1 INTRODUCTION

1. It is the analysis of the social characteristics of the Nazi Movement's rank and file *membership* which is the focus of attention in the present work. The allied question of the Nazi Party's *electorate* will not be evaluated.

2. A good example of this trend is Peter Manstein's recent book *Die Mitglieder und Wähler der NSDAP 1919-1933. Untersuchungen zu ihrer schichtmäßigen Zusammensetzung* (Frankfurt a.M./Bern, 1988). Although the author provides a comprehensive review of the literature dealing with the membership and electorate of the NSDAP and makes a number of valid criticisms of work that has been done on the theme, one does get irritated at times by the advice proffered on how to tackle a number of problems facing the researcher which suggests that Manstein has not been near archival material (such as membership lists of the Nazi Party or *Stammrollen* of the SA or SS), and has no real idea as to the practical difficulties involved in processing the type of data which is available. See also the advice provided by Herbert D. Andrews, 'The Social Composition of the NSDAP: Problems and Possible Solutions', *German Studies Review*, 9 (1986), pp. 293-318.

3. One set - based on the NSDAP Master File in the Berlin Document Center - was provided by Michael Kater in 1977, which involves 18,255 members who had joined the Nazi Party in the period 1925 to 1945: Michael H. Kater, 'Quantifizierung und NS-Geschichte. Methodologische Überlegungen über Grenzen und Möglichkeiten einer EDV-Analyse der NSDAP-Sozialstruktur von 1925 bis 1945', *Geschichte und Gesellschaft*, 3 (1977), pp. 543-84, here p. 458, Table 1. An analysis of a much larger sample involving 55,582 members who had joined the Nazi Party between 1919 and 1932, has recently been published by Paul Madden, 'The Social Class Origins of Nazi Party Members as Determined by Occupations, 1919-1933', *Social Science Quarterly*, 68 (1987), pp. 263-80, here pp. 272-3, Table 2.

4. Much new ground was broken by Michael Kater in his pioneering study 'Zur Soziographie der frühen NSDAP', *Vierteljahreshefte für*

210

Zeitgeschichte, 19 (1971), pp. 124–59. Cf. Paul Madden, 'Some Social Characteristics of Early Nazi Party Members, 1919–23', *Central European History*, 15 (1982), pp. 34–56.
5. Lawrence D. Stokes, 'The Social Composition of the Nazi Party in Eutin, 1925–32', *International Review of Social History*, 23 (1978), pp. 1–32; Detlef Mühlberger, 'The Occupational and Social Structure of the NSDAP in the Border Province Posen – West Prussia in the early 1930s', *European History Quarterly*, 15 (1985), pp. 281–311.
6. *Partei-Statistik Stand 1. Januar 1935*. Herausgeber Der Reichsorganisationsleiter der NSDAP (3 vols, Munich, n.d.).
7. These figures are taken from J. Paul Madden, 'The Social Composition of the Nazi Party, 1919–1930' (Ph.D. thesis, University of Oklahoma, 1976), p. 311.
8. This is the estimate made by Michael H. Kater, 'Quantifizierung und NS-Geschichte', p. 454, n. 4.
9. Michael Kater was able to find a number of Nazi branch membership lists in various German archives in the 1970s, which he incorporated in his major study on the sociology of the NSDAP: Michael H. Kater, *The Nazi Party. A Social Profile of Members and Leaders 1919–1945* (Oxford, 1983), pp. 242–3, Table 2; pp. 246–7, Table 4; pp. 250–1, Table 6. See also my essay on 'Germany', in Detlef Mühlberger (ed.), *The Social Basis of European Fascist Movements* (London, 1987), pp. 54–7, Table 2.2; pp. 78–81, Table 2.6; pp. 91–3, Table 2.7.
10. Jeremy Noakes relied on the *Partei-Statistik* as a guide to the social make-up of the NSDAP in Lower Saxony in his valuable study on *The Nazi Party in Lower Saxony 1921–1933* (Oxford 1971). The membership lists available on *Gau* South-Hanover-Brunswick (which form the basis of chapter 5 of this volume) at the *Niedersächsisches Hauptstaatsarchiv* in Hanover were probably not accessible in the 1960s. Eberhard Schön's study *Die Entstehung des Nationalsozialismus in Hessen* (Meisenheim am Glan, 1972) hardly deals with the question of the sociology of the Hessian NSDAP at all, yet the Hessian archives are (now?) the richest by far in terms of data on Nazi Party members. Wilfried Böhnke seems to have been unaware of (or did he ignore?) the existence of a number of membership lists on various towns of the Ruhr for the mid-1920s in the files which he consulted in the *Nordrhein-Westfälisches Hauptstaatsarchiv* in Düsseldorf while working on his book *Die NSDAP im Ruhrgebiet 1920–1933* (Bonn-Bad Godesberg, 1974).
11. Eike Hennig (ed.), *Hessen unterm Hakenkreuz. Studien zur Durchsetzung der NSDAP in Hessen* (Frankfurt a. M., 1983). The use of archival material is hardly in evidence in Ulrich Schneider (ed.), *Hessen vor 50 Jahren – 1933: Naziterror und antifaschistischer Widerstand zwischen Kassel und Bergstraße 1932/33* (Frankfurt a. M., 1983). It is surprising that Rudi Koshar, in his very detailed local study on the development of Nazism in Marburg entitled *Social Life, Local Politics and Nazism. Marburg 1880–1935* (Chapel Hill/

London, 1986), did not use the archival material on the occupational background of members of the NSDAP and the SA in Marburg available in the *Hessisches Hauptstaatsarchiv* in Wiesbaden.

12. I am currently working on the reconstruction of the social make-up of the Nazi Movement in Hesse for the period 1925-1945 using the extensive data available in the Hessian archives on *Gaue* Hesse-Nassau and Hesse-Darmstadt.

1 HISTORIOGRAPHICAL AND METHODOLOGICAL ASPECTS

1. On the historiography of the sociology of Nazism see J. Paul Madden, 'The Social Composition of the Nazi Party, 1919-1930' (Ph.D. thesis, University of Oklahoma, 1976), pp. 3-33; Mathilde Jamin, *Zwischen den Klassen. Zur Sozialstruktur der SA-Führerschaft* (Wuppertal, 1984), pp. 11-37; and Peter Manstein, *Die Mitglieder und Wähler der NSDAP 1919-1933. Untersuchungen zu ihrer schichtmäßigen Zusammensetzung* (Frankfurt a. M./Bern, 1988), *passim*.

2. Madden, 'Social Composition', pp. 3-8.

3. See especially the pioneering efforts published in the early 1930s by Werner Stephan, 'Zur Soziologie der Nationalsozialistischen Deutschen Arbeiterpartei', *Zeitschrift für Politik*, 20 (1931), pp. 793-800; 'Grenzen des nationalsozialistischen Vormarsches. Eine Analyse der Wahlziffern seit der Reichstagswahl 1930', *Zeitschrift für Politik*, 21 (1932), pp. 570-8; 'Die Parteien nach den großen Frühjahrswahlkämpfen. Eine Analyse der Wahlziffern des Jahres 1932', *Zeitschrift für Politik*, 22 (1933), pp. 110-18; 'Die Reichstagswahlen vom 31.Juli 1932', *Zeitschrift für Politik*, 22 (1933), pp. 353-60.

4. Theodor Geiger, *Die soziale Schichtung des deutschen Volkes* (Stuttgart, 1932).

5. Especially important in popularizing the middle-class thesis of Nazism was the work by Seymour Martin Lipset, *Political Man* (New York, 1960). Cf. Heinrich August Winkler, *Mittelstand, Demokratie und Nationalsozialismus. Die politische Entwicklung von Handwerk und Kleinhandel in der Weimarer Republik* (Cologne, 1972).

6. The notion of the NSDAP as a *Volkspartei* or *Sammlungspartei* transcending class and religious cleavages in German society is suggested by Rudolf Billung, *NSDAP. Die Geschichte einer Bewegung* (Munich, 1931); Sigmund Neumann, *Die politischen Parteien in Deutschland* (Berlin, 1932); Theodor Heuß, *Hitler's Weg. Eine historisch-politische Studie über den Nationalsozialismus* (Stuttgart, 1932); Paul Sering, 'Der Faschismus', *Zeitschrift für den Sozialismus*, 24-5 (1936), pp. 765-92.

7. In the immediate post-war period the *Volkspartei* nature of Nazism was pointed to by Reinhard Bendix, 'Social Stratification and Political Power', *American Political Science Review*, (1952), pp. 357-

75; Wilhelm Ehrenstein, *Dämon Masse* (Frankfurt a. M., 1952); Raymond Martin, *Le National Socialisme hitlerien* (Paris, 1959).

8. Konrad Heiden, *A History of National Socialism* (New York, 1935).

9. Daniel Lerner, *The Nazi Elite* (Stanford, 1951).

10. Jacob Banaszkiewicz, 'German Fascism and People of the Social Fringe', *Polish Western Affairs*, 8 (1967), pp. 251-88.

11. Peter Loewenberg, 'The Psychohistorical Origins of the Nazi Youth Cohort', *American Historical Review*, 75 (1971), pp. 1457-502. Peter Merkl, *Political Violence under the Swastika: 581 Early Nazis* (Princeton, 1975); cf. Michael H. Kater, 'Generationskonflikt als Entwicklungsfaktor in der NS-Bewegung vor 1933', *Geschichte und Gesellschaft*, 11 (1985), pp. 217-43.

12. Cf. Charles P. Loomis and J. Allan Beegle, 'The Spread of German Nazism in Rural Areas', *The American Sociological Review*, 11 (1946), pp. 724-34; Rudolf Heberle, *From Democracy to Dictatorship* (Baton Rouge, 1945); Werner T. Angress, 'The Political Role of the Peasantry in the Weimar Republic', *The Review of Politics*, 21 (1959), pp. 530-49; Gerhard Stoltenberg, *Politische Strömungen im schleswig-holsteinischen Landvolk 1918-1933. Ein Beitrag zur politischen Meinungsbildung in der Weimarer Republik* (Düsseldorf, 1962).

13. For example, the works by Karl Dietrich Bracher, *Die Deutsche Diktatur. Entstehung, Struktur und Folgen des Nationalsozialismus* (Cologne/Berlin, 1969); Martin Broszat, *Der Staat Hitlers: Grundlegung und Entwicklung seiner inneren Verfassung* (Munich, 1969); Dietrich Orlow, *The History of the Nazi Party. Volume 1: 1919-1933* (Pittsburgh, 1969).

14. See Harold D. Lasswell, 'The Psychology of Hitlerism', *Political Quarterly*, 19 (1934), pp. 812-21; R. Palme Dutt, *Fascism and Social Revolution* (New York, 1935); Talcott Parsons, 'Some Sociological Aspects of the Fascist Movements', *Social Forces*, 21 (1942), pp. 138-47; Lipset, *Political Man*; Herman Lebovics, *Social Conservatism and the Middle Classes in Germany, 1914-1933* (Princeton, 1969); Winkler, *Mittelstand, Demokratie und Nationalsozialismus*; Barbara Heimel, 'Mittelschichten - Brutstätten des Faschismus? Zum Verhältnis von objektiver Lage und politischem Bewußtsein', in Reinhard Kühnl and Gerd Hardach (eds), *Die Zerstörung der Weimarer Republik*, (Cologne, 1977); Kater, *Nazi Party*. For a thorough review of the literature see Peter Manstein, *Mitglieder und Wähler*, pp. 46-89.

15. Theodore Abel, *The Nazi Movement: Why Hitler Came to Power* (New York, 1935).

16. *Partei-Statistik. Stand 1. Januar 1935. Band 1 Parteimitglieder.* Herausgeber Der Reichsorganisationsleiter der NSDAP (Munich, n.d.).

17. Hans Volz, *Daten der Geschichte der N.S.D.A.P.* (Berlin, 1938).

18. Hans Gerth, 'The Nazi Party: Its Leadership and Composition', *American Journal of Sociology*, 45 (1940), pp. 517-41.

19. For example by Wolfgang Schäfer, *NSDAP. Entwicklung und*

Struktur der Staatspartei des Dritten Reiches (Hanover, 1957); also Broszat, *Staat Hitlers*.

20. The data provided by the *Partei-Statistik* for the *Gaue* has been used as the sole or major source for the evaluation of the social structure of the NSDAP at the regional level by Jeremy Noakes, *The Nazi Party in Lower Saxony 1921–1933* (Oxford, 1971), pp. 141 and 159; Geoffrey Pridham, *Hitler's Rise to Power. The Nazi Movement in Bavaria 1923–1933* (London, 1973), p. 187, Table 2; Wilfried Böhnke, *Die NSDAP im Ruhrgebiet 1920-1933* (Bonn-Bad Godesberg, 1974), pp. 195, 198-9. See also Karl-Heinz Rothenberger, 'Die NSDAP in der Pfalz. Sozialstruktur der Partei nach der Parteistatistik von 1935', *Jahrbuch Westdeutscher Landesgeschichte*, 12 (1986), pp. 199-211.

21. For example, Geoffrey Pridham, *Hitler's Rise to Power*, p. 187, questions the value of statistical data produced by any party, especially that put together by the Nazis, who had a vested interest in proving that the NSDAP was a *Volkspartei* drawing support from all social classes. Albrecht Tyrell, *Führer befiehl . . . Selbstzeugnisse aus der Kampfzeit der NSDAP. Dokumente und Analyse* (Düsseldorf, 1969), p. 379, claims that the Nazis falsified the degree of support secured from the working class. Cf. the critiques by Reinhard Kühnl, *Formen bürgerlicher Herrschaft. Liberalismus - Faschismus* (Hamburg, 1971), p. 82; Eike Hennig, *Bürgerliche Gesellschaft und Faschismus in Deutschland: Ein Forschungsbericht* (Frankfurt a. M., 1977), pp. 164-5, p. 394, n. 281; Böhnke, *NSDAP im Ruhrgebiet*, p. 199.

22. In his thorough review of the utility of the *Partei-Statistik*, Peter Manstein concludes that this source has 'considerable value'; Manstein, *Mitglieder und Wähler*, pp. 143-52. Cf. Jamin, *Zwischen den Klassen*, pp. 17-18, 31-2; Detlef Mühlberger, 'Germany', in Detlef Mühlberger (ed.), *The Social Basis of European Fascist Movements* (London, 1987), pp. 40-139, here pp. 82-3.

23. *Partei-Statistik*, 1, pp. 11 and 56.

24. Cf. Gerhard Schulz, *Aufstieg des Nationalsozialismus* (Frankfurt a. M./Berlin/Vienna, 1975), pp. 550, 858-9; Detlef Mühlberger, 'The Sociology of the NSDAP: The Question of Working-Class Membership', *Journal of Contemporary History*, 15 (1980), pp. 493-511, here p. 507, n. 23; Manstein, *Mitglieder und Wähler*, pp. 149-51.

25. See Mühlberger, 'Germany', pp. 83-4.

26. The charge of vagueness and lack of precision is above all often applied to the 'worker' category to be found in the *Partei-Statistik*. Thomas Childers has it that 'the NSDAP's official statistics are . . . extraordinarily vague about what constituted a worker'; Thomas Childers, *The Nazi Voter. The Social Foundations of Fascism in Germany, 1919-1933* (Chapel Hill, 1983), p. 253. This view is echoed by Eberhard Kolb when he writes that 'it is not clear how the term "worker" is defined by the party statisticians'; Eberhard Kolb, *Die Weimarer Republik* (Munich/ Vienna), (1984), p. 118. In the *Partei-Statistik* the Nazi statisticians do make an effort to define the 'worker' category: a bar chart is provided which divides the category

into five groups comprising skilled workers in the metallurgical industry, other skilled workers, (workers in the) mining industry, agricultural workers, and (the) unskilled; *Partei-Statistik*, 1, p. 55.

27. Georg Franz-Willing, *Die Hitlerbewegung: Der Ursprung, 1919–1922* (Hamburg, 1962), pp. 129–30; Werner Maser, *Die Frühgeschichte der NSDAP. Hitlers Weg bis 1924* (Frankfurt a.M., 1965), pp. 254–5. Neither provided a representative sample and both employed odd occupational classification systems, especially Maser, who did not differentiate between skilled workers and artisans, and placed shopkeepers into three different occupational subgroups.

28. Michael Kater, 'Zur Soziographie der frühen NSDAP', *Vierteljahrshefte für Zeitgeschichte*, 19 (1971), pp. 124–59.

29. Also important among Professor Kater's prolific output on the social dimensions of Nazism are 'Zum gegenseitigen Verhältnis von SA und SS in der Sozialgeschichte des Nationalsozialismus von 1925 bis 1939', *Vierteljahrschrift für Sozial- und Wirtschaftsgeschichte*, 62 (1975), pp. 339–79; 'Sozialer Wandel in der NSDAP im Zuge der nationalsozialistischen Machtergreifung', in Wolfgang Schieder (ed.), *Faschismus als soziale Bewegung. Deutschland und Italien im Vergleich* (Hamburg, 1976), pp. 25–67; 'Ansätze zu einer Soziologie der SA bis zur Röhmkrise', in Ulrich Engelhardt, Volker Sellin and Horst Stuke (eds), *Soziale Bewegung und politische Verfassung. Beiträge zur Geschichte der modernen Welt* (Stuttgart, 1976), pp. 798–831; 'Methodologische Überlegungen über Möglichkeiten und Grenzen einer Analyse der sozialen Zusammensetzung der NSDAP von 1925 bis 1945', in Reinhard Mann (ed.), *Die Nationalsozialisten. Analysen faschistischer Bewegungen* (Stuttgart, 1980), pp. 155–85.

30. This change can be seen in Michael Kater, 'Quantifizierung und NS-Geschichte. Methodologische Überlegungen über Grenzen und Möglichkeiten einer EDV-Analyse der NSDAP-Sozialstruktur von 1925 bis 1945', *Geschichte und Gesellschaft*, 3 (1977), p. 477, Table 10.

31. Kater, *Nazi Party*, p. 236.

32. Donald M. Douglas, 'The Parent Cell: Some Computer Notes on the Composition of the First Nazi Party Group in Munich, 1919–1921', *Central European History*, 10 (1977), pp. 55–72; Paul Madden, 'Some Social Characteristics of Early Nazi Party Members, 1919–1923', *Central European History*, 15 (1982), pp. 34–56.

33. Lawrence D. Stokes, 'The Social Composition of the Nazi Party in Eutin, 1925–32', *International Review of Social History*, 23 (1978), pp. 1–32; Detlef Mühlberger, 'The Occupational and Social Structure of the NSDAP in the Border Province Posen–West Prussia in the early 1930s', *European History Quarterly*, 15 (1985), pp. 281–311.

34. See especially Conan Fischer, *Stormtroopers. A Social, Economic and Ideological Analysis, 1929–1935* (London, 1983); Jamin, *Zwischen den Klassen*.

35. Mühlberger, 'Germany', pp. 40–139.

36. In the *Partei-Statistik* the Nazis claimed that 'workers' accounted for 26.3 per cent of the Nazi Party's membership before 14 September 1930, and for 35.5 per cent in the period 15 September 1930 to 30

January 1933. For a summary of the *Partei-Statistik* data see Jeremy Noakes and Geoffrey Pridham (eds), *Nazism 1919–1945. 1: The Rise to Power 1919–1934* (Exeter, 1983), pp. 84–5.

37. Franz Josef Heyen, *Nationalsozialismus im Alltag. Quellen zur Geschichte des Nationalsozialismus vornehmlich im Raum Mainz-Koblenz-Trier* (Boppard am Rhein, 1967), pp. 52–6. For a summary of the data see Mühlberger, 'Germany', pp. 95–6.

38. Harold J. Gordon Jr., *Hitler and the Beer Hall Putsch* (Princeton, 1972), p. 82.

39. Madden, 'Social Composition of the Nazi Party', p. 267.

40. Detlef Mühlberger, 'The Sociology of the NSDAP: The Question of Working-Class Membership', *Journal of Contemporary History*, 15 (1980), pp. 493–511.

41. Mühlberger, 'NSDAP in the Border Province Posen-West Prussia', and Mühlberger, 'Germany'.

42. Madden, 'Social Class Origins', p. 237.

43. Kater, 'Quantifizierung und NS-Geschichte', p. 477, Table 10, II.

44. Kater, *Nazi Party*, p. 246, Table 4; p. 250, Table 6.

45. ibid., pp. 244–5, Table 3.

46. Madden, 'Social Class Origins', pp. 272–3, Table 2.

47. On this problem see Christoph Schmidt, 'Zu den Motiven "alter Kämpfer" in der NSDAP', in Detlev Peukert and Jürgen Renlecke (eds), *Die Reihen fast geschloßen. Beiträge zur Geschichte des Alltags unterm Hakenkreuz* (Wuppertal, 1981), pp. 21–43, here pp. 22–6. It seems, however, that Schmidt exaggerates the differences that he argues exist between the occupational-social reality and the self-assigned job descriptions of individual members as recorded in their files in the BDC. See the re-working of the material Schmidt used by Andrews, 'Social Composition of the NSDAP', p. 307. Cf. also Manstein, *Mitglieder und Wähler*, pp. 141–2.

48. This does not usually apply to police records on Nazi members, in which the data on the occupational status of individual Nazis is probably accurate since it is unlikely that Nazis subjected to police investigation would have lied about the nature of their jobs.

49. In the personal files of SA and SS members, the data given on individuals is often quite extensive (including information on income, father's occupation, marital status, religion). However, even within a set of files dealing with the same unit, there is no consistency of entries recording such aspects. Thus if one does collate the information on those individuals for whom the complete data is provided, one is faced with the question of how representative such a 'sample' would be.

50. Wage rates differed not only between various regions of Germany but also *within* the same region. For example, in Rhineland-Westphalia, especially the Ruhr (where wage tariffs were near the top in comparison with other parts of Germany), an unskilled worker (*Bauhilfsarbeiter*) in the building industry was earning an average of 43.20 RM for a 48-hour week in Essen and Dortmund and an unskilled worker (*Hilfsarbeiter*) in the timber industry in

Dortmund was taking home on average 41.28 RM for a 48-hour week in July 1925. In contrast to these rates, skilled workers were often receiving much lower wages in a variety of industrial sectors. Thus an artisan (*Handwerker*) in the chemical industry was taking home on average 37.20 RM for a 48-hour week in Essen and 37.14 RM in Elberfeld, and a skilled worker in the confectionary and baking industry received on average 36.24 RM in Essen, also for a 48-hour week. The wages received by skilled male workers such as weavers (*Weber*) in the textile industry in Barmen, which averaged 31.07 RM for a 48-hour week, were very much lower than those earned by unskilled workers in the metal, chemical or building industries in Essen or Düsseldorf or Dortmund or Bochum. In June 1926 Ruhr miners were being paid 8.53 RM per shift, almost double the rate being paid to miners in Silesia, who averaged 4.65 RM per shift. Data taken from *StJDR*, 45 (Berlin, 1926), pp. 276–90.

51. The average monthly salary paid to (married) Reich civil servants in April 1926 in the lowest salary groups I and II (which included line workers and guards on the State railway) ranged from 151.50 RM to 179 RM, incomes below the monthly earnings received by skilled blue-collar workers in many industrial sectors at that time. Data on civil servants salary rates taken from *StJDR*, 45 (Berlin, 1926), p. 291. Similarly, the average monthly salaries for (married) commercial employees in the textile industry in Mönchen–Gladbach stood at 151 RM and white-collar staff in the insurance industry in the Emscher region of Westphalia were receiving 166.82 RM in February 1928, incomes which compared unfavourably even with the average wage being paid to unskilled labourers in the timber industry in the Düsseldorf area in March 1928, which stood at 53.78 RM for a 54 hour week (including 3.4 hours of overtime), never mind the incomes being secured by skilled workers (*Facharbeiter*) in the same industrial sector in the same area, which averaged out at 69.81 RM for a 49.5 hour week. Data taken from *StJDR*, 47 (Berlin, 1928), pp. 360–1, 374.

52. This is most effectively demonstrated by Jürgen Genuneit, 'Methodische Probleme der quantitativen Analyse früher NSDAP-Mitgliederlisten', in Mann (ed.), *Die Nationalsozialisten*, pp. 34–66. Cf. Kater, 'Quantifizierung und NS-Geschichte', p. 477.

53. On the problems involved in the assignment of occupations to specific social classes see John H. Goldthorpe and Keith Hope, *The Social Grading of Occupations. A New Approach and Scale* (Oxford, 1974); A. P. M. Coxon and C. L. Jones, *The Images of Occupational Prestige* (London, 1978), and A. P. M. Coxon and C. L. Jones, *Class and Hierarchy: Social Meaning of Occupations* (London, 1979); L. S. Lewis, 'Class and Perceptions of Class', *Social Forces*, 42 (1964), pp. 336–40. At present not even self-professed Marxist scholars are agreed on the issue of which occupational categories should be deemed 'bourgeois' and which 'proletarian'. See Nicos Poulantzas, 'The New Petty Bourgeoisie', and Alan Hunt, 'Theory and Politics in the Identification of the Working Class', both in Alan Hunt (ed.),

Class and Class Structure (London, 1977).

54. For example Kater, 'Soziographie', p. 134; Kater, 'Sozialer Wandel', p. 27.
55. Kater changed his classification system in the late 1970s. For his current approach see Kater, *Nazi Party*, pp. 5–7.
56. Cf. Madden, 'Social Class Origins', p. 270, Table 1. A similar approach is advocated by Andrews, 'Social Composition', p. 312, Table 6.
57. Gordon, *Hitler and the Beer Hall Putsch*, p. 73; Max Kele, *Nazis and Workers. National Socialist Appeals to German Labor, 1919–1933* (Chapel Hill, 1972), pp. 69–73.
58. Douglas, 'Parent Cell', p. 66.
59. This would, of course, increase markedly the social and occupational groups employed in tabulating data. Andrews suggests a classification model divided into seven social categories and 38 occupational subgroups; Andrews, 'Social Composition', pp. 312–16. Cf. Genuneit, 'Methodische Probleme', p. 64, Appendix 5; Mühlberger, 'NSDAP in the Border Province Posen-West Prussia', pp. 29–23, Table 4.
60. Such a triple division of German society is used by all scholars working on the problem of the sociology of Nazism with the exception of Donald Douglas, who does not specifically refer to an élite or upper class in his analysis of the early Nazi membership; Douglas, 'Parent Cell', pp. 667. Cf. Manstein, *Mitglieder und Wähler*, p. 106.
61. The proximity of the official statisticians to the social and historical context of the time, as well as their experience in the field of occupational classification, shaped by value judgements (admittedly not infallible) concerning occupational and social prestige current at the time, suggests that it would be ill-judged to ignore their guidelines. On the approach taken by the statisticians compiling the 1925 and 1933 censuses, see *StDR*, 402, I (Berlin, 1927), pp. 3–16, and *StDR*, 453, I (Berlin, 1936), pp. 5–27. In appendix 14 of *StDR*, 402, I, pp. 177–212, thousands of occupational titles (and indications as to where these should be placed in social class terms) are listed alphabetically; occupations to be found in 160 economic branches are also given in appendix 12, pp. 46–118. Cf. the detail provided in the 1933 census, *StDR*, 453, I, pp. 36–263.
62. For example, Madden includes *Eisenbahner* and *Ladeschaffner* in the semi- and unskilled labourers subgroup of the lower class; Madden, 'Social Class Origins', p. 270. Kater includes some categories (e.g. *Schaffner, Lokomotivführer, Weichenwärter*) in the lower and intermediary civil servants subgroup, but assigns *Telegraphisten* and *Funker*, for example, to the lower class; Kater, *Nazi Party*, p. 285, n. 42.
63. Thus engine drivers and railway guards are deemed to be white-collar employees (*Angestellten*) in the 1925 census; *StDR*, 402, I (Berlin, 1929), p. 11. The income groups to which *Bahnwärter, Eisenbahnschaffner, Lokomotivheizer, Zugführer*, and *Loko-*

motivführer belonged within the salary scales of civil servants (*Reichsbeamten*) are noted in *StJDR*, 45 (Berlin, 1926), p. 293. Cf. Conan Fischer, *Stormtroopers. A Social, Economic and Ideological Analysis, 1929-35* (London, 1983), p. 16.

64. Douglas, 'Parent Cell', p. 66; Madden, 'Social Class Origins', p. 270, Table 1.
65. Kater, *Nazi Party*, pp. 7-8.
66. Cf. *StDR*, 402, I (Berlin, 1927), p. 11; *StDR*, 453, I (Berlin, 1936), p. 20.
67. According to the SPD's own analysis of the occupational status of its membership, skilled and semi-skilled workers accounted for 53 per cent of the membership in 1930; R. N. Hunt, *German Social Democracy 1918-1933* (New Haven/London, 1964), p. 103. Skilled workers made up 40 per cent of the KPD's membership in 1927; H. Weber, *Die Wandlung des deutschen Kommunismus. Die Stalinisierung der KPD in der Weimarer Republik* (Frankfurt a. M., 1969), p. 282.
68. The information on the social profile of the KPD in Bavaria is taken from Hartmut Mehringer, 'Die KPD in Bayern 1919-1945. Vorgeschichte, Verfolgung und Widerstand', in Martin Broszat and Helmut Mehringer (eds), *Bayern in der NS-Zeit. Die Parteien KPD, SPD, BVP in Verfolgung und Widerstand* (Munich/Vienna, 1983), pp. 1-286, here pp. 23-5, 63-6, 97, 99-100, 107-8, 131-2, 136-8, 175, 181, 189-90, 203, 219-30, 282-5. On the SPD in Bavaria see Hartmut Mehringer's essay 'Die bayerische Sozialdemokratie bis zum Ende des NS-Regimes. Vorgeschichte, Verfolgung und Widerstand' in the same work, pp. 287-432, here p. 331, Table 18.
69. See *StDR*, 453, I (Berlin, 1936), p. 16; *StDR*, 453, II (Berlin, 1936), pp. 14-15.
70. Kater, *Nazi Party*, p. 241, Table 1.
71. For the following see *StDR*, 453, II (Berlin, 1936), p. 25.
72. *StDR*, 402, III (Berlin, 1929), p. 433.
73. According to the *Partei-Statistik*, 65.5 per cent of the total Nazi membership was under 40 in late 1934; Kater, *Nazi Party*, p. 261, Table 13.
74. Fischer notes that an independent artisan only rarely omitted 'to describe himself as a master or make his independent status perfectly clear in some other way in his job description'; Fischer, *Stormtroopers*, p. 19.
75. For example, Kater's placement of foremen in mines (*Steiger*) into the 'other skilled workers' subgroup of the working class is mistaken; Kater, *Nazi Party*, p. 6. In the 1925 census, *Steiger* are assigned to the supervisory personnel (*Angestellten*) category; *StDR*, 402, I (Berlin, 1927), p. 48.
76. For a useful, concise overview see Kater, *Nazi Party*, pp. 4-5, 10-12. Cf. Ralf Dahrendorf, *Gesellschaft und Demokratie in Deutschland* (Munich, 1971), pp. 233-312.
77. The occupations listed under the '*a3 Personen*' in the *StDR*, 402, I (Berlin, 1927), pp. 137-8, were deemed members of the 'elite'. Cf.

StDR, 453, I (Berlin, 1936), pp. 62–193.

78. Madden, 'Social Class Origins', p. 270, Table 1.
79. Kater, *Nazi Party*, p. 12.
80. Madden, 'Social Class Origins', p. 270, Table 1.
81. Kater, *Nazi Party*, p. 12.
82. In the early 1930s just over one-third of (male) students came from the *Oberschicht*, and just under two-thirds from the ranks of the *Mittelschicht*. Students with a working-class background accounted for a mere 3.2 per cent; Manstein, *Mitglieder und Wähler*, p. 91.
83. The suggestion made by Manstein, *Mitglieder und Wähler*, p. 127, that it might be possible to separate workers into the various economic or industrial branches in which they were active is not practicable since the sort of information required to produce such a differentiation is only given in rare instances. The data presented in the 1933 census returns in *StDR*, 453, II (Berlin, 1936), p. 20, indicates the problems faced in the type of detailed classification Manstein thinks is possible. Although it is feasible to apportion all brewers and maltsters to economic branch 358 (the brewing industry), since 100 per cent of all dependent brewers and maltsters were employed in this branch, or to be almost one hundred per cent accurate in placing weavers into the textile industry (99.8 per cent of all weavers were employed in economic sector 28), it would be impossible to be accurate in the case of the ubiquitous *Schloßer*, 66.6 per cent of whom were in the metal industry (economic sectors 22–6), while the rest were scattered across 95 industrial branches.
84. *StDR*, 453, II (Berlin, 1936), p. 14.
85. Andrews, 'Social Composition', p. 316.
86. Cf. Ludwig Preller, *Sozialpolitik in der Weimarer Republik* (reprint, Kronberg/Ts., 1978), pp. 99–100.
87. In the 1933 census 'servants' were assigned to both the '*Arbeiter*' and '*Angestellten*' category, depending on their function and position within the household in which they were employed; see *StDR*, 453, I (Berlin, 1936), pp. 20 and 192. In the *Partei-Statistik* the *Hausangestellten* were included in the 'Others' subgroup; *Partei-Statistik*, 1, p. 335, Table J. Genuneit includes *Hausangestellte* in his second and third definition of the occupational types comprising the working class; Genuneit, 'Methodologische Probleme', pp. 44–5.

2 THE WESTERN RUHR, 1925-6

1. On the development of Nazism in the Ruhr see the study by Wilfried Böhnke, *Die NSDAP im Ruhrgebiet 1920-1933* (Bonn–Bad Godesberg, 1974). Cf. Detlef Mühlberger, 'The Rise of National Socialism in Westphalia 1920-1933' (Ph.D. thesis, University of London, 1975), which deals with the eastern half of the Ruhr.
2. A report on the formation of the Dortmund branch is entered on 5 June 1920 in the *Brieftagebuch DAP München von 2. Juni 1920-16. April 1921*, in HA, reel 1A, folder 222. The precise date of the

founding of the Dortmund branch is not given. There are two entries in the list *Adolf Hitler's Mitkämpfer 1919–1921*, of members resident in Dortmund, member no. 1502 (a 'miner' resident in Dortmund/Mengede) and member no. 1503 (an 'electro-technician'), both of whom joined on 1 May 1920. The list is in HA, 2A/230. The 1 May 1920 was probably the date on which the branch was founded, as asserted in the Nazi account of the origins and development of Nazism in southern Westphalia by Friedrich Alfred Beck, *Kampf und Sieg. Geschichte der NSDAP im Gau Westfalen-Süd von den Anfängen bis zur Machtübernahme* (Dortmund, 1938), p. 301.

3. Cf. Alfred Milatz, *Wähler und Wahlen in der Weimarer Republik* (Bonn, 1965), p. 112.

4. Böhnke, *NSDAP im Ruhrgebiet*, pp. 91–105; Mühlberger, 'National Socialism in Westphalia', pp. 192–217.

5. The membership of the branches established at Essen and Langerfeld was relatively stable. Of the 267 people recruited in Essen in the latter half of 1925 only ten had left by December. The small Mettmann branch attracted a more volatile group of supporters, with 26 per cent of those listed in November 1925 no longer in the party by February 1926. The various lists relating to the branches are in NWHStAD, RW 23, No. 38 (Essen); RW 23, No. 85 (Barmen-Langerfeld); and RW 23, No. 55 (Mettmann).

6. According to the census data of 1925 the *Regierungsbezirke* of Düsseldorf and Arnsberg had a population density of 703.39 and 354.07 people per square kilometre respectively, well above the average for Prussia (130.68) and Germany (133.15, excluding the Saar). Düsseldorf was the most densely populated *Regierungsbezirk* in Germany. Data taken from *StJDR*, 46 (Berlin, 1927), pp. 5–6.

7. According to the census returns of 1925, 41.24 and 30.94 per cent of the population of the Rheinprovinz and Westphalia respectively lived in cities with a population of 100,000 and over (the figures for Prussia and Germany were 29.24 and 26.78 respectively). The Rheinprovinz had the highest percentage share of the population resident in cities of 100,000 and over for any Prussian province or for any German *Land*. Data taken from *StJDR*, 46 (Berlin, 1927), pp. 12–13.

8. In his analysis of the regional distribution of the working class in the Ruhr region, Heinz-Günther Steinberg notes that in many Ruhr towns the lower class made up 70 per cent or more of the working population; Heinz-Günter Steinberg, 'Sozialräumliche Entwicklung und Gliederung des Ruhrgebietes', *Forschungen zur Deutschen Landeskunde*, 166 (1967), p. 174. According to Böhnke workers accounted for 60 to 75 per cent of the working population of the Ruhr towns; Böhnke, *NSDAP im Ruhrgebiet*, p. 140.

9. Unskilled workers accounted for 49.3 per cent of the working population, and skilled workers for a further 16.8 per cent. Percentages taken from Ingrid Buchloh, *Die Nationalsozialistische Machtergreifung in Duisburg* (Duisburg, 1980), p. 12.

10. This becomes clear when one looks at the data on the 23 economic

groups into which the working population of these towns is divided in the *Berufszählung* of 1925, *StDR*, 404, part 15 (Berlin, 1928), pp. 92-6, 110-14.

11. ibid., pp. 104-9.
12. ibid., pp. 86-90.
13. See Steinberg, 'Sozialräumliche Entwicklung', p. 175; also Herbert Kühr, *Parteien und Wahlen im Stadt- und Landkreis Essen in der Weimarer Republik* (Düsseldorf, 1973), pp. 47-9.
14. Data (based on the 1925 census) on Germany, Prussia, the Rheinprovinz and Westphalia taken from *StJDR*, 47 (Berlin, 1928), p. 25. The percentages for the *Regierungsbezirke* and the towns were calculated on the basis of data provided in *StDR*, 404, part 15 (Berlin, 1928), pp. 72 and 90; and 404, part 16 (Berlin, 1928), pp. 86, 92, 98, 104-5, and 110.
15. On the performance of the SPD and KPD in these electoral districts see data in Milatz, *Wähler und Wahlen*, pp. 90 and 108.
16. Electoral district Westphalia-South contained a number of counties in which agriculture and forestry were still major employers. Cf. Mühlberger, 'National Socialism in Westphalia', p. 19.
17. For an overview of this aspect see Karl Rohe, 'Vom alten Revier zum heutigen Ruhrgebiet. Die Entwicklung einer regionalen politischen Gesellschaft im Spiegel der Wahlen', in Karl Rohe and Herbert Kühr (eds), *Politik und Gesellschaft im Ruhrgebiet* (Königstein/Ts., 1979), pp. 32-7. On the significance of political Catholicism in Essen see Kühr, *Parteien und Wahlen*, pp. 57-89.
18. *StJFP*, 23 (Berlin, 1927), pp. 238-9.
19. Percentages taken from Johannes Schauff, *Das Wahlverhalten der Deutschen Katholiken im Kaiserreich und in der Weimarer Republik* (Mainz, 1975), pp. 198-9.
20. This is emphasized by Böhnke, *NSDAP im Ruhrgebiet*, *passim*; Mühlberger, 'National Socialism in Westphalia', *passim*. Cf. the influence of religion on the electoral behaviour of the Essen voters in Kühr, *Parteien und Wahlen*, pp. 257-82.
21. Beck, *Kampf und Sieg*, p. 301.
22. According to a report in *VB*, 8 March 1922.
23. On the weakness of Nazism in the Ruhr from 1920 to 1922 see Böhnke, *NSDAP im Ruhrgebiet*, pp. 38-53. In some Ruhr towns, such as Duisburg, 'unofficial' Nazi branches were established, which led a very shadowy existence; see Buchloh, *Nationalsozialistische Machtergreifung in Duisburg*, p. 43.
24. Böhnke, *NSDAP im Ruhrgebiet*, pp. 48-52; Mühlberger, 'National Socialism in Westphalia', pp. 139-40.
25. In those parts of the western Ruhr which were occupied by the Allies after the First World War, the occupation authorities had already prohibited radical right-wing organizations before the general Prussian ban of 15 November 1922. In Duisburg and Hamborn, occupied since March 1921, a ban on right-wing groups was already in place in 1921; see Buchloh, *Nationalsozialistische Machtergreifung in Duisburg*, p. 39.

26. Böhnke, *NSDAP im Ruhrgebiet*, pp. 54-7; Mühlberger, 'National Socialism in Westphalia', pp. 146-8.
27. Böhnke, *NSDAP im Ruhrgebiet*, pp. 44 and 54.
28. In a report by the Hagen police the size of the membership of the Hagen NSDAP is given as 304; police report, Hagen, 1 May 1922, StAM, 1 PA/398.
29. Böhnke, *NSDAP im Ruhrgebiet*, p. 197.
30. Police report, Hagen, 1 May 1922, StAM, 1 PA/398.
31. Report by the *Landrat*, Dortmund, 9 May 1922, StAM, 1 PA/398; also *VB*, 17 June 1922. Cf. H. Graf, *Die Entwicklung der Wahlen und politischen Parteien in Groß Dortmund* (Frankfurt a. M., 1958), pp. 35-6.
32. The changes in the structure of the Dortmund branch leadership are made clear in the Dortmund police reports dated 10 May and 22 September 1922, StAM, 1 PA/398.
33. *Adolf Hitler's Mitkämpfer 1919-1921*, copy in HA, 2A/230.
34. The membership list recording those who joined the Nazi Party between 28 September and 9 November 1923 is in HA, 10/215.
35. Surprisingly the lower-class percentage was lower, and that for the lower- and middle-middle class very much higher than that for the total number joining the party at that time, even though the great bulk of these recruits came from the less industrialized Bavaria. For a breakdown of the social background of the recruits see Detlef Mühlberger, 'Germany', in Detlef Mühlberger (ed.), *The Social Basis of European Fascist Movements* (London, 1987), pp. 62-8.
36. The general growth pattern of the NSDAP in the Ruhr in 1925 is discussed in Böhnke, *NSDAP im Ruhrgebiet*, pp. 98-100.
37. See the membership lists of the Essen branch covering July 1925 to March 1926 in NWHStAD, RW 23, No. 38.
38. This figure is given by Peter Hüttenberger, *Die Gauleiter. Studie zum Wandel des Machtgefüges in der NSDAP* (Stuttgart, 1969), p. 34, n. 65.
39. The total strength is calculated from data given in *Gau Ruhr der N.S.D.A.P. Mitgliederstand vom 31. Mai 1926*, in BA, NS1/342.
40. ibid.
41. In the urban and rural districts of Essen, for example, the Nazi Party had a membership of 508 by the end of May 1926, as against the (estimated) 15,000-20,000 membership which the Centre Party generally had in the early 1920s, or the (estimated) 1,500 to 2,500 strong SPD (the figure applies to the urban district): Kühr, *Parteien und Wahlen*, p. 104.
42. The KPD, which had acquired a membership of around 21,000 in the Ruhr region by 1924, had managed to lose much of its support by the beginning of 1926, by which time it was down to around 4,000 paid-up members; see Siegfried Bahne, 'Die KPD im Ruhrgebiet in der Weimarer Republik', in Jürgen Reulecke (ed.), *Arbeiterbewegung an Rhein und Ruhr. Beiträge zur Geschichte der Arbeiterbewegung in Rheinland-Westfalen* (Wuppertal, 1974), pp. 323 and 326.

43. The figure is suggested by Buchloh, *Nationalsozialistische Machtergreifung in Duisburg*, p. 46, n. 268. Some 27,000 people joined the Nazi Party in 1925 and a further 22,000 in 1926. Some 16.2 per cent of the 1925 recruits left the party in 1926. Figures taken from J. Paul Madden, 'The Social Composition of the Nazi Party, 1919-1930' (Ph.D. thesis, University of Oklahoma, 1976), pp. 137, 150 and 156. In a letter to Munich party headquarters in July 1926 the Ruhr *Gauleitung* asserted that it represented 'the strongest *Gau*' of the movement; see *Gauleitung Ruhr an Parteileitung, Elberfeld 1. Juli 1926*, in BA, Sammlung Schumacher 203.

44. The data is based on membership lists in NWHStAD, RW 23, No. 38 (Essen); RW 23, No. 41 (Mörs); RW 23, No. 44 (Hamborn); RW 23, No. 45 (Oberhausen/Rheinland); RW 23, No. 47 (Hammerthal); RW 23, No. 49 (Barmen); RW 23, Nos. 50-1 (Mülheim/Ruhr); RW 23, No. 55 (Mettmann); RW 23, No. 63 (Rheinhausen); RW 23, No. 85 (Barmen-Langerfeld).

45. In the Essen branch 3.5 per cent of the membership was unemployed by the end of July 1925, a figure which rose to 11.8 per cent by the end of August. Percentages calculated from data in *Abrechnung für Monat August 1925*, NWHStAD, RW 23, No. 38. According to a letter from the Hammerthal branch to the *Gau* headquarters of the NSDAP at Elberfeld, dated 27 December 1925, more than half (54.5 per cent) of the branch members were unemployed by the end of 1925: NWHStAD, RW 23, No. 47.

46. See *Mitgliederliste der Ortsgruppe Essen. Monat Juli* and *Nachtrag. Mitgliederliste Ortsgruppe Essen. Monat August. 1925*, in which the contributions paid by the members are recorded; NWHStAD, RW 23, No. 38.

47. The party functionaries included were the branch committee members (branch leader and deputy leader, treasurer and secretary or business manager and - in some branches - their deputies).

48. The *a* columns are based on the membership of the branches, the *b* columns on the working population of the cities or towns (county Hattingen in the case of the Hammerthal branch) in which the branches were situated. The percentages in the *b* columns were calculated on the basis of data in *StDR*, 404, part 15 (Berlin, 1928), p. 103; and 404, part 16 (Berlin, 1928), pp. 86, 92, 98, 104-5 and 110.

49. The information on the social profile of the districts is taken from Kühr, *Parteien und Wahlen*, p. 47.

50. Goebbels to Frl. B., Elberfeld, 15 September 1925, in NWHStAD, RW 23, No. 41.

51. Fortunately the specific districts of Essen (e.g. Essen-West, Essen-Borbeck, Altenessen) in which the members lived were regularly entered in the membership lists. A small percentage of the members lived in county Essen (primarily in Katernberg), which was included in the city from 1929.

52. The percentages of the age structure of the male working population in the Rheinprovinz are calculated on the basis of data in *StDR*, 404, part 16 (Berlin, 1928), pp. 4-5; the figures for Prussia are based on

data in *StDR*, 403, part 1 (Berlin, 1929), and for Germany on the basis of data in *StDR*, 402, III (Berlin, 1929), p. 424.

53. Cf. Richard F. Hamilton, *Who voted for Hitler?* (Princeton, 1982), pp. 160-1.
54. Of the first 144 members recruited in Essen by the end of August 1925, 23.6 per cent were married. Of the 46 members enrolled in the Mülheim/Ruhr branch in 1925, only 13 per cent were married.
55. Goebbels' attitude and resentment are reflected in his diary entries from 7 to 21 June 1926; see Helmut Heiber (ed.), *The Early Goebbels Diaries. The Journal of Joseph Goebbels from 1925-1926* (London, 1962), pp. 89-92.
56. Kaufmann's problems are surveyed in Hüttenberger, *Die Gauleiter*, pp. 46-9.
57. For example, in the coal-mining district of Gelsenkirchen-Recklinghausen the membership of Nazi branches declined by some 42 per cent between January 1927 and December 1928: see police report, *Polizeibezirk* Recklinghausen, 12 January 1929, in StAM, VII-2, Band 6.
58. In the May *Reichstag* election the NSDAP secured 2.6 per cent nationally. In the electoral districts covering the Ruhr the party secured 1 per cent in Westphalia-North, 1.6 per cent in Westphalia-South, 1.8 per cent in Düsseldorf-East and 1.2 per cent in Düsseldorf-West. The poor performance of the party in the Ruhr towns and cities emerges from the figures provided by Böhnke, *NSDAP im Ruhrgebiet*, p. 132.
59. Figures from Kühr, *Parteien und Wahlen*, p. 149.
60. Figures from Buchloh, *Nationalsozialistische Machtergreifung in Duisburg*, pp. 44-5.
61. Police report, Bochum, 3 October 1930, in StAM, VII - 67 Band 1.
62. The first figure is cited in a report by the police president, Bochum, 9 January 1930, in StAM, VII - 67 Band 1. The second figure was claimed by the Westphalian *Gauleiter* Wagner in a report to the organizational section of the *Reichsleitung* of the NSDAP, dated 7 November 1930: copy in StAM, VII - 67 Band 1. Wagner's high figure probably included a sizeable percentage of members who were not contributing regular membership dues; cf. Mühlberger, 'National Socialism in Westphalia', pp. 296-7.
63. Data taken from *Partei-Statistik. Stand 1. Januar 1935. Band I Parteimitglieder*. Herausgeber Der Reichsorganisationsleiter der NSDAP (Munich, n.d.), pp. 146-7.
64. The lower class provided 50 per cent of the district's functionaries at branch level; see Mühlberger, 'Germany', p. 99, Table 2.8, column g.
65. The report is analysed by Böhnke, *NSDAP im Ruhrgebiet*, p. 199.
66. For the following see *An die RL der NSDAP-Organisationsabteilung*, NSDAP *Gau* Westphalia, Bochum, 7 November 1930. Copy in StAM, VII-67 Band 1. Böhnke, although he consulted this file, makes no reference to Wagner's figures.
67. See Michael H. Kater, *The Nazi Party. A Social Profile of Members and, Leaders, 1919-1945* (Oxford, 1983), Table 5, p. 248.

68. Böhnke, *NSDAP im Ruhrgebiet*, p. 225.
69. In his study on Bochum, Johannes Wagner claims that the *Mittelschichten* carried the party in the city. No evidence is advanced to support this assertion. See Johannes Volker Wagner, *Hakenkreuz über Bochum. Machtergreifung und Nationalsozialistischer Alltag in einer Revierstadt* (Bochum, 1983), p. 111.
70. Böhnke, *NSDAP im Ruhrgebiet*, p. 201.
71. Buchloh, *Nationalsozialistische Machtergreifung in Duisburg*, *passim*.
72. Hamilton, in his examination of voting behaviour in five Ruhr cities, notes that the majority of the votes cast for the NSDAP in Essen in the July 1932 *Reichstag* election came from the lower class. See Hamilton, *Who voted for Hitler?*, p. 162.
73. Böhnke, *NSDAP im Ruhrgebiet*, pp. 183-9.

3 *GAU* WÜRTTEMBERG, 1928-30

1. On the history of the NSDAP in Bavaria see Geoffrey Pridham, *Hitler's Rise to Power. The Nazi Movement in Bavaria, 1923-1933* (London, 1973); cf. the study by Rainer Hambrecht, *Der Aufstieg der NSDAP in Mittel- und Oberfranken, 1925-1933* (Nuremberg, 1976). On the Nazi Party in the Palatinate see Jürgen Poschick, 'Die Entwicklung der NSDAP der Pfalz von 1926 bis 1932' (*Diplom-Arbeit*, University of Mannheim, 1985); and H. Fenske, 'Die pfälzische NSDAP 1921-1932', *Mitteilungen des Historischen Vereins der Pfalz*, 85 (1987), pp. 347-81.
2. Johnpeter Horst Grill, *The Nazi Movement in Baden 1920-1945* (Chapel Hill, 1983). An overview is provided by Ernst Otto Bräunche, 'Die NSDAP in Baden 1928-1933. Der Weg zur Macht', in Thomas Schnabel (ed.) *Die Machtergreifung in Südwestdeutschland. Das Ende der Weimarer Republik in Baden und Württemberg 1928-1933* (Stuttgart, 1982), pp. 15-48.
3. Gerhard Paul, *Die NSDAP des Saargebietes 1920-1935. Der verspätete Aufstieg der NSDAP in der katholischen-proletarischen Provinz* (Saarbrücken, 1985).
4. An outline history of the NSDAP's development in Württemberg is provided by Thomas Schnabel, 'Die NSDAP in Württemberg 1928-1933. Die Schwäche einer regionalen Parteiorganisation', in Thomas Schnabel (ed.), *Machtergreifung in Südwestdeutschland*, pp. 49-81. Cf. the local studies on Mühlacker by Bernd Burkhardt, *Eine Stadt wird Braun. Die nationalsozialistische Machtergreifung in der schwäbischen Provinz* (Hamburg, 1980), and on Balingen by Wilhelm Foch, 'Die letzten Jahre der Weimarer Republik und die Machtergreifung der NSDAP in Balingen', *Heimatkundliche Blätter für den Kreis Balingen*, 18 (1968). Some insight into the situation of the Nazi Party in Tübingen is provided by Rudy Koshar, 'Two "Nazisms": the social context of Nazi mobilization in Marburg and Tübingen', *Social History*, 7 (1982), pp. 27-42.
5. The Nazi *Gau* Württemberg included both *Land* Württemberg and

the small Prussian province of Hohenzollern (*Regierungsbezirk Sigmaringen*). Electoral District 31 (Württemberg) also included Hohenzollern.

6. On the early history of Nazism in the Stuttgart area see Jürgen Genuneit, *Völkische Radikale in Stuttgart: Zur Vorgeschichte und Frühphase der NSDAP 1920–1925* (Stuttgart, 1982). Cf. the reminiscences by Eugen Haub, one of the founding members of the branch, *Aufzeichnungen zur Vorgeschichte der Entstehung der NSDAP in Stuttgart* (written just before the Second World War), copy in HA, 8/166.

7. This is especially so if one subscribes to the view found in many accounts of the history of the Nazi Party that it mobilized strong support from the late 1920s primarily in rural and small-town Protestant regions. Cf. Lipset's well-known characterization of the 'ideal-typical Nazi voter in 1932' as being 'a middle-class self-employed Protestant who lived either on a farm or in a small community'; Seymour M. Lipset, *Political Man* (London, 1960), p. 149.

8. Data taken from *StJDR*, 46 (Berlin, 1927), p. 9.

9. The following data is from Thomas Schnabel, 'Tabellen und Übersichten', in Schnabel (ed.), *Machtergreifung in Südwestdeutschland*, p. 318, Table 1.

10. Data taken from *Einzelschriften zur Statistik des Deutschen Reichs. Nr. 7: Die Steuerkraft der Finanzbezirke* (Berlin, 1929), p. 136.

11. In Hohenzollern the owner-occupiers farmed 88.8 per cent of the land and tenant-farmers 7.4 per cent. The respective figures for Germany were 86.6 and 12.4 per cent. Data from *StJDR*, 46 (Berlin, 1927), p. 42.

12. For the following see Thomas Schnabel, 'Warum geht es in Schwaben besser? Württemberg in der Weltwirtschaftskrise 1928–33', in Schnabel (ed.), *Machtergreifung in Südwestdeutschland*, pp. 184–218, here pp. 186–8.

13. Adapted from a map in Schnabel, 'Tabellen', p. 317.

14. Adapted from maps in Alfred Milatz, *Wähler und Wahlen in der Weimarer Republik* (Bonn, 1965), Appendix, Maps 3 and 4.

15. Data taken from *StJDR*, 46 (Berlin, 1927), p. 24.

16. The calculations are based on data in *Vierteljahrshefte zur Statistik des Deutschen Reichs*, 34, part 2 (Berlin, 1925), p. 95.

17. Cf. Schnabel, 'Warum geht es in Schwaben besser?', p. 188.

18. Workers in the trade and transport sector accounted for 2.2 per cent of the working population of Württemberg and 4.5 per cent of the German working population. Percentages calculated from data in *StDR*, 402, II (Berlin, 1927), pp. 228 and 230, and *StDR*, 405, part 32 (Berlin, 1928), pp. 2 and 4.

19. Organizationally the NSDAP had had some success in Württemberg before 1923. Although 155 of the Nazi Party's 347 branches were in Bavaria, Württemberg followed with 37, ahead of Saxony (27) and Thuringia (14). See Wolfgang Schäfer, *NSDAP. Entwicklung und Struktur der Staatspartei des Dritten Reiches* (Hanover, 1956), p. 11.

In a police report on the state of the Nazi Party in Württemberg in 1928, its slow development in the late 1920s is compared with 'its rapid growth ... before the Hitlerputsch'. The report, dated 11.4.1928, is in HA, 58/1401.

20. The return of 9.4 per cent secured by the Württemberg Nazi Party in the 1930 *Reichstag* election was the worst performance by the NSDAP in any of the 35 electoral districts, and half the party's national average of 18.3 per cent. Cf. Milatz, *Wähler und Wahlen*, p. 110. See also the analysis by Eberhard Schanbacher, 'Das Wählervotum und die "Machtergreifung" im deutschen Südwesten', in *Machtergreifung in Südwestdeutschland*, pp. 295–308.

21. Details in Schnabel, 'Die NSDAP in Württemberg', pp. 49–74, *passim*; and Schnabel, 'Warum geht es in Schwaben besser', pp. 184–209, *passim*.

22. Accounts of various squabbles among the Nazi hierarchy are a constant theme in the situation reports (*Lageberichte*) dealing with the political situation in Württemberg drawn up by the *Staatspolizei*. The reports dealing with the period 1927 to 1930 are in HA, 58/1400 (1927); 58/1401 (1928); 58/1402 (1929); and 58/1403 (1930). These reports give a useful insight into the broad development pattern of the Württemberg NSDAP, as well as a more detailed picture of the affairs of the Stuttgart branch. The factionalism within the Württemberg Nazi movement is also hinted at by *Gauleiter* Murr in his *Bericht über die Lage des Gaues Württemberg*, reprinted in Schnabel 'NSDAP in Württemberg', pp. 75–7, here p. 76.

23. See Gerhard Schildt, 'Die Arbeitsgemeinschaft Nord-West. Untersuchungen zur Geschichte der NSDAP 1925/26', (Phil. Diss., Albert-Ludwigs-Universität zu Freiburg im Breisgau, 1966), p. 34.

24. A major row developed in the *Gau* in October 1927 over which Nazis were to be on the electoral slate in the forthcoming *Landtag* elections, and in which order the names were to appear on the party list. Munder thought he ought to head the list, a suggestion questioned by Mergenthaler, who turned to Hitler for support in advancing his own candidature. When Mergenthaler succeeded in getting the premier slot, Munder resigned. The quarrel is given much attention in the *Lageberichte* of 11.4.1928 (p. 3) and 9.5.1928 (p. 7), in HA, 58/1401.

25. For example, see his *Rundschreiben Nr. 1*, dated 28 September 1925, in HA, 8/166. Cf. Peter Hüttenberger, *Die Gauleiter. Studie zum Wandel des Machtgefüges in der NSDAP* (Stuttgart, 1969), pp. 14–15.

26. *Lagebericht*, 23.1.1929 (p. 3), in HA, 58/1402.

27. ibid., pp. 4–5.

28. Schnabel, 'NSDAP in Württemberg', p. 53.

29. *Lagebericht*, 3.4.1929 (p. 4), in HA, 58/1402.

30. See the situation reports of 5.3.1930 (p. 6) and 19.3.1930 (p. 5), in HA, 58/1403.

31. *Lagebericht*, 16.7.1930 (p. 5), in HA, 58/1403.

32. The lack of organizational talent even in the large Stuttgart branch is indicated by Wilhelm Dreher's description of the branch as a 'shambles' at the time of his appointment as *Ortsgruppenleiter* in 1927. See *Lagebericht*, 13.7.1927 (p. 2), in HA, 58/1400.

33. Noted by *Gauleiter* Murr in his *Bericht über die Lage des Gaues Württemberg*, reprinted in Schnabel, 'NSDAP in Württemberg', p. 75.

34. For example, in December 1928 both the branch leader and the treasurer of the Stuttgart branch resigned, as did the *Gauführer* of the *Hitlerjugend*. See *Lagebericht*, 23.1.1929 (p. 4), in HA, 58/1402.

35. This emerges from the report on the financial position of the *Gau* by the *Gaukassenwart* at the *Gautagung* of 25 September 1927; in *Lagebericht*, 5.10.1927 (p. 5), in HA, 58/1400. See also Murr's *Bericht über die Lage des Gaues Württemberg*, reprinted in Schnabel, 'NSDAP in Württemberg', p. 75.

36. In a branch circular dated 2 October 1928, the Stuttgart leadership was appealing to the membership for funds to cover the cost of past elections and to finance the forthcoming local election campaign. Copy of the circular in HA, 8/166.

37. See *Bericht über die Lage des Gaues Württemberg*, reprinted in Schnabel, 'NSDAP in Württemberg', p. 75.

38. One of the speakers at the *Gautagung* held in Stuttgart on 24 September 1927, to which the Stuttgart branch members had been invited, complained that few had attended due to the rival attraction of a *Volksfest*. See *Lagebericht*, 5.10.27 (p. 4), in HA, 58/1400.

39. The *Gaukassenwart* threatened to ask the Munich *Parteileitung* to dissolve branches with large arrears; *Lagebericht*, 5.10.1927 (p. 5), in HA, 58/1400.

40. Based on *Neuaufnahmenerklärungen* sent by the *Gaukassenwart* to the *Reichsleitung* of the NSDAP in the period from 27 March 1928 to 30 September 1930. The lists usually noted the surname and first name, the date of birth, place of birth and place of residence of the new member, and the name of the *Ortsgruppe* which he or (more rarely) she joined. The lists are virtually complete, barring a gap in January and early February 1930. Presumably due to the pressure of work occasioned by the run-up to the September 1930 *Reichstag* election, there were no lists compiled after 1 September until 22 and 30 September 1930. The names in the latter lists have been included on the assumption that these lists record those enrolling before the election and thus do not involve the *Septemberlinge* who jumped on the Nazi bandwagon in Württemberg, as elsewhere in Germany, after the Nazi electoral breakthrough. The lists are in StAL, PL 501/ 93–4.

41. Attendance figures at Nazi meetings are regularly given in the *Lageberichte* covering the years 1927 to 1930, in HA, 58/1400–1403.

42. See especially the negative picture of the development of the party emerging from the *Lageberichte* of 12.12.1928 (p. 3), in HA, 58/1401; 12.6.1929 (p. 4) and 13.11.1929 (p. 1), in HA, 58/1402; and 5.3.1930 (p. 5), in HA, 58/1403.

43. Cf. *Lageberichte* of 24.4.1930 (p. 7) and 7.5.1930 (p. 5), in HA, 58/1403.
44. Schnabel, 'NSDAP in Württemberg', p. 52. The police, in general well-informed on the overall development pattern of the Nazi movement in Württemberg, consistently overstated the numeric strength of the party. Thus the report on the strength of the Württemberg NSDAP at the beginning of 1929 grossly over-estimated the membership at between 2,500 to 2,800; see *Lagebericht*, 6.2.1929 (p. 3), in HA, 58/1402.
45. The claim made by Murr in his report on the *Gau* at the end of 1929, that the party was recruiting an average of 47 members per month during 1928 is confirmed by the *Neuaufnahmen*. See *Bericht über die Lage des Gaues Württemberg*, reprinted in Schnabel, 'NSDAP in Württemberg', p. 75.
46. ibid.
47. There are no copies of lists recording new members who joined in January and early February (the first list for 1930 is dated 14 February listing nine members recruited by the Owen Teck branch). However, replies from Munich speak of 78 membership cards issued in January and 115 in February. The correspondence is in StAL, PL 501/94.
48. *Partei-Statistik. Stand 1. Januar 1935*. Herausgeber Der Reichsorganisationsleiter der NSDAP (Munich, n.d.), p. 26. The police again exaggerated the total strength of the Nazi Party's membership in the region, suggesting that it stood at 5,000 paid-up members by May 1930; see *Lagebericht* 16.7.1930 (p. 4), in HA, 58/1403. The same report is even wider off the mark in suggesting that between 1 April and 15 May 1930 *Gau* Württemberg had enrolled 1,104 new members! The real figure was 396; see lists dated 14 and 24 April and 7 and 9 May in StAL, PL 501/94.
49. The figure for 1925 is taken from Schäfer, *NSDAP*, p. 11. Figures for 1928 and 1930 are from volume III of the *Partei-Statistik* quoted in Schnabel, 'NSDAP in Württemberg', p. 56.
50. This is also clearly in evidence when one looks at the electoral performance of the NSDAP in the Catholic parts of Württemberg-Hohenzollern. On this aspect see Eberhard Schanbacher, 'Das Wählervotum und die "Machtergreifung" im deutschen Südwesten', in Schnabel (ed.), *Machtergreifung in Südwestdeutschland*, pp. 295–308, here especially pp. 306–7.
51. Details taken from a list recording 4,786 members who joined the NSDAP between September and November 1923, in HA, 10/215.
52. The following percentages are calculated on basis of data in *StDR*, 382, II (Berlin, 1932), pp. 66–70.
53. I am at present processing the data listing members who joined *Gau* Württemberg-Hohenzollern between September 1930 and January 1933 and will publish the results in a forthcoming article.
54. As suggested by J. Paul Madden, 'The Social Composition of the Nazi Party, 1919–1930', (Ph.D. thesis, University of Oklahoma, 1976), p. 202.

55. The data is calculated on the basis of the *Neuaufnahmen* lists in StAL, PL 501/93-4.
56. See, for example, the situation in Lower Saxony in Jeremy Noakes, *The Nazi Party in Lower Saxony 1921-1933* (Oxford, 1971), pp. 121-7, 148-55. Agrarian support in Protestant areas for Nazism by the late 1920s is also emphasized by Johnpeter Horst Grill, *The Nazi Movement in Baden 1920-1945* (Chapel Hill, NC, 1983), pp. 148-50, 164-9, and 190. Cf. Gerhard Stoltenberg, *Politische Strömungen im schleswig-holsteinischen Landvolk 1918-1933. Ein Beitrag zur politischen Meinungsbildung in der Weimarer Republik* (Düsseldorf, 1962), pp. 141-64.
57. Cf. Detlef Mühlberger, 'Germany', in Detlef Mühlberger (ed.), *The Social Basis of European Fascist Movements* (London, 1987), p. 54, Table 2.2, column E. The social profile of the Stuttgart branch on the eve of the Munich Putsch provided in this work on p. 68, Table 2.3, column PP, is misleading, given that virtually all of the Nazi recruits recorded as entering the branch were not resident in Stuttgart.
58. Quote taken from Hüttenberger, *Die Gauleiter*, p. 14.
59. In Heilbronn, for example, the SPD had a membership of 1,000 at a time when the entire Nazi membership in Württemberg-Hohenzollern stood at just over the 1,000 mark. Membership strength of Heilbronn branch cited in Schnabel, 'NSDAP in Württemberg', p. 52.
60. A strong hint of class friction in the Stuttgart NSDAP membership is evident from the remark made by Dreher when he took over the branch in 1927 that 'the man in the stand-up collar, the academic, must not avoid sitting next to a craftsman'. See *Lagebericht*, 13.7.1927 (p. 2), in HA, 58/1400.
61. On this aspect see Schnabel, 'Warum geht es in Schwaben besser?', p. 191.
62. The data on Württemberg, Hohenzollern and Germany is taken from *StJDR* 46 (Berlin, 1927), pp. 12-13.
63. The data in column 1 is taken from *Partei-Statistik*, p. 147; the data in column 6 is calculated on the basis of information in *StDR*, 405, part 32 (Berlin, 1928), pp. 2-4.

4 *GAU* HESSE-NASSAU-SOUTH, 1929-31

1. The general development pattern of the NSDAP in Hesse has been evaluated by Eberhard Schön, *Die Entstehung des Nationalsozialismus in Hessen* (Meisenheim am Glan, 1972). Schön's account deals with the Nazi Movement's emergence and growth in both *Land* Hesse and in the Prussian province of Hesse-Nassau.
2. Among the local studies dealing with the Nazi Party's history in the region before 1933 see Franz Josef Heyen, *Nationalsozialismus im Alltag. Quellen zur Geschichte des Nationalsozialismus vornehmlich im Raum Mainz-Koblenz-Trier* (Boppard am Rhein, 1967), which contains documentary material on the NSDAP's development in

county Wetzlar; Ulrich Meyer, *Das Eindringen des Natio-nalsozialismus in die Stadt Wetzlar* (Wetzlar, 1970); Rosemarie Mann, 'Entstehung und Entwicklung der NSDAP in Marburg bis 1933', *Hessisches Jahrbuch für Landesgeschichte*, 22 (1972), pp. 254–342; Henner Pingel, *Das Jahr 1933. NSDAP – Machtergreifung in Darmstadt und im Volkstaat Hessen* (Darmstadt, 1978); Gabriele Müller, 'Die Machtübernahme 1933 im Landkreis Dieburg', *Archiv für hessische Geschichte und Altertumskunde*, 38 (1980); Ulrich Lange (ed.), *1932 in der Provinz* (Bad Camberg, 1982), which deals with county Limburg; Eike Hennig (ed.), *Hessen unterm Hak-enkreuz. Studien zur Durchsetzung der NSDAP in Hessen* (Frankfurt a.M., 1983); Ulrich Schneider (ed.), *Hessen vor 50 Jahren–1933 Naziterror und antifaschistischer Widerstand zwischen Kassel und Bergstraße 1932/33* (Frankfurt a. M., 1983); Wolf-Arno Kropat, 'Die nationalsozialistische Machtergreifung in Wiesbaden und Nassau', *Nassauische Annalen*, 94 (1983), pp. 245–77; Hubertus Seibert, 'Der Aufstieg des Nationalsozialismus im Kreis St. Goarshausen (1926–1933)', *Nassauische Annalen*, 95 (1984), pp. 299–307; Rudy Koshar, *Social Life, Local Politics, and Nazism. Marburg, 1880–1935* (Chapel Hill/London, 1986).

3. See especially Alexander Weber, 'Soziale Merkmale der NSDAP-Wähler. Eine Zusammenfassung bisheriger empirischen Untersu-chungen und eine Analyse in den Gemeinden der Länder Baden und Hessen' (Diss. phil., University of Freiburg im Breisgau, 1969); David Eugene Arns, 'Grassroots politics in the Weimar Republic: Long-term structural change and electoral behavior in Hessen-Darmstadt to 1930' (Ph.D. thesis, State University of New York, 1979). Electoral trends at the local level are dealt with in many of the studies listed under note 2. See also Eike Hennig, 'Die Wahlent-wicklung im Landkreis Kassel (1928–33)', *Zeitschrift des Vereins für hessische Geschichte*, 92 (1982), pp. 205–45; Richard Hamilton, *Who Voted for Hitler?* (Princeton, 1982), deals with Nazi electoral support in Frankfurt (pp. 199–204).

4. Some empirical evidence on the social background of Nazi members in a number of Hessian communities has been examined by Heidi Fogel and Dieter Rebentisch, 'Organisation und Struktur der NSDAP in südhessischen Arbeiterwohngemeinden 1928–1932', in Hennig (ed.), *Hessen unterm Hakenkreuz*, pp. 328–31. A detailed analysis of the social characteristics of the NSDAP in Marburg is provided by Koshar, *Social Life*, pp. 237–43. The extensive data on the social background of the Marburg NSDAP and SA available in HHStAW, especially files 483/4642a, 4209b and 4209f, was not used by Koshar. An insight into the occupational and class background of the 'old fighters' (*alte Kämpfer* – that is individuals who had joined the NSDAP before 1928) of *Gau* Hesse-Nassau – is given by Christoph Schmidt, 'Zu den Motiven alter Kämpfer in der NSDAP', in Detlev Peukert and Jürgen Reulecke (eds), *Die Reihen fast geschloßen. Beiträge zur Geschichte des Alltags unterm Natio-nalsozialismus* (Wuppertal, 1981), pp. 21–43. The data used by

Schmidt has been re-evaluated by Herbert D. Andrews, 'The Social Composition of the NSDAP: Problems and Possible Solutions', *German Studies Review*, 9 (1986), pp. 293–318. The nature of the Nazi cadre in Hesse is examined by Dieter Rebentisch, 'Persönlichkeitsprofil und Karriereverlauf der nationalsozialistischen Führungskader in Hessen 1928–1945', *Hessisches Jahrbuch für Landesgeschichte*, 33 (1983), pp. 293–331.

5. I am at present re-constructing the social profile of the membership and leadership of the NSDAP, SA and SS in Hesse (that is, in the *Gaue* Hesse-Nassau-North and Hesse-Nassau-South, and Hesse-Darmstadt) for the period 1925 to 1945.

6. The lists of newly recruited individuals (along with the relevant enrolment fee) were regularly submitted by the *Gau* officials to the *Kassenverwaltung* of the NSDAP in Munich. The lists have survived as from 11 September 1929 onwards and appear to be complete. The data provided in the majority of the lists is restricted to the surname and first name, occupation and address (usually precise, but sometimes merely the town or village in which the applicant was resident is provided – a few of the 1929 lists omit the address completely) of the new members, as well as the branch which recruited them. Only a few of the 1929 lists provide limited additional detail, namely the date and place of birth of the applicants (it is therefore not possible to establish the age profile of the membership), while one list records the actual date on which the application to join the party was made. The lists are in HHStAW, 483/10605-6.

7. Schön, *Nationalsozialismus in Hessen*, p. 78.

8. The data is taken from *StDR*, 401, II (Berlin, 1930), p. 611.

9. The percentages are calculated on the basis of data in *StDR*, 405, part 26 (Berlin, 1928), pp. 24 and 84.

10. *StDR*, 401, II (Berlin, 1930), p. 610.

11. *Einzelschriften zur Statistik des Deutschen Reichs*, No. 7: Die Steuerkraft der Finanzbezirke (Berlin, 1929), p. 104.

12. Cf. W. Hardtke, *Pendelwanderung und kulturgeographische Raumbildung im Rhein-Main Gebiet* (Frankfurt a.M., 1938).

13. A sketch of the economy of Frankfurt is provided by Eike Hennig in the preface to the essay by Dieter Rebentisch, 'Zwei Beiträge zur Vorgeschichte und Machtergreifung des Nationalsozialismus in Frankfurt', in Hennig (ed.), *Hessen unterm Hakenkreuz*, p. 279.

14. Cf. Mayer, *Nationalsozialismus in Wetzlar*, pp. 16–22.

15. The over-reliance on the tourist and 'health' industry (given that it was particularly sensitive to changing economic conditions) of many of the spa towns in the region was to produce great difficulties for many of these resorts in the late 1920s with the onset of the economic depression. On the impact of the recession on the tourist and 'health' industry of even such a sizeable city as Wiesbaden, which was adversely affected by the decline of visitors (and the declining purchasing power of its middle-class clientele) even before the recession of the late 1920s, see Wolf-Arno Kropat, 'Die nationalsozialistische Machtergreifung in Wiesbaden und Nassau', in

Hennig (ed.), *Hessen unterm Hakenkreuz*, pp. 260–78, here p. 260.
16. A further 7.3 per cent lived in small towns, and 42.9 per cent in communities with populations of under 5,000. Percentages for 1933 calculated on the basis of data in *StDR*, 453, part 25 (Berlin, 1936) p. 44. The 1933 data includes county Wetzlar, which became part of *Regierungsbezirk* Wiesbaden in 1932.
17. The first Nazi Party branch in Hesse was formed in Frankfurt on 26 May 1922; Schön, *Nationalsozialismus in Hessen*, pp. 21–73.
18. ibid., pp. 78–9.
19. ibid., pp. 86–94. Cf. Dieter Rebentisch, 'Zwei Beiträge zur Vorgeschichte und Machtergreifung des Nationalsozialismus in Frankfurt: Von der Splittergruppe zur Massenpartei', in Hennig (ed.), *Hessen unterm Hakenkreuz*, pp. 280–90; Seibert, 'Nationalsozialismus im Kreis St Goarshausen', pp. 299–300.
20. Schön, *Nationalsozialismus in Hessen*, pp. 92–5.
21. The figures are taken from Alfred Milatz, *Wähler und Wahlen in der Weimarer Republik* (Bonn, 1965), p. 112.
22. The percentages are calculated on the basis of data in *StDR*, 372, II (Berlin, 1930), pp. 43–4.
23. *Völkischer Beobachter*, 10/11 June 1928 and 13 June 1928.
24. On the rural/urban voting pattern see Eike Hennig, 'Der Hunger naht – Mittelstand wehr Dich – Wir Bauern misten aus. Über angepaßtes und abweichendes Wahlverhalten in hessischen Agrarregionen', in Hennig (ed.), *Hessen unterm Hakenkreuz*, pp. 379–432, here p. 409.
25. For example, the Herborn branch in the Dillkreis, one of the oldest established branches in the region, is not noted as recruiting in the September to December period covered by the 1929 *Neuaufnahmen*; cf. Schön, *Nationalsozialismus in Hessen*, p. 96. The Wetzlar branch, in existence since 1925, which Mayer suggests had a probable membership of 60 by 1928, is also not noted as recruiting in the last quarter of 1929; see Mayer, *Nationalsozialismus in Wetzlar*, pp. 31–2.
26. In their press the Nazis claimed that the party had formed 118 branches in *Gaue* Hesse-Nassau-South and Hesse-Darmstadt by April 1930; Schön, *Nationalsozialismus in Hessen*, p. 99.
27. For an account of the campaign see Schön, *Nationalsozialismus in Hessen*, pp. 170–7.
28. The following percentages are calculated on the basis of data in *StDR*, 382, II (Berlin, 1932), pp. 42–4.
29. Cf. Schön, *Nationalsozialismus in Hessen*, pp. 181–2.
30. By the time the census was taken, *Gau* Hesse-Nassau-South had been merged with *Gau* Hesse-Darmstadt once more to form *Gau* Hesse-Nassau. The membership figures given in the *Partei-Statistik* for *Gau* Hessen-Nassau record that of the members still in the party by the time of the census, 6,570 had joined the NSDAP by 14 September 1930, while a further 38,061 had subsequently joined by the 30 January 1933; *Partei-Statistik. Stand 1. Januar 1935*. Herausgeber Der Reichsorganisationsleiter der NSDAP (Munich, n.d.), p. 26. The

actual number enrolled, given the high turnover of the party membership before 1930/33, was probably 30–40 per cent higher.

31. By November 1931 *Gau* Hesse-Nassau-South had a membership of 9,000; Schön, *Nationalsozialismus in Hessen*, p. 140.

32. The list is headed *Adolf Hitlers Mitkämpfer 1919–1921* and is in HA, 2A/230.

33. A breakdown of the occupational and class background of the members resident in Hesse is provided in my essay 'Germany', in Detlef Mühlberger (ed.), *The Social Basis of European Fascist Movements* (London, 1987), pp. 40–139, here p. 62, Table 2.3, column G.

34. The following is based on data provided by the 1923 membership list which is in HA, 10/215.

35. The lower- and middle-middle class provided 52.9 per cent of the membership of the Bad Nauheim branch following its re-formation in March 1925, while the upper-middle class and upper class accounted for a further 35.3 per cent (primarily due to the large number of university students who joined the NSDAP in the town). A full breakdown of the occupational and social structure of the branch membership is provided by Mühlberger, 'Germany', p. 78, Table 2.6, column A. Wolfgang Egerer was obviously unaware of the existence of the 1925 membership list when he wrote that 'unfortunately there is no information relating to the social background of the appproximately twenty members who joined the NSDAP branch formed in Friedberg-Bad Nauheim led by the druggist Ernstberger after the ban (on the party) was lifted'. See Wolfgang Egerer, 'Die Entwicklung des Nationalsozialismus im Kreis Friedberg und seine Beziehungen zu den bäuerlichen Organisationen', in Hennig (ed.), *Hessen unterm Hakenkreuz*, pp. 199–222, here pp. 202–3.

36. Cf. Mayer, *Nationalsozialismus in Wetzlar*, pp. 31–5.

37. Rebentisch, 'Zwei Beiträge', pp. 280–4.

38. According to the 1933 census the male working population of Frankfurt was made up as follows:

Workers	50.4%
White-collar employees	23.9%
Self-employed	16.6%
Assisting family members	0.6%
Civil servants	8.5%

Percentages calculated on the basis of data in *StDR*, 456, part 25 (Berlin, 1936), p. 37.

39. Cf. Rebentisch, 'Zwei Beiträge', pp. 280–2.

40. In November 1931, when the total strength of the NSDAP in *Gau* Hesse-Nassau-South stood at 9,000, the SPD had over 11,000 members in Frankfurt alone; figure cited by James Wickham, 'Working-class movement and working-class life: Frankfurt am Main during the Weimar Republic', *Social History*, 8 (1983), pp. 315–43, here p. 343, n. 83.

41. According to the 1925 census workers formed 63.4 per cent of the

male working population in Höchst. Percentage calculated on the basis of data in *StDR*, 405, part 26 (Berlin, 1928), p. 84.

42. This suspicion cannot be verified as such given that the *Neuaufnahmen* lists, with the exception of two lists relating to Frankfurt dated 5 October and 7 November 1929, do not provide any data on the age of the individuals recruited. Of the 34 recruits who are described as 'Kaufmann' in the 1929 lists, 18 were in their twenties and thus probably commercial employees rather than independent merchants. The lists are in HHStAW, 483/10,605.

43. The report is reprinted by Klaus Schönekäs, 'Hinweise auf die soziopolitische Verfassung Hessens in der Weimarer Zeit', in Hennig (ed.) *Hessen unterm Hakenkreuz*, pp. 45–55, here pp. 52–3.

44. On the role played by anti-Semitism in generating Nazi support in Frankfurt see Hamilton, *Who voted for Hitler?*, p. 203.

45. According to the 1933 census the male working population of Wiesbaden was made up as follows:

Workers	49.8%
White-collar employees	19.2%
Self-employed	19.0%
Assisting family members	3.5%
Civil servants	8.5%

Percentages calculated on the basis of data in *StDR*, 456, part 25 (Berlin, 1936), p. 41.

46. Wiesbaden's function as a 'Kur- und Pensionärsstadt' made it particularly vulnerable to the recessionist forces unleashed by the World Economic Crisis. On the impact of the depression on the city see Kropat, 'Die nationalsozialistische Machtergreifung in Wiesbaden und Nassau', pp. 260–5.

47. The percentages of the population dependent on agriculture in these villages relate to 1933 and are taken from *StDR*, 456, part 25 (Berlin, 1936), pp. 48, 52–5.

48. The percentage values for *Gau* Hesse-Nassau-South (made up by the *Reg.-Bez.* Wiesbaden, *Stadtkreis* Hanau and the counties of Hanau, Gelnhausen, Schlüchtern and Wetzlar) relate to the 1925 census returns and are calculated on the basis of data in *StDR*, 372, II (Berlin, 1930), pp. 42–4. The percentages for *Provinz* Hesse-Nassau, *Land* Prussia and Germany are taken from *StJDR*, Jg. 46 (Berlin, 1927), pp. 11–13.

49. The percentages in column 1 are taken from *Partei-Statistik*, p. 146. The percentages in column 6 are calculated on the basis of data in *StDR*, 405, part 26, p. 84.

50. *Gau* Hesse-Darmstadt was by far the more successful of the two in terms of membership recruitment. By October 1931 the *Gau* had a membership of 15,000, while *Gau* Hesse-Nassau-South had a total strength of only 9,000 by November 1931; figures in Schön, *Nationalsozialismus in Hessen*, p. 140.

NOTES

5 *GAU* SOUTH-HANOVER-BRUNSWICK, 1925-33

1. On the history of the Nazi Party in Lower Saxony as a whole see the excellent study by Jeremy Noakes, *The Nazi Party in Lower Saxony 1921-1933* (Oxford, 1971). A detailed examination of the relationship between Munich party headquarters and *Gau* South-Hanover-Brunswick is provided by Hanna Behrend, *Die Beziehungen zwischen der NSDAP-Zentrale und dem Gauverband Süd-Hannover-Braunschweig 1921-1933. Ein Beitrag zur Führungsstruktur der nationalsozialistischen Partei* (Frankfurt a. M./Bern, 1981). On the development of Nazism in Brunswick, see Ernst-August Roloff, *Bürgertum und Nationalsozialismus 1930-1933. Braunschweigs Weg ins Dritte Reich* (Hanover, 1961); Ernst-August Roloff, 'Zur Entstehungsgeschichte des Nationalsozialismus im Lande Braunschweig', in Michael Künne (ed.), *Anpassung und Widerspruch (Vortragsreihe zur Geschichte des Helmstedter Landes)* Cf. Klaus Kaiser, *Braunschweiger Presse und Nationalsozialismus: Der Aufstieg der NSDAP im Lande Braunschweig im Spiegel der Braunschweiger Tageszeitungen 1930 bis 1933* (Brunswick, 1970). A Nazi account was written by Kurt Schmalz, *Nationalsozialisten ringen um Braunschweig* (Brunswick, 1934).

2. There are a number of local studies which deal with the development of the NSDAP in *Gau* South-Hanover-Brunswick. On Northeim there is the pioneering study by William Sheridan Allen, *The Nazi Seizure of Power. The Experience of a Single German Town 1930-1935* (London, 1966). An outline history of the Nazi Party in Clausthal-Zellerfeld is to be found in Sigurd Plesse, *Die nationalsozialistische Machtergreifung im Oberharz. Clausthal-Zellerfeld 1929-1933* (Clausthal-Zellerfeld, 1970). An overview of the Nazi Party's development in Göttingen is provided by Helga-Maria Kühn, 'Die nationalsozialistische Bewegung in Göttingen von ihren Anfängen bis zur Machtergreifung (1922-1933)', in Jens-Uwe Brinkman and Hans-Georg Schmeling (eds), *Göttingen unterm Hakenkreuz: Nationalsozialistischer Alltag in einer deutschen Stadt* (Göttingen, 1983). The impact of Nazism on Göttingen is also evaluated by Barbara Marshall, 'The Political Development of German University Towns: Göttingen and Münster 1918-1933' (Ph.D. thesis, University of London, 1972); cf. Barbara Marshall, 'Politics in Academe: Göttingen University and the growing impact of political issues, 1918-33', *European History Quarterly*, 18 (1988), pp. 291-320. The origins and growth of Nazism in the Hildesheimer region has been sketched out by Anne-Gret Politz, 'Die NSDAP im Raum Hildesheim. Anfänge und Entwicklung bis 1933', *Alt-Hildesheim*, 42 (1971), pp. 42-55. There are a number of works in which the electoral performance of the Nazi Party in various parts of the region is analysed. The Nazi Party's performance in *Land* Brunswick is evaluated by Martin Schumacher, *Stabilität und Instabilität. Wahlentwicklung und Parlament in Baden und Braunschweig* (Düsseldorf, 1974). Aspects of the basis of Nazi

237

support in the city of Brunswick are dealt with by Richard F. Hamilton, 'Braunschweig 1932: Further Evidence on the Support for National Socialism', *Central European History*, 17 (1984), pp. 3-35; and by Ernst-August Roloff, 'Die bürgerliche Oberschicht in Braunschweig und der Nationalsozialismus: Eine Stellungnahme', ibid., pp. 37-44. On the electoral geometry of the NSDAP in Hanover see Richard F. Hamilton, *Who voted for Hitler?* (Princeton, 1982), pp. 204-9. The electoral support of the Nazi Party in Goslar is reviewed by Lieselotte Krull, *Wahlen und Wahlverhalten in Goslar während der Weimarer Republik* (Goslar, 1982); see also the study on Göttingen by Fritz Hasselhorn, *Wie wählte Göttingen? Wahlverhalten und die soziale Basis der Parteien in Göttingen 1924-1933* (Göttingen, 1983).

3. The data relating to *Land* Brunswick and to the province of Hanover is taken from *StJDR*, 46 (Berlin, 1927), p. 24. Other percentages for 1925 are calculated on the basis of data in *StDR*, 404, part 14 (Berlin, 1928), pp. 74 and 80. The percentages for 1933 are calculated on the basis of data in *StDR*, 455, parts 14 and 20 (Berlin, 1936), pp. 467 and 367 respectively.

4. The data is taken from *StDR*, 401, II (Berlin, 1927), pp. 608-9.

5. For the following see Noakes, *Nazi Party in Lower Saxony*, p. 4; Roloff, 'Nationalsozialismus im Lande Braunschweig', p. 11.

6. The percentages are taken from *StDR*, 404, part 14 (Berlin, 1936), pp. 50-4.

7. The percentages are calculated on the basis of data in *StDR*, 404, part 14 (Berlin, 1936), pp. 2-3; and *StDR*, 404, part 20 (Berlin, 1936), pp. 2-3.

8. The data relating to *Land* Brunswick and to the province of Hanover is taken from *StJDR*, 46 (Berlin, 1927), p. 24. Other percentages for 1925 are calculated on the basis of data in *StDR*, 404, part 14 (Berlin, 1928), pp. 74 and 80. The percentages for 1933 are calculated on the basis of data in *StDR*, 455, parts 14 and 20 (Berlin, 1936), pp. 467 and 367 respectively.

9. Cf. Alfred Milatz, *Wähler und Wahlen in der Weimarer Republik* (Bonn, 1965), p. 112.

10. *Partei-Statistik. Stand 1. Januar 1935. Band 1 Parteimitglieder.* Herausgeber Der Reichsorganisationsleiter der NSDAP (Munich, n.d.), p. 35.

11. For a detailed account of the early history of the NSDAP in *Gau* South-Hanover-Brunswick see Behrend, *Gauverband Süd-Hannover-Braunschweig*, pp. 39-82; cf. Noakes, *Nazi Party in Lower Saxony*, pp. 14-55. There are two Nazi 'histories' written in 1934, one by Bruno Wenzel, *Zur Frühgeschichte der NSDAP in Niedersachsen*, the other by Gustav Seifert, *Die Treue ist die Mark der Ehre. Beginn und Entwicklung der ersten norddeutschen Kämpfe der NSDAP in Hannover und Niedersachsen*; copies of MS. in HA, 6/141.

12. Noakes, *Nazi Party in Lower Saxony*, pp. 17 and 28.

13. Behrend, *Gauverband Süd-Hannover-Braunschweig*, p. 42.

14. Noakes, *Nazi Party in Lower Saxony*, pp. 22, 34 and 40.
15. The breakdown for the Hanover branch as in December 1921 (by which time it had 25 members) is taken from my essay 'Germany', in Detlef Mühlberger (ed.), *The Social Basis of European Fascist Movements* (London, 1987), p. 55, Table 2.2, column K. It is based on the *Mitgliederliste der alten Ortsgruppe Hannover der N.S.D.A.P.*, a copy of which is in HA, 6/141.
16. The percentages are calculated on the basis of data in Noakes, *Nazi Party in Lower Saxony*, p. 23.
17. This largest membership fragment of the pre-1923 NSDAP is in HA, 10/215.
18. For a breakdown of the social and occupational status of Nazi recruits in province Hanover and *Land* Brunswick see Mühlberger 'Germany', pp. 62 and 64, Table 2.3, columns D, F and S.
19. For an analysis of the development of Nazism in the region from November 1923 to 1925 see Behrend, *Gauverband Süd-Hannover-Braunschweig*, pp. 66–82; Noakes, *Nazi Party in Lower Saxony*, pp. 41–55.
20. For details see Behrend, *Gauverband Süd-Hannover-Braunschweig*, pp. 91–3.
21. ibid., pp. 118 and 158; Noakes, *Nazi Party in Lower Saxony*, p. 104.
22. Noakes, *Nazi Party in Lower Saxony*, pp. 89 and 104.
23. ibid., pp. 89–90.
24. Behrend, *Gauverband Süd-Hannover-Braunschweig*, p. 119.
25. ibid., p. 168.
26. ibid., p. 174. Cf. Noakes, *Nazi Party in Lower Saxony*, pp. 89–101.
27. This point is emphasized by Noakes, *Nazi Party in Lower Saxony*, p. 95.
28. For the following see Behrend, *Gauverband Süd-Hannover-Braunschweig*, pp. 176–9; Noakes, *Nazi Party in Lower Saxony*, pp. 139–40.
29. Noakes, *Nazi Party in Lower Saxony*, pp. 140–1.
30. Behrend, *Gauverband Süd-Hannover-Braunschweig*, p. 228.
31. *Partei-Statistik*, p. 26. These figures relate to those members who were still in the party by the time the census was taken in 1934. Given the high turnover (around the 40 per cent mark) in Nazi membership before 1933, the actual total membership figures were very much higher.
32. Behrend, *Gauverband Süd-Hannover-Braunschweig*, p. 256.
33. ibid., pp. 228 and 257.
34. Milatz, *Wähler und Wahlen*, p. 112.
35. On the basis of the *Partei-Statistik*, Jeremy Noakes reached the conclusion that the Nazi Party in Lower Saxony was made up primarily by 'some members of the younger generation of the *Mittelstand*' before September 1930, with 'a slight broadening of its social base' in the period September 1930 to January 1933, in which more working-class members joined the party; Noakes, *Nazi Party in Lower Saxony*, pp. 141 and 159.
36. Access to the 'NSDAP Mitgliederkartei (1936–1942)', specifically the

'Mitgliederkartei Kreisleitung Braunschweig-Land', is still barred. This material was transferred from the Berlin Document Center to the Niedersächsisches Hauptstaatsarchiv in Hanover in 1978 and is now catalogued under NHStAH, Hann. 310 I/O Nos. 2-24.
37. In Anderten 9.5 per cent – and in county Hanover 18.3 per cent – of the total population was still dependent on agriculture in 1933. In the 1933 census the occupational breakdown of the population (including those recorded as unemployed) in county Hanover was as follows:

	%
Workers	56.8
Domestic workers	2.6
White-collar employees	9.3
Civil servants	3.4
Self-employed	13.0
Working family members	14.8

Percentages calculated on the basis of data in *StDR*, 455, part 14 (Berlin, 1936), pp. 46-7, 51. Where it is possible, given that the Nazi Party was essentially a male movement, the proportion of males in the social make-up of the working population will be established. The 1933 census only provides data which permits a separation of the male and female workforce for communities with a population of 10,000 and over.
38. The two membership lists are in NHStAH, Hann. 310 I/E No. 1. Neither is dated, but record members joining between 1 July 1930 and 25 April 1933.
39. There are lists of Brunswick Nazi Party branch members (listed cell by cell) who were paying dues in June 1932, but with no details about their occupational status, which would need to be discovered by reference to the city's address directory. The lists are in NHStAH, Hann. 310 I/E No. 6. Some (undated) membership fragments of OG Braunschweig-Giersberg are in NHStAH, Hann. 310 I/E No. 7. A list of members – but again without any information on their occupational status – of OG Braunschweig-Fallerslebertor (this branch had 236 members in November 1932) is in NHStAH, Hann. 310 I/E No. 5.
40. Percentages calculated on the basis of data in *StDR*, 455, part 20 (Berlin, 1936), pp. 34-5.
41. ibid., p. 35.
42. According to the 1933 census the occupational breakdown of the population in Brunswick-City was as follows:

	% of male working population	% of total population
Workers	53.1	48.6
Domestic workers	0.02	5.4
White-collar employees	21.9	23.7
Civil servants	10.3	7.5

Self-employed	14.1	12.5
Working family members	0.5	2.3

ibid., p. 35.

43. For a social geography of Brunswick in the early 1930s see Richard Hamilton, 'Braunschweig 1932', pp. 8–13.
44. The *Mitgliederliste/-verzeichnis c. 1925–1933. OG Braunschweig-Steintor* is in NHStAH, Hann. 310 I/E No. 8.
45. The percentage for *Gau* South-Hanover-Brunswick relates to the period 1925 to 31 January 1933; it is calculated on the basis of data in *Partei-Statistik*, pp. 26 and 30.
46. Percentage taken from *StDR*, 455, part 14 (Berlin, 1936), p. 55. The occupational breakdown of the working population in county Zellerfeld in 1933 was as follows:

	%
Workers	53.4
Domestic workers	5.7
White-collar employees	9.8
Civil servants	4.4
Self-employed	15.0
Working family members	11.7

ibid., pp. 46–7.

47. Cf. Plesse, *Nationalsozialistische Machtergreifung im Oberharz*, pp. 30–41.
48. The list is headed *Die Mitglieder der NSDAP. Stand 15 März 1941. OG Clausthal-Zellerfeld*, and is in NHStAH, Hann. 310 I/O No. 176.
49. The percentages are calculated on the basis of data in *StDR*, 382, II (Berlin, 1932), p. 34.
50. Plesse, *Nationalsozialistische Machtergreifung im Oberharz*, p. 91.
51. The two lists are in NHStAH, Hann. 310 I/O No. 183.
52. *Mitgliederstandsliste 12.II.36 der NSDAP, Ortsgruppe Sieber*, in NHStAH, Hann. 310 I/O No. 185.
53. Some 50.2 per cent of the total population of Sieber was dependent on agriculture and forestry for a living in 1933; percentage taken from *StDR*, 455, part 14 (Berlin, 1936), p. 55.
54. The occupational breakdown of the working population of Clausthal-Zellerfeld in 1933 was as follows:

	% of male working population	% of total working population
Workers	63.1	50.7
Domestic workers	0	6.9
White-collar employees	13.5	13.7
Civil servants	7.7	5.9
Self-employed	15.0	13.5
Working family members	0.6	9.3

The percentages are calculated on the basis of data in *StDR*, 455, part 14 (Berlin, 1936), p. 37.

55. Cf. Noakes, *Nazi Party in Lower Saxony*, pp. 159–60.

56. See chapter 7, p. 187, Table 7.1, column 4.
57. Percentage taken from *StDR*, 455, part 14 (Berlin, 1936), p. 54.
58. The list is in NHStAH, Hann. 310 I/O No. 171.
59. The percentages are calculated on the basis of data in *StDR*, 455, part 14 (Berlin, 1936), pp. 46-7.
60. The occupational breakdown of the working population of county Göttingen in 1933 was as follows:

	%
Workers	44.0
Domestic workers	2.4
White-collar employees	5.1
Civil servants	2.3
Self-employed	16.1
Working family members	30.0

The percentages are calculated on the basis of data in *StDR*, 455, part 14 (Berlin, 1936), pp. 46-7.

61. The list for OG Friedland-Leine (dated 16 February 1936) is in NHStAH, Hann. 310 I/O No. 35; that for OG Hetjershausen (dated 23 February 1936) is in NHStAH, Hann. 310 I/O No. 36; and that for OG Nikolausberg (dated 10 November 1936) is in NHStAH, Hann. 310 I/O No. 37.
62. In Nikolausberg the figure was 38.3 per cent, and in Friedland only 28.2 per cent; percentages taken from *StDR*, 455, part 14 (Berlin, 1936), p. 53.
63. The percentages are calculated on the basis of data in *StDR*, 455, part 14 (Berlin, 1936), pp. 38-9. The same source is used in providing the following occupational breakdown of the working population of Goslar in 1933:

	% of male working population	% of total working population
Workers	48.8	43.2
Domestic workers	0.03	6.8
White-collar employees	14.6	16.6
Civil servants	19.5	14.3
Self-employed	16.1	14.6
Working family members	0.9	4.4

64. This is clear from the 1925 census of the town's artisanal enterprises and industrial concerns in *StDR*, 416, part 7a (Berlin, 1929), pp. 41 and 43.
65. The *Mitgliedergrundbuch Goslar-Ost* is in NHStAH, Hann. 310 I/E No. 11.
66. The party claimed to have 700 members in Göttingen by 1924; Marshall, 'Politics in Academe', p. 312.
67. The percentage is calculated on the basis of data in *StDR*, 455, part 14 (Berlin, 1936), pp. 38-9.
68. Cf. Marshall, 'Politics in Academe', p. 293.

69. These and the following percentages are calculated on the basis of data in *StDR*, 455, part 14 (Berlin, 1936), pp. 38–9. The occupational breakdown of the working population of Göttingen in 1933 was as follows:

	% of male working	% of total population
Workers	45.9	38.7
Domestic workers	0.01	8.5
White-collar employees	18.0	21.7
Civil servants	19.4	13.8
Self-employed	16.0	14.3
Working family members	0.6	3.4

70. Noakes, *Nazi Party in Lower Saxony*, p. 90.
71. These and the following percentages are calculated on the basis of data in *StDR*, 455, part 14 (Berlin, 1936), pp. 46–7. The occupational breakdown of the working population of county Peine (excluding the town of Peine) in 1933 was as follows:

	%
Workers	43.6
Domestic workers	1.8
White-collar employees	5.2
Civil servants	1.4
Self-employed	19.0
Working family members	28.9

72. ibid., p. 54.
73. The first membership list is dated 16 February 1931; another list (not dated) records members in the branch by 1 May 1931; the largest list, again undated, gives a membership breakdown as in January 1932. The lists, along with correspondence dealing with membership aspects, are in NHStAH, Hann. 310 I/E No. 16.
74. Among the 9,250 newly recruited members in *Gau* South-Hanover-Brunswick in December 1931 were 2,000 who joined the Nazi Party in Hanover.
75. In the September 1930 *Reichstag* election the NSDAP polled 20.7 per cent of the vote in Hanover and became the second strongest party in the city, though admittedly a long way behind the SPD, which secured 45.2 per cent of the votes cast. The percentages are calculated on the basis of data in *StDR*, 382, II (Berlin, 1932), p. 33.
76. On the social geography of various districts of Hanover see Hamilton, *Who voted for Hitler?*, pp. 304–6.
77. The following percentages are calculated on the basis of data in *StDR*, 455, part 14 (Berlin, 1936), pp. 38–9. The same source is used in calculating the occupational breakdown of the working popula-tion of Hanover in 1933, which was as follows:

	% of male	% of total
	working population	
Workers	53.0	47.9
Domestic workers	0.02	5.2
White-collar employees	21.7	23.9
Civil servants	10.1	7.6
Self-employed	14.4	12.4
Working family members	0.6	2.8

78. The membership book is in NHStAH, Hann. 310 I/E No. 12.
79. Cf. Politz, 'NSDAP im Raum Hildesheim', p. 44.
80. The percentages are taken from *StDR*, 455, part 14 (Berlin, 1936), p. 52.
81. *OG Hüpede-Oerie Mitgliederbuch (1931-35)*, in NHStAH, Hann. 310 I/E No. 15.
82. According to the census of 1933, 54.3 per cent of the total population in county *Grafschaft* Hoya was dependent on agriculture; the percentage is taken from *StDR*, 455, part 14 (Berlin, 1936), p. 50.
83. The percentage is calculated on the basis of data in *StDR*, 382, II (Berlin, 1932), p. 33.
84. The percentages are taken from *StDR*, 455, part 14 (Berlin, 1936), p. 50.
85. Cf. Noakes, *Nazi Party in Lower Saxony*, pp. 99-100 and 117.
86. *OG Nordholz bzw. Brebber: Kleines Mitgliederbuch 1931-34*, in NHStAH, Hann. 310 I/E No. 21.
87. The percentages are calculated on the basis of data in *StDR*, 455, part 20 (Berlin, 1936), pp. 36-7.
88. Only 7.9 per cent of the town's population depended on agriculture for a living; ibid., p. 38.
89. The lists and correspondence are in NHStAH, Hann. 310 I/E No. 31.
90. The lowest party number listed is 447,623, which suggests that the member was recruited into the NSDAP around November 1930.
91. Copy of *Einwohnerverzeichnis Stadtoldendorf*, not dated, is in NHStAH, Hann. 310 I/E No. 32.
92. In 1933 county Alfeld had a mixed economy. Agriculture employed 42.1 per cent of the working population, industry and crafts 37.2 per cent, and trade and transport 12.4 per cent. The percentages are calculated on the basis of data in *StDR*, 455, part 14 (Berlin, 1936), pp. 46-7.
93. Details taken from *OG Wetteborn. Mitgliederliste am 13 März 1932*, in NHStAH, Hann. 310 I/E No. 36.
94. *Partei-Statistik*, p. 148.
95. The data on Brunswick is taken from *StJDR*, 46 (Berlin, 1927), pp. 12-13. The percentages for the *Regierungsbezirke* of Hanover and Hildesheim are calculated on the basis of data in *StDR*, 382, II (Berlin, 1932), pp. 33-4.

6 THE SA

1. The literature on the SA is now relatively extensive. The overall development of the organization is dealt with by Heinrich Bennecke, *Hitler und die SA* (Munich, 1962); Wolfgang Sauer, *Die Mobilmachung der Gewalt* (Frankfurt a.M., 1974), pp. 194–364; Andreas Werner, 'SA und NSDAP. SA: "Wehrverband", "Parteitruppe", oder "Revolutionsarmee" ? Studien zur Geschichte der SA und der NSDAP' (Phil. Diss., University of Erlangen, 1964). More specific aspects of the development of the SA are dealt with by Otis C. Mitchell, 'An Institutional History of the National Socialist SA: A Study of the SA as a Functioning Organization within the Party Structure (1931–1934)' (Ph.D thesis, University of Kansas, 1964); Peter H. Merkl, *The Making of a Stormtrooper* (Princeton, 1980). A number of excellent studies on the SA have appeared in recent years which break new ground: Conan Fischer, *Stormtroopers. A Social, Economic and Ideological Analysis, 1929–1935* (London 1983); Richard Bressel, *Political Violence and the Rise of Nazism. The Storm Troopers in Eastern Germany 1925–1934* (New Haven/London, 1984); Mathilde Jamin, *Zwischen den Klassen. Zur Sozialstruktur der SA-Führerschaft* (Wuppertal, 1984); and the local study by Eric G. Reiche, *The Development of the SA in Nürnberg, 1922–1934* (Cambridge, 1986).
2. Jamin, *Zwischen den Klassen*, p. 1.
3. Extract from a speech on the purpose of the SA by SA Leader Voss at the NSDAP *Bezirksvertretertagung* of Groß-Dortmund, 2 February 1930; a copy of the speech is in StAM, VII-67, Band 1.
4. See especially Bessel, *Political Violence*, and his essay 'Violence as propaganda: The Role of the Storm Troopers in the Rise of National Socialism', in Thomas Childers (ed.), *The Formation of the Nazi Constituency 1919–1933* (London, 1986), pp. 131–46; Peter H. Merkl, *Political Violence under the Swastika. 581 Early Nazis* (Princeton, 1975).
5. The essential role played by the SA in the urban centres of Westphalia is strongly underlined in the Nazi account of the history of the NSDAP in southern Westphalia; see Friedrich Alfred Beck, *Kampf und Sieg. Geschichte der NSDAP im Gau Westfalen-Süd von den Anfängen bis zur Machtübernahme* (Dortmund, 1938), especially pp. 99–100.
6. Figures taken from Bennecke, *Hitler und die SA*, p. 126; Fischer, *Stormtroopers*, p. 5; Jamin, *Zwischen den Klassen*, p. 1.
7. Figures taken from Fischer, *Stormtroopers*, p. 6, and Jamin, *Zwischen den Klassen*, pp. 1–2. Excluding the Motor-SA, the strength of the SA (according to figures produced by the Nazis themselves) stood at 427,692 in December 1932; see Conan Fischer, 'The SA of the NSDAP: Social Background and Ideology of the Rank and File in the Early 1930s', *Journal of Contemporary History*, 17 (1982), pp. 651–70, here p. 660.
8. Cf. Jamin, *Zwischen den Klassen*, pp. 2–3.

9. ibid., p. 1.
10. Fischer, *Stormtroopers*, pp. 19 and 23, n. 37.
11. Jamin, *Zwischen den Klassen*, p. 72, n. 31.
12. The files are in StAL, PL/505/34 Nos. 1–5.
13. The files are in NHStAH, Hann. 310 I/N Nos. 13–14.
14. The files are in GLAK, 465c Nos. 2181–2, 2187–8.
15. The *Stammrollen* are in HHStAW, 483/702 a–d.
16. In his analysis of the Eutin SA Lawrence Stokes found that 87.5 per cent of the SA members were simultaneously also enrolled in the Nazi Party in 1929; Lawrence D. Stokes, 'The Social Composition of the Nazi Party in Eutin, 1925–1932', *International Review of Social History*, 23 (1978) pp. 1–32, here p. 27.
17. Jamin, *Zwischen den Klassen*, text and Tables II–9 and II–10, pp. 73–6.
18. For a useful historiographical review of the debate on the SA see Jamin, *Zwischen den Klassen*, pp. 37–45.
19. Eric G. Reiche, 'The Development of the SA in Nuremberg, 1922 to 1934' (Ph.D. thesis, University of Delaware, 1972). Published subsequently under the title *The Development of the SA in Nürnberg, 1922–1934*.
20. Reiche, *SA in Nürnberg*, p. 30, Table 2.4; p. 68, Table 3.3; and Table 4.5, p. 108.
21. Merkl, *Political Violence*, p. 595, Table VI–7. In Merkl's second re-working of the Abel data, unskilled and skilled workers account for 38.5 per cent of the 'Abel SA'; Merkl, *The Making of a Stormtrooper*, Table II–3, p. 99.
22. Michael H. Kater, 'Ansätze zu einer Soziologie der SA bis zur Röhmkrise', in Ulrich Engelhardt/Volker Sellin/Horst Stuke (eds), *Soziale Bewegung und politische Verfassung. Beiträge zur Geschichte der modernen Welt* (Stuttgart, 1976), pp. 798–831, here p. 802. Cf. Michael H. Kater, 'Zum gegenseitigen Verhältnis von SA und SS in der Sozialgeschichte des Nationalsozialismus von 1925 bis 1939', *Vierteljahrschrift für Sozial- und Wirtschaftsgeschichte*, 62, part 3 (1975), pp. 339–79, here p. 343.
23. Michael H. Kater, 'Zur Soziographie der frühen NSDAP', *Vierteljahrshefte für Zeitgeschichte*, 19 (1971), pp. 124–59, here pp. 140–1.
24. Conan Fischer, 'The Occupational Background of the SA's Rank and File Membership during the Depression years, 1929 to mid-1934', in Peter D. Stachura (ed.), *The Shaping of the Nazi State* (London, 1978), pp. 131–59, here pp. 137 and 155, n.54.
25. ibid., p. 138.
26. ibid., Figures 2a and 2b, p. 140.
27. ibid., p. 152.
28. Stokes, 'Nazi Party in Eutin', pp. 27–8.
29. Mathilde Jamin, 'Zwischen den Klassen. Eine quantitative Untersuchung zur Sozialstruktur der SA-Führerschaft' (Phil. Diss., Ruhr-Universität Bochum, 1982), published in 1984 under the title *Zwischen den Klassen. Zur Sozialstruktur der SA-Führerschaft*.

30. Richard Bessel, 'The S.A. in the Eastern Regions of Germany, 1925–1934' (D.Phil. thesis, Oxford University, 1980), published in 1984 under the title *Political Violence and the Rise of Nazism. The Storm Troopers in Eastern Germany 1925–1934.*

31. Cf. Richard Bessel and Mathilde Jamin, 'Nazis, Workers and the Uses of Quantitative Evidence', *Social History*, 4 (1979), pp. 111–16. Reply by Conan Fischer and Carolyn Hicks, 'Statistics and the Historian: the Occupational Profile of the SA of the NSDAP', *Social History*, 5 (1980), pp. 131–8; cf. the reply by Richard Bessel and Mathilde Jamin, 'Statistics and the Historian: A Rejoinder', *Social History*, 5 (1980), pp. 139–40.

32. Bessel and Jamin, 'Nazis, Workers', p. 113, Table 1.

33. Fischer, *Stormtroopers*, pp. 25–37.

34. ibid., pp. 31, 36.

35. Bessel, *Political Violence*, pp. 36–7. See also his summary of reports on the nature of SA members in county Johannisberg in *Regierungsbezirk* Allenstein, pp. 38–9.

36. If this approach is adopted on the assumption that those listed in this category were not of independent status, the share of the lower-class members in the SA rises to 40.5 per cent in *Regierungsbezirk* Königsberg and to 41 per cent in *Regierungsbezirk* Allenstein. Cf. Fischer, *Stormtroopers*, p. 30; Jamin, *Zwischen den Klassen*, pp. 42–3.

37. Jamin, *Zwischen den Klassen*, pp. 166–9, Tables IV–1–3 and IV–1–4. Cf. Fischer, *Stormtroopers*, pp. 59–61; also Bessel, *Political Violence*, pp. 39–41.

38. Bessel, *Political Violence*, p. 39; Fischer, *Stormtroopers*, p. 59.

39. Detlef Mühlberger, 'Germany', in Detlef Mühlberger (ed.), *The Social Basis of European Fascist Movements* (London, 1987), pp. 40–139, here pp. 116–21, Table 2.12.

40. ibid., p. 116, Table 2.12, columns A, C and D.

41. ibid., pp. 115 and 122, and pp. 118–120, Table 2.12, columns S to AA.

42. Bessel, *Political Violence*, pp. 36–7; Mühlberger, 'Germany', pp. 118–20, Table 2.12, columns S to AA.

43. The sources used in Table 6.1 are the following — Column 1: Membership list of SA *Sturm 1/112 Eberbach* and *Verzeichnis der in der Zeit 4.1 – 5. November 1933 angemeldeten . . . SA Anwärter*, dated Eberbach, 13 December 1933, in GLAK, 465d/No. 1307. Column 2: *Stammrolle SA Sturmbann III/R.63* (only those who had joined the *Sturmbann* by the end of 1933 are evaluated), in HHStAW, 483/702 a-d. Column 3: SA members recorded in membership list of *Ortsgruppe* Groß Ilsede (n.d., probably late 1932 on the basis of membership numbers recorded in the file), in NHStAH, Hann. 310 I/E No. 16. Column 4: *Personalakten der SA (überwiegend des Sturmbanns II/251 in Adelebsen)*, in NHStAH, Hann. 310 I/N Nos 13–14. Column 5: *Stammrollen SA Standarte 110/SA Brigade 153-Unterbaden*, in GLAK, 465c, Nos 2181–2 and 2187–8. Columns 6-7: *Stammrolle des SA Sturmes 2/258 (1930–*

1934), in NWHStAD, NW 1069–87, HA LK Paderborn. Columns 8–9: Lists compiled by police, dated 18.4.1932, in StAF, Landratsamt Villingen Zug. 1979/82, No. 1245. Column 10: *SA Personalakten Kr. Waiblingen*, in StAL, PL 505/34, Nos 1–5. Column 11: *SA Sturm 23/R.224 Wetzlar* (data on *Trupp* Hochelheim and *Trupp* Niederwetz), in HHStAW, 483/4519a. Columns 12–13: various lists relating to *SA Sturm 41/83 Großalmerode, SA Reserve, Sturm 41/83 Großalmerode, Mannschaftsliste des Sturmes 45/83, Mannschaftsliste des Trupps Großalmerode vom Motorsturm V/83* and *Mannschaftsliste des Trupps Witzenhausen vom Motorsturm V/83*, in HHStAW, 483/4800 e–f. The data in column 14 is based on the various sources listed under columns 1 to 13.

44. In the case of the SA in Groß Ilsede (Province of Hanover), the SA membership is based on the NSDAP *Ortsgruppe* list which also recorded which party members were in the SA. The SA in county Villingen (*Land* Baden) involves those individuals positively identified as members of *Sturmbann* IV/113 by the police authorities at the time of the ban on the SA in April 1932.

45. In 1933 industry and crafts employed 34.6 per cent of the working population in Eberbach, and trade and transport 27.7 per cent. Workers made up 51.5 per cent of the working population. In county Heidelberg (excluding the towns of Heidelberg and Eberbach), industry and crafts employed 35.3 per cent of the working population, trade and transport 9.7 per cent, and agriculture 27.3 per cent. Workers formed 51.5 per cent of the workforce, and independents and assisting family members (predominantly employed in agriculture) 37.5 per cent. The percentages are calculated on the basis of 1933 census returns in *StDR*, 456, part 32 (Berlin, 1936), pp. 46–7. On the general development of Nazism in Eberbach see Johnpeter Horst Grill, *The Nazi Movement in Baden, 1920–1945* (Chapel Hill, 1983), pp. 66–7, 154–7.

46. In county Villingen agriculture employed 30.8 per cent of the working population, while the industry and crafts and trade and transport sectors combined employed 33 per cent. Workers accounted for 43.7 per cent of the working population, and independents and assisting family members (the majority in agriculture) for 38.2 per cent. The percentages are calculated on basis of data in *StDR*, 456, part 32 (Berlin, 1936), pp. 44–5.

47. The data tabulated in Table 6.1, columns 8 and 9, is based on those individuals whom the police recorded as being 'members of the SA'. Only 37 out of 128 individuals suspected of being in the SA (that is, their homes were searched for any incriminating evidence following the ban on the SA in April 1932) were deemed to be SA members (including nine whose occupations were not recorded), the bulk of whom were resident in the small towns of Villingen, St Georgen, Triberg and Schonach, and the villages of Königsfeld, Mönchweiler and Schabenhausen.

48. Frequency *N*: 87. Excludes those identified as members of the NSDAP or the SS, and those whose occupations are not given.

NOTES

49. The breakdown of the membership of *Sturm* 82/6, based in Donaueschingen, is attached to a report by the Landespolizeiamt *Außenstelle* Villingen, dated 29 July 1931, in StAF, Landratsamt Donaueschingen, Zug. 1977/52, No. 345.
50. Copy of *Personalien der SA Eisenbach*, dated 4 July 1931 in StAF, Landratsamt Donaueschingen, Zug. 1977/52, No. 345.
51. The percentages are calculated on the basis of data in *StDR*, 456, section 32 (Berlin, 1936), p. 41.
52. This 'combination' was apparently not uncommon among SA units in cities; see Fischer, *Stormtroopers*, p. 28 and p. 69, n. 18.
53. Lack of time permitted only 5 of the 23 folders containing the individual files on SA men in *Kreise* Waiblingen and Schorndorf to be worked through. The members are listed alphabetically and the data relates to those entered under the letters A to E. The complete set of files is in StAL, PL 505/34, Nos. 1-23.
54. The percentages are calculated on the basis of data in *StDR*, 456, part 31 (Berlin, 1936), pp. 46-9.
55. ibid., pp. 53 and 57.
56. ibid., pp. 46-9.
57. Administratively Wetzlar belonged to *Regierungsbezirk* Koblenz (part of the *Rheinprovinz*) until 1.10.1932, when it was incorporated into *Regierungsbezirk* Wiesbaden (province of Hesse-Nassau); cf. Ulrich Mayer, *Das Eindringen des Nationalsozialismus in die Stadt Wetzlar* (Wetzlar, 1970), p. 12.
58. On the nature of the reserve SA see Fischer, *Stormtroopers*, pp. 63-7.
59. See ch. 4, p. 204, n. 38.
60. Fischer, *Stormtroopers*, p. 64.
61. The percentages are calculated on the basis of data in *StDR*, 456, part 25 (Berlin, 1936), pp. 44-5.
62. ibid., p. 55.
63. These and the following percentages are calculated on the basis of data in *StDR*, 456, part 25 (Berlin, 1936), pp. 42-3. Cf. Eberhart Schön, *Die Entstehung des Nationalsozialismus in Hessen* (Meisenheim am Glan, 1972), pp. 4-5.
64. On the difficulties encountered by the NSDAP in its efforts to penetrate the Catholic communities in Westphalia see Detlef Mühlberger, 'The Rise of National Socialism in Westphalia 1920-1933' (Ph.D. thesis, University of London, 1975), especially pp. 330, 379-81. Cf. Beck, *Kampf und Sieg, passim*.
65. The percentages are calculated on the basis of data in *StDR*, 455, section 15 (Berlin, 1936), p. 53.
66. The percentage is taken from *StDR*, 455, section 14 (Berlin, 1936), p. 54.
67. See ch. 5, p. 135, Table 5.3, column 8.
68. The percentages are calculated on the basis of data in *StDR*, 455, part 14 (Berlin, 1936), pp. 46-7. In 1933 some 33.1 per cent of the total population in the county was still dependent on agriculture for a living; percentage taken from ibid., p. 54.
69. This is clear from the information given in the personal files of most

of the SA men, which also notes the occupational status of their fathers. Twenty-nine out of thirty-five SA men with lower-class occupations were the sons of unskilled or skilled workers.

70. Karl Rohe has shown that functional reasons determined that the largely lower-class *Reichsbanner* also had a leadership corps made up primarily of middle-class types; Karl Rohe, *Das Reichsbanner Schwarz Rot Gold* (Stuttgart, 1965), p. 272.

71. Cf. Fischer, *Stormtroopers*, p. 59.

72. ibid., pp. 32 and 36.

73. Cf. Günther Mai, 'Zwischen den Klassen? Zur Soziographie der SA', *Archiv für Sozialgeschichte*, 25 (1985), p. 639.

7 THE SS

1. On the history of the SS see Hans Buchheim, 'Die SS – das Herrschaftsinstrument. Befehl und Gehorsam', in Hans Buchheim, Martin Broszat, Hans-Adolf Jacobsen and Helmut Krausnick, *Anatomie des SS-Staates* (Olten/Freiburg im Breisgau, 1965); Heinz Höhne, *The Order of the Death's Head. The Story of Hitler's SS* (London, 1969) trans. of *Der Orden unter dem Totenkopf* (Gütersloh, 1967); Bernd Wegner, *Hitlers Politische Soldaten: Die Waffen-SS, 1933–1945* (Paderborn, 1982).

2. My analysis of a police report listing 44 members of the *Stosstrupp Hitler* shows that it recruited heavily from the lower- and middle-middle class, which provided two-thirds of its membership; see Detlef Mühlberger, 'Germany', in Detlef Mühlberger (ed.), *The Social Basis of European Fascist Movements* (London, 1987), p. 116, Table 2.12, column d.

3. These figures are taken from Gerhard Rempel, *Hitler's Children. The Hitler Youth and the SS* (Chapel Hill/London, 1989), p. 266, Table 1.1. According to figures compiled by the *Inspekteur für Statistik*, submitted to the *Reichsführer-SS* in March 1943, the SS had about 280 men in January 1929 and around 1,000 by the end of the year; cf. Wegner, *Hitlers Politische Soldaten*, pp. 80–1, n. 8. Michael Kater notes that calculations made by the Bavarian police authorities gave the SS a strength of at least 1,200 men by the end of February 1929, and of 1,400 by mid-April; Michael Kater, 'Zum gegenseitigen Verhältnis von SA und SS in der Sozialgeschichte des Nationalsozialismus von 1925 bis 1939', *Vierteljahrschrift für Sozial- und Wirtschaftsgeschichte*, 62 (1975), pp. 339–79, here p. 349.

4. Figures cited by Wegner, *Hitlers Politische Soldaten*, pp. 80–1, n. 8. Cf. Rempel, *Hitler's Children*, p. 266, Table 1.1.

5. For example, Karl O. Paetel, 'Die SS. Ein Beitrag zur Soziologie des Nationalsozialismus', *Vierteljahrshefte für Zeitgeschichte*, 2 (1954), pp. 1–33.

6. Robert Koehl, 'The Character of the Nazi SS', *Journal of Modern History*, 34 (1962), pp. 275–83, here p. 281.

7. Höhne, *Order of the Death's Head*, p. 54.

8. Kater, 'SA und SS', p. 344.

9. ibid., pp. 358–60.

10. ibid. pp. 372-3. The size of the sample used by Kater is not given.
11. Gunnar C. Boehnert, 'A Sociography of the SS Officer Corps, 1925–1939' (Ph.D. thesis, University of London, 1977). Parts of the thesis have now been published: Gunnar C. Boehnert, 'An Analysis of the Age and Education of the SS-Führerkorps', *Historical Social Research. Historische Sozialforschung*, 12 (1979), pp. 4–17; Gunnar C. Boehnert, 'The Jurists in the SS-Führerkorps, 1925–1939', in Gerhard Hirschfeld and Lothar Kettenacker (eds), *Der 'Führerstaat': Mythos und Realität. Studien zur Struktur und Politik des Dritten Reiches* (Stuttgart, 1981), pp. 361–74. Cf. Herbert Friedrich Ziegler, 'The SS-Führerkorps. An Analysis of its Socioeconomic and Demographic Structure 1925-1939' (Ph.D. thesis, Emory University, 1980).
12. Only 7.4 per cent of the *SS-Führerkorps* came from the lower class, whereas 52.6 per cent was drawn from the lower *Mittelstand* and 40 per cent from the upper *Mittelstand*; Boehnert, 'Jurists', p. 362.
13. Some 44 per cent of SS leaders who joined in the period February 1933 to June 1934 were academics; the percentage fell to 34 per cent in the period July 1934 to September 1939; Boehnert, 'SS Corps', p. 124.
14. Friedrich Zipfel, 'Gestapo and the SD: A Sociographic Profile of the Organizers of Terror', in Stein Ugelvik Larsen, Bernt Hagtvet and Jan Petter Myklebust (eds), *Who were the Fascists? Social Roots of European Fascism* (Bergen/Oslo/Tromso, 1980), pp. 301–11. Ruth Bettina Birn, *Die Höheren SS- und Polizeiführer. Himmlers Vertreter im Reich und in den besetzten Gebieten* (Düsseldorf, 1986).
15. See Mühlberger, 'Germany', pp. 117–20, Table 2.12, columns J, M, P, R, CC and EE.
16. Rempel notes that his percentage for the lower-middle class is much lower than that suggested by Michael Kater in his breakdown of the social structure of the General-SS. Rempel seems unaware that Kater has made significant changes in his occupational and class model since the appearance of Kater's article in 1976, which undoubtedly accounts for the difference given that Rempel, in his analysis, employs the amended classification system used by Kater in his later work on the subject; Rempel, *Hitler's Children*, pp. 15–16 and p. 266, Table 1.1.
17. The sources on which Table 7.1 is based are – Column 1: *SS-Stammrolle des 3.SS Sturmes 3/I/24 (Brake)*, compiled in September 1933, in StAB, provisionally catalogued as 7,1066-315/316 (previously catalogued by the BDC under D-423, 1 and 2). Column 2: *SS-Stammrolle des SS-Sturm 1/II/24 (Bremen)*, in StAB, 7,1066-321 (previously BDC, D-825, 6); *SS-Stammrolle des 3.SS Sturmes 3/II/24 (Bremen)*, in StAB, 7,1066-318/319, and 322 (previously BDC, D-825, 23, and 7); *SS-Stammrolle des Spielmannszuges S.Z./II/24 (Bremen)*, in StAB, 7,1066-317 (previously BDC, D-825, 1). Column 3: *Stammmrolle des SS-Sturmes 1/II/M/XI (Burgbrohl)*, HHStAW, 483/1935. Column 4: *OG Clausthal-Zellerfeld, SS-Sturm 4/II/12 Trupp Clausthal (SS-Männer und SS-Anwärter)*, dated 20 March 1932, in NHStAH, Hann. 310 I/O No. 176. Column 5: *SS-Stammkarten 8/35 SS-Standarte (Dillkreis)*, in HHStAW, 483/4207d.

Column 6: SS-Stammrollen des P./II/2 SS (Frankfurt a. M.), in
HHStAW, 483/668-9; *SS-Stammrollen SS-Motorstaffel II/2
(Frankfurt a. M.)*, in HHStAW, 483/1735-9. Column 7: *SS-
Stammrolle 2.SS Sturmes 2/I/24 (Großenmeer)*, in StAB, 7,1066-314
(previously BDC, D-423, 3). Column 8: Based on a list of persons
identified as belonging to the SS in Ludwigshafen at the time of the
ban on the SS on 13 April 1932; the list is in HA, 87/1816. Column 9:
SS members listed in *Mitgliedergrundbuch Ortsgruppe Schwabing*
(1929), in HA, 8/182; *Angehörige der SS.München, Sturm 69*, police
reports, dated 2. and 28.6.1930, in HA, 72/1546; *Mitglieder der
SS.München*, police report, dated 14.10.1930, in HA, 72/1546;
(Recruits of) *Sturm 2. Sturmbann II*, listed in Munich police report,
dated 5 May 1931, in HA, 72/1546; *Mitglieder der SS, Sturm 1,
Sturmbann I*, Munich police report, dated 17 November 1931, in
HA, 72/1546; *Angehörige des SS-Motorsturms 2/II/1*, Munich
police report, dated 8.8.1932, in HA, 72/1546; *Verzeichnis der
Standarte 1. Sturm 3. Trupp Pasing* (1932), in HA,
72/1546; *Verzeichnis der Führer der SS-Standarte München nach
dem Stande vom 1. Dezember 1932*, in HA, 72/1546. Column 10: list
of members of *Motorsturm I/10* and *II/10* compiled by Palatinate
police authorities (April 1932), in HA, 28A/1774. Column 11: list of
SS-leadership corps, Palatinate (as on 1.3.1932), compiled by the
Palatinate police authorities, in HA, 28A/1774. Column 12: *SS-
Stammrollen. Standarte 33 (Mainz-Worms-Bingen)*, 1933-8, in
StAD, N1/1917. Column 13: *Stammrolle. SS-Sturms 3/II/M/XI
(Trier)*, HHStAW, 483/1936. Column 14: *SS-Stammrollen des SS M/
I/2 (Wiesbaden)*, dated 20 and 24.9.1933, in HHStAW, 483/1933.

18. The total strength of the *1. SS-Standarte München* on 31 December
    1932 was 889 and 881 on 31 January 1933 (includes both members
    and leaders); see *Stärkemeldung für Monat Januar 1933*, dated
    5.2.1933, in HA, 72/1546.

19. Percentages of the male working population of Munich are
    calculated on the basis of data in *StDR*, 456, part 28 (Berlin, 1936), p.
    39.

20. Some 52.1 per cent of 773 SA members resident in Munich in the
    summer of 1932 were from the lower class; see Conan Fischer,
    *Stormtroopers. A Social, Economic and Ideological Analysis, 1929–
    35* (London, 1983), p. 26, Table 3.1. The lower class provided 21.7
    per cent of the SA leadership (Frequency *N*: 46) in November 1932,
    as against the 29.2 per cent of the leadership of the SS (Frequency *N*:
    24) in December 1932; see Mühlberger, 'Germany', p. 120, Table
    2.12, columns DD and EE.

21. The class structure of the NSDAP, SA and SS in Schwabing at the
    end of 1929 was as follows:

	NSDAP	SA	SS
Lower Class	17.1	45.2	46.7
Lower- & middle-Middle Class	38.9	30.5	15.5
Upper-Middle Class & Upper Class	14.4	14.6	18.7
Status Unclear	29.4	9.3	18.7

Total (%)	100	100	100
Frequency (N)	836	75	32

The high percentage in the 'Status Unclear' category probably distorts the breakdown of the NSDAP and, to a lesser extent, that of the SS. Data taken from Mühlberger, 'Germany', p. 80, Table 2.6, column R; and p. 117, Table 2.12, columns I and J.

22. The data roughly involves between 10 to 15 per cent of the total SS membership in the Rhenish Palatinate. At the beginning of 1932 there were 573 SS members in Standarte 10; see *Gesamt-Stärkemeldung der SS für den Monat Dezember 1931, Der Reichs-führer-SS*, Munich, 25.1.1932, in HA, 72/1546.

23. The lower class was marginally under-represented in the SS in comparison with the social structure of the male working population in the Palatinate, in which the category 'workers' accounted for 54.6 per cent. The percentage is calculated on the basis of data in *StDR*, 456, part 30 (Berlin, 1936), p. 3.

24. The percentage is calculated on the basis of data in *StDR*, 456, part 30 (Berlin, 1936), p. 39.

25. In the material on the SS in Bremen there are quite a few individual files where no indication is given as to whether the applicant became an SS-probationer, never mind a fully-fledged SS-man. These files have been omitted in the data presented here.

26. When the 111 members are removed from the data presented in Table 7.1, column 3, the percentage values of the SS membership resident in Bremen itself are only marginally affected, with the lower class accounting for 58.7 per cent, the lower- and middle-middle class for 38.5 per cent, and the upper-middle class and upper class for 1.2 per cent. Those listed in the 'Status Unknown' category account for a further 1.2 per cent. The data on the SS resident in Delmenhorst will be looked at in the section dealing with the SS in Oldenburg.

27. It does seem that the SS had made little progress in recruiting members in the Bremen region by the end of 1931. Standarte 24 (Weser–Ems), to which the Bremen SS belonged, had only 197 members by the end of December 1931; see *Gesamt-Stärkemeldung der SS für den Monat Dezember 1931, Der Reichsführer-SS*, dated Munich, 25 January 1932, in HA, 72/1546.

28. These and the following percentages are calculated on the basis of data in *StDR*, 455, part 21 (Berlin, 1936), p. 34.

29. Few craftsmen below the age of thirty-five secured their independence, while sons of shopkeepers or farmers were unlikely to have inherited the family business or farm while they were in their twenties or early thirties. The upper age limit appears to have been increasingly vigorously enforced for the rank and file applicants after January 1933 (when the entry *Abgelehnt wegen Altersgrenze* begins to appear more frequently in SS files), though it was generally waived, it would seem, for 18 to 23 year-old recruits provided that they met other requirements, such as height and physique.

30. According to Michael Kater, the percentage of Nazi Party recruits drawn from the elite (which according to his calculations made up 2.8 per cent of German society) accounted for 12.2 per cent in 1933, 9.7 per cent in the period 1934 to 1936, and 8 per cent in 1937; Michael H. Kater, *The Nazi Party. A Social Profile of Members and Leaders, 1919-1945* (Oxford, 1983), p. 241, Table 1; p. 252, Table 7, columns A, B and C. Cf. Boehnert, 'Jurists', p. 363, Table 1.

31. The category 'workers' represented 52.6 per cent of the male working population in Hesse in 1933, 49.9 per cent of the total working population in province Starkenburg and 39 per cent in province Rheinhessen. The percentages are calculated on the basis of data in *StDR*, 453, part 33 (Berlin, 1936), pp. 3 and 4. It is not always possible to differentiate between the male and female share in the workforce. The census returns of 1933 provide information on how many males and females made up the *Selbständige, Mithelfende Familienangehörige, Beamte, Angestellte, Arbeiter* and *Hausangestellte* categories in the workforce of the various *Länder* (and in the case of Prussia, of the various provinces) and the communities with a population of 10,000 or over within the *Länder* or provinces. But no such separation is made for the *Regierungsbezirke* (or in the case of *Land* Hesse, provinces), counties or communities with a population of less than 10,000, for which only the global figure for each category is available, without differentiation along gender lines.

32. Agriculture employed 20.9 and 19.6 per cent of the working population in the provinces of Starkenburg and Rheinhessen respectively; the percentages are calculated on the basis of data in *StDR*, 453, part 33 (Berlin, 1936), p. 33.

33. The category *Angestellte* made up 11.6 per cent of the workforce in province Starkenburg, and 12.7 per cent in province Rheinhessen; ibid., p. 33.

34. The percentages are calculated on the basis of data in *StDR*, 455, part 19 (Berlin, 1936), pp. 36-7.

35. The Nazi branch at Golzwarden was very active by the late 1920s and was instrumental in forming the first Nazi cell in Brake in 1930; see W. Günther, 'Die Zeit der Krisen vom Ersten zum Zweiten Weltkrieg (1910-1945)', in Albert Eckhardt *et al.*, *Brake. Geschichte der Seehafenstadt an der Unterweser* (Oldenburg, 1981), p. 268.

36. The percentage is calculated on the basis of data in *StDR*, 455, part 19 (Berlin, 1936), p. 35.

37. The severity of the depression in Clausthal-Zellerfeld and the interrelationship between socio-economic insecurity and the growth in Nazi support is well illustrated by Sigurd Plesse, *Die nationalsozialistische Machtergreifung im Oberharz. Clausthal-Zellerfeld 1929-1933* (Clausthal-Zellerfeld, 1970).

38. See ch. 5, p. 135, Table 5.3, column 3.

39. The percentage is calculated on the basis of data in *StDR*, 455, part 19 (Berlin, 1936), p. 37.

40. On the social structure of the male working population of Frankfurt

see ch. 4, p.235, n. 38.

41. The data presented in Table 7.1, column 14, is based on approximately half of the membership recorded in the *Stammrollen* relating to SS–M/I/2 (Wiesbaden).

42. On the social structure of Wiesbaden's male working population see p. 236, n. 45.

43. The percentages are calculated on the basis of data in *StDR*, 456, part 25 (Berlin, 1936), pp. 44–5.

44. With a mere 9,732 members, *Gau* Koblenz-Trier was among the *Gaue* with the lowest number of Nazi members by the time of the *Machtergreifung* in January 1933. See *Partei-Statistik. Stand 1.Januar 1935. Band 1: Parteimitglieder*. Herausgeber: Der Reichsorganisationsleiter der NSDAP (Munich, n.d.), p. 19.

45. An insight into the social structure of the NSDAP branches in the counties is provided in a report by the *Regierungspräsident* of Koblenz, dated 14 February 1931, reprinted in Franz Josef Heyen, *Nationalsozialismus im Alltag. Quellen zur Geschichte des Nationalsozialismus vornehmlich im Raum Mainz-Koblenz-Trier* (Boppard am Rhein, 1967), pp. 52–5.

46. The percentage is calculated on the basis of data in *StDR*, 455, part 16 (Berlin, 1936), pp. 64–5.

47. *Partei-Statistik*, p. 150.

48. Cf. Kater, 'SA und SS', pp. 363–4. See also Jeremy Noakes, *The Nazi Party in Lower Saxony 1921–1933* (Oxford, 1971), pp. 188–9.

49. The ability to play a musical instrument rather than the need to conform with the age requirement laid down by the SS leadership may also have conditioned the recruitment policy of *SS-Musikzüge*. The average age of the 21 members identified by the police as belonging to the *SS-Musikzug* in Ludwigshafen in 1932 was 35.5, with several members in their forties and quite a few in their fifties. The list is in HA, 75/1557.

50. On this aspect see the examples cited by Gunnar C. Boehnert, 'The Third Reich and the Problem of "Social Revolution": German Officers and the SS', in Volker R. Berghahn and Martin Kitchen (eds), *Germany in the Age of Total War* (London, 1981), pp. 203–17, *passim*.

51. The lower- and middle-middle class consistently provided around half of the new members enrolled by the NSDAP in the late 1920s and early 1930s – see Kater, *Nazi Party*, pp. 244–5, Table 3, columns G and I; p. 250, Table 6, column A.

52. On the SA see Fischer, *Stormtroopers*, p. 31, Table 3.3; cf. ch. 6, Table 6.2, p. 178, column 5.

CONCLUSION

1 This is the line of argument advanced by Richard J. Overy in his review article 'Fascist Societies', *Social History Society Newsletter*, 13 (1988), p. 13.

2. According to statistics produced by the KPD in 1927, unskilled and

skilled workers made up 80 per cent of its membership; see H. Weber, *Die Wandlung des deutschen Kommunismus. Die Stalinisierung der KPD in der Weimarer Republik* (Frankfurt a. M., 1969), p. 282. In the occupational breakdown of its membership provided by the SPD in 1930 (based on a sample of 100,000 members), 'workers' accounted for 59.5 per cent, the 'petty bourgeoisie' for 17.3 per cent, 'intellectuals' for 1.5 per cent, and 'others' for 21.7 per cent; figures cited in R. N. Hunt, *German Social Democracy 1918–1933* (New Haven/London, 1964), p. 103.

3. On 1 January 1931 the SPD's membership was 1,037,384 (including approximately 100,000 members drawn from the middle class); see Hunt, *German Social Democracy*, p. 100. The KPD had a paid-up membership of 259,155 (and a registered membership of 381,000) in December 1931; see Weber, *Wandlung des deutschen Kommunismus*, p. 364.

4. Cf. Tim Mason, *Sozialpolitik im Dritten Reich. Arbeiterklasse und Volksgemeinschaft* (Opladen, 1978), pp. 56 and 62.

5. Figures taken from Jürgen Falter, Thomas Lindenberger and Siegfried Schumann, *Wahlen und Abstimmungen in der Weimarer Republik. Materialien zum Wahlverhalten 1919–1933* (Munich, 1986), p. 41.

6. For example, 7 per cent of the 'old fighters' analysed by Theodore Abel had been members of left-wing movements; cited by Mason, *Sozialpolitik*, p. 54, n. 21.

7. Gerhard Schulz has argued that the Nazi Party may well have ranked second behind the SPD in its ability to mobilize working-class support in the early 1930s; see Gerhard Schulz, *Aufstieg des Nationalsozialismus. Krise und Revolution in Deutschland* (Frankfurt a. M./Berlin/Vienna, 1975), p. 551.

8. Some 42.2 per cent of the members who joined the Nazi Party before 31 January 1933 (and were still in the party by 1 January 1935) were aged between 18 and 30; a further 27.8 per cent were in the 31 to 40 age group. Figures taken from *Partei-Statistik. Stand 1. Januar 1935. Band 1: Mitglieder*. Herausgeber Der Reichsorganisationsleiter der NSDAP (Munich, n.d.), p. 204.

9. Cf. *Partei-Statistik*, p. 56.

10. The size of the 'elite' in Weimar society ranges from the 0.84 per cent suggested by Theodor Geiger to 3.3 per cent noted by Carl Dreyfuss. Michael Kater's calculations based on the 1933 census returns result in an elite component of 2.78 per cent (Kater includes managers, higher civil servants, academic professionals, students and entrepreneurs in the 'elite' category); see Michael Kater, *The Nazi Party. A Social Profile of Members and Leaders, 1919–1945* (Oxford, 1983), pp. 12–13 and p. 241, Table 1. Paul Madden, who bases his calculations of the size of the elite on the 1925 census returns, suggests a figure of 1.1 per cent (Madden includes only capitalists, industrialists, large landowners, and persons with private incomes in the 'elite' category); see Paul Madden, 'The Social Class Origins of Nazi Party Members as Determined by Occupations, 1919–1933',

Social Science Quarterly, 68 (1987), pp. 272–3, Table 2.

11. According to Michael Kater the elite made up 9.2 per cent of Nazi recruits (*N*: 2,186) in the period 1925–32, and 12.2 per cent of Nazi recruits (*N*: 3,316) in 1933; see Michael Kater, 'Quantifizierung und NS-Geschichte. Methodologische Überlegungen über Grenzen und Möglichkeiten einer EDV-Analyse der NSDAP-Sozialstruktur von 1925 bis 1945', *Geschichte und Gesellschaft*, 3 (1977), p. 477, Table 10. Cf. Kater's re-working of material provided by Werner Studentkowski and Paul Madden for the period 1925 to 1930 shows that the 'elite' component among Nazi recruits ranged between 6.3 and 8.8 per cent according to Studentkowski's data, and between 4.8 and 8.4 per cent according to Madden's data; see Kater, *Nazi Party*, pp. 244–5, Table 3.

12. Kater, *Nazi Party*, p. 236.

13. Peter Stachura, 'The Nazis, the Bourgeoisie and the Workers during the *Kampfzeit*', in Peter D. Stachura (ed.), *The Nazi Machtergreifung* (London, 1983), p. 28.

14. Peter Stachura characterizes the membership of the HJ as 'predominantly working class', with 65 to 70 per cent of its membership being drawn from the working class before 1933. Stachura does not analyse any raw material on the social structure of the HJ's membership as such, but uses summaries of the social background of HJ members contained in Nazi reports on *Gaue* Munich–Upper Bavaria, Hamburg, South Bavaria, and the Rhineland. See Peter Stachura, *Nazi Youth in the Weimar Republic* (Santa Barbara/Oxford, 1975), pp. 58–62. My own breakdown of the HJ in the Palatinate, based on a complete membership record of 2,053 members who joined the organization between 1928 and April 1932, also points to the strong lower-class base (57.4 per cent were recruited from the lower class) of the HJ in this region; see Detlef Mühlberger, 'Germany', in Detlef Mühlberger (ed.), *The Social Basis of European Fascist Movements* (London, 1987), p. 110, Table 2.11. It seems that this high incidence of lower-class support was not universal, however. A report on the HJ membership in *Gau* South-Hanover-Brunswick (*N*: 1,200) as in February 1931 listed the following groupings:

Young workers	37%
Commercial apprentices	14%
Farmers	11%
Free occupations	15%
School children, students	23%

Taken from *Führer zum Gautag der Nationalsozialistischen Deutschen Arbeiter-Partei am 21. und 22. Februar 1931 in der Stadt Braunschweig*. Herausgeber: Propaganda-Abteilung der Gauleitung Südhannover-Braunschweig, p. 31; copy in NHStAH, Hann. 310 I/G No. 17/1.

15. Among the extensive literature dealing with the social background of the Nazi electorate see especially Thomas Childers, *The Nazi Voter. The Social Foundations of Fascism in Germany, 1919–1933* (Chapel Hill/London, 1983); Dirk Hänisch, *Sozialstrukturelle*

Bestimmungsgründe des Wahlverhaltens in der Weimarer Republik. Eine Aggregatdatenanalyse der Ergebnisse der Reichstagswahlen 1924-1933 (Duisburg, 1983); and Richard Hamilton, *Who voted for Hitler?* (New York, 1982). Especially important among the enormous output on this question by Jürgen W. Falter in the last decade are the following: 'Wer verhalf der NSDAP zum Sieg? Neuere Forschungsergebnisse zum parteipolitischen und sozialen Hintergrund der NSDAP-Wähler 1924-1933', *Aus Politik und Zeitgeschichte*, B 28/29 (1979), pp. 3-21; 'Wählerbewegung zur NSDAP 1924-1933. Methodologische Probleme - Empirisch abgesicherte Erkenntnisse - Offene Fragen', in Otto Büsch (ed.), *Wählerbewegung in der europäischen Geschichte* (Berlin, 1980), pp. 159-202; 'Die Wähler der NSDAP 1928-1933: Sozialstruktur und parteipolitische Herkunft', in Wolfgang Michalka (ed.), *Die nationalsozialistische Machtergreifung* (Paderborn/Munich/Vienna/Zürich, 1984); (with Dirk Hänisch) 'Die Anfälligkeit von Arbeitern gegenüber der NSDAP bei den Reichstagswahlen 1928-1933', *Archiv für Sozialgeschichte*, 26 (1986), pp. 179-216; 'Der Aufstieg der NSDAP in Franken bei den Reichstagswahlen 1924-1933. Ein Vergleich mit dem Reich unter besonderer Berücksichtigung landwirtschaftlicher Einflußfaktoren', *German Studies Review*, 9 (1986), pp. 319-59; (with Reinhard Zintl) 'The Economic Crisis of the 1930s and the Nazi Vote', *Journal of Interdisciplinary History*, 18 (1988), pp. 55-85. All these studies demonstrate the broad social base on which the electoral support of the NSDAP rested. For a review of the debate on the sociology of the Nazi electoral constituency see Peter Manstein, *Die Mitglieder und Wähler der NSDAP 1919-1933. Untersuchungen zu ihrer schichtmäßigen Zusammensetzung* (Frankfurt a. M./Bern/New York/Paris, 1988), pp. 165-93.

16. See, for example, Seymour Martin Lipset's characterization of 'the ideal-typical Nazi voter in 1932' as being 'a middle-class self-employed Protestant who lived either on a farm or in a small community'; Seymour Martin Lipset, *Political Man* (New York, 1960), p. 149.

17. According to the *Partei-Statistik*, females accounted for 5.9 per cent of the Nazi membership before 14.9.1930, 7.8 per cent of those who joined between 15.9.1930 and 30.1.1933, and 4.4 per cent of those who rushed to join the party after the 30.1.1933. Percentages calculated on the basis of data in *Partei-Statistik*, pp. 26 and 30.

18. See n. 8.

19. Regional studies on the Nazi Party produced by East German scholars, such as Gerhard Neuber's study on Berlin entitled 'Entwicklung und Wirken der NSDAP und ihrer Organisationen in der Reichshauptstadt 1920-1934' (Dr. phil. thesis, Humboldt-Universität Berlin, 1976), are not very illuminating on the class basis of the Nazi Party.

20. I am at present working on this aspect, dealing with the membership fluctuations of the Nazi Party in *Gaue* Württemberg and Hesse-Nassau-South.

BIBLIOGRAPHY

PRIMARY SOURCES

Archival sources

Bundesarchiv, Koblenz (BA)
  Sammlung Schumacher 203
  NS 1/342.
Generallandersarchiv Karlsruhe (GLAK)
  Abt. 465 c: Nos 2181-2, 2187-8.
  Abt. 465 d: No 1307.
Hessisches Hauptstaatsarchiv Wiesbaden (HHStAW)
  Abt. 483: Nos 668-9, 702a-d, 1735-8, 1933, 1935-6, 4207d, 4519a,
  4800e-f, 10605-6.
Niedersächsisches Hauptstaatsarchiv Hannover (NHStAH)
  Hann. Des. 310 I/E: Nos   1, 5-8, 11-12, 16, 21, 31-2, 36.
  Hann. Des. 310 I/G: No   17/1.
  Hann. Des. 310 I/N: No   13-14.
  Hann. Des. 310 I/O: Nos   35-7, 171, 176, 183, 185.
Nordrhein-Westfälisches Hauptstaatsarchiv Düsseldorf (NWHStAD)
  RW 23: Nos 38, 41, 44-5, 47, 49-51, 55, 63, 85.
  NW 1069-87, HA LK Paderborn.
Staatsarchiv Bremen (StAB)
  Rep. 7,1066: Nos 314-19, 321.
Staatsarchiv Darmstadt (StAD)
  N1: No 1917.
Staatsarchiv Freiburg (StAF)
  Landratsamt Donaueschingen, Zug. 1977/52: No 345.
  Landratsamt Villingen, Zug. 1979/82: No 1245.
Staatsarchiv Ludwigsburg (StAL)
  PL 501: Nos 93-4.
  PL 505: No 34/1-5.
Staatsarchiv Münster (StAM)
  1 PA/398.
  VII - 2, Bd 6.
  VII - 67, Bd 1.

Microfilmed Documents

NSDAP Hauptarchiv - Hoover Institution Microfilm Collection (HA)

Reel	1A	Folder	222.
	2A		230.
	6		141.
	8		166.
	8		182.
	10		215
	28A		1774.
	58		1400-3.
	72		1546.
	75		1557.
	87		1816.

Published Sources

Einzelschriften zur Statistik des Deutschen Reichs
  No 7: Die Steuerkraft der Finanzbezirke (Berlin, 1929).
Partei-Statistik. Stand 1. Januar 1935. Herausgeber Der Reichsorganisationsleiter der NSDAP (Munich, n.d.).
Statistik des Deutschen Reichs (StDR)
  Bde.: 372 (Berlin, 1930); 382 (Berlin, 1932); 401 (Berlin, 1927); 402 (Berlin, 1927-9); 404 (Berlin, 1928); 405 (Berlin, 1928); 453 (Berlin, 1936); 455 (Berlin, 1936); 456 (Berlin, 1936).
Statistisches Jahrbuch für das Deutsche Reich (StJDR)
  Jg. 45 (Berlin, 1926).
  Jg. 46 (Berlin, 1927).
  Jg. 47 (Berlin, 1928).
Statistisches Jahrbuch für den Freistaat Preußen (StJFP)
  Jg. 23 (Berlin, 1927).
Vierteljahrshefte zur Statistik des Deutschen Reichs
  Jg. 34 (Berlin, 1925).
Völkischer Beobachter 1922-32.

SECONDARY SOURCES

Select bibliography

Listed is literature dealing specifically with the sociology of the rank and file membership and leadership of the National Socialist Movement and with methodological and interpretational aspects of the debate on the sociology of the Nazi Movement. Articles and books dealing primarily with the electoral support of the NSDAP are not included.

Abel, Theodore, *The Nazi Movement: Why Hitler came to Power* (New York, 1935).

Allen, William Sheridan, 'Farewell to Class Analysis in the Rise of Nazism: Comment', *Central European History*, 17 (1984), pp. 54-62.

Andrews, Herbert D., 'The Social Composition of the NSDAP: Problems and Possible Solutions', *German Studies Review*, 9 (1986), pp. 293-318.

Banaszkiewicz, Jacob, 'German Fascism and People of the Social Fringe', *Polish Western Affairs*, 8 (1967), pp. 251-88.

Bergmann, Jürgen and Megerle, Klaus, 'Wer unterstützte die Nationalsozialisten? Das Verhältnis der gesellschaftlichen Gruppen zur nationalsozialistischen Bewegung', in Klaus Megerle (ed.), *Warum gerade die Nationalsozialisten?* (Berlin, 1983), pp. 146-95.

Bessel, Richard and Jamin, Mathilde, 'Nazis, Workers and the Use of Quantitative Evidence', *Social History*, 4 (1979), pp. 111-16.

Bessel, Richard and Jamin, Mathilde, 'Statistics and the Historian: A Rejoinder', *Social History*, 5 (1980), pp. 139-40.

Bessel, Richard, 'The S.A. in the Eastern Regions of Germany, 1925-1934' (D.Phil. thesis, Oxford University, 1980).

Bessel, Richard, *Political Violence and the Rise of Nazism. The Storm Troopers in Eastern Germany 1925-1934* (New Haven, 1984).

Birn, Ruth Bettina, *Die Höheren SS- und Polizeiführer. Himmlers Vertreter im Reich und in den besetzten Gebieten* (Düsseldorf, 1986).

Boehnert, Gunnar C., 'A Sociography of the SS Officer Corps, 1925-1939', (Ph.D. thesis, University of London, 1977).

Boehnert, Gunnar C., 'An Analysis of the Age and Education of the SS Führerkorps, 1925-1939', *Historical Social Research*, 12 (1979), pp. 4-17.

Boehnert, Gunnar C., 'The Third Reich and the Problem of 'Social Revolution': German Officers and the SS', in Volker R. Berghahn and Martin Kitchen (eds), *Germany in the Age of Total War* (London, 1981), pp. 203-17.

Boehnert, Gunnar C., 'The Jurists in the SS-Führerkorps, 1925-1939', in Gerhard Hirschfeld and Lothar Kettenacker (eds), *Der 'Führerstaat': Mythos and Realität. Studien zur Struktur und Politik des Dritten Reiches* (Stuttgart, 1981), pp. 361-74.

Böhnke, Wilfried, *Die NSDAP im Ruhrgebiet 1920-1933* (Bonn–Bad Godesberg, 1974).

Douglas, Donald M., 'The Early Ortsgruppen: The Development of National Socialist Local Groups 1919-1923' (Ph.D. thesis, University of Kansas, 1968).

Douglas, Donald M., 'The Parent Cell: Some Computer Notes on the Composition of the First Nazi Party Group in Munich, 1919-1921', *Central European History*, 10 (1977), pp. 55-72.

Fischer, Conan, 'The Occupational Background of the SA's Rank and File Membership during the Depression Years 1929 to mid-1934', in Peter D. Stachura (ed.), *The Shaping of the Nazi State* (London, 1978), pp. 131-59.

Fischer, Conan, 'The SA of the NSDAP: Social Background and

Ideology of the Rank and File in the Early 1930s', *Journal of Contemporary History*, 17 (1982), pp. 651-70.

Fischer, Conan, *Stormtroopers. A Social, Economic and Ideological Analysis, 1929-1935* (London, 1983).

Fischer, Conan and Hicks, Carolyn, 'Statistics and the Historian: The Occupational Profile of the SA of the NSDAP', *Social History*, 5 (1980), pp. 131-8.

Fogel, Heidi and Rebentisch, Dieter, 'Organisation und Struktur der NSDAP in südhessischen Arbeiterwohngemeinden 1928-1932', in Eike Hennig (ed.), *Hessen unterm Hakenkreuz. Studien zur Durchsetzung der NSDAP in Hessen* (Frankfurt a. M., 1983), pp. 318-49.

Friters, Gerhard, 'Who are the German Fascists?', *Current History*, 35 (1932), pp. 532-6.

Fritz, Stephen G., 'The NSDAP as Volkspartei? A Look at the Social Basis of the Nazi Voter', *The History Teacher*, 20 (1987), pp. 379-99.

Geiger, Theodor, *Die soziale Schichtung des deutschen Volkes. Soziographischer Versuch auf statistischer Grundlage* (Stuttgart, 1932).

Gellately, Robert, 'German Shopkeepers and the Rise of National Socialism', *The Wiener Library Bulletin*, 28 (1975), pp. 31-40.

Genuneit, Jürgen, 'Methodische Probleme der quantitativen Analyse früher NSDAP-Mitgliederlisten', in Reinhard Mann (ed.), *Die Nationalsozialisten. Analysen faschistischer Bewegungen* (Stuttgart, 1980), pp. 34-66.

Gerth, Hans, 'The Nazi Party: Its Leadership and Composition', *American Journal of Sociology*, 45 (1940), pp. 517-41.

Gordon, Harold, J., Jr., *Hitler and the Beer Hall Putsch* (Princeton, 1972).

Hänisch, Dirk and Strasser, Hermann, 'Die Klassenbasis der NSDAP und anderer NS-Organisationen im Lichte neuer Untersuchungen', paper presented at the Ad-hoc Conference 'Soziologie des Nationalsozialismus' on the occasion of the 24th German Sociology Day in Zürich, 4-7 October 1988.

Hardach, Gerd, 'Klassen und Schichten in Deutschland 1848-1970: Probleme einer historischen Sozialstrukturanalyse', *Geschichte und Gesellschaft*, 3 (1977), pp. 503-24.

Haupt, Heinz-Gerhard, 'Mittelstand und Kleinbürgertum in der Weimarer Republik. Zu Problemen und Perspektiven ihrer Erforschung', *Archiv für Sozialgeschichte*, 26 (1986), pp. 217-38.

Heimel, Barbara, 'Mittelschichten - Brutstätten des Faschismus? Zum Verhältnis von objektiver Lage und politischem Bewußtsein', in Reinhard Kühnl and Gerd Hardach (eds), *Die Zerstörung der Weimarer Republik* (Cologne, 1977), pp. 181-213.

Hennig, Eike (ed.), *Hessen unterm Hakenkreuz. Studien zur Durchsetzung der NSDAP in Hessen* (Frankfurt a. M., 1984).

Jamin, Mathilde, 'Zur Kritik an Michael Katers Überlegungen über Quantifizierung und NS-Geschichte', *Geschichte und Gesellschaft*, 4 (1978), pp. 536-41.

Jamin, Mathilde, 'Methodische Konzeption einer quantitativen Analyse zur sozialen Zusammensetzung der SA', in Reinhard Mann (ed.), *Die Nationalsozialisten. Analysen faschistischer Bewegungen* (Stuttgart, 1980), pp. 84-97.

Jamin, Mathilde, 'Zwischen den Klassen. Eine quantitative Untersuchung zur Sozialstruktur der SA-Führerschaft' (Phil. Diss., Ruhr-Universität Bochum, 1982).

Jamin, Mathilde, *Zwischen den Klassen. Zur Sozialstruktur der SA-Führerschaft* (Wuppertal, 1984).

Jarausch, Konrad H. and Arminger, Gerhard, 'The German Teaching Profession and Nazi Party Membership: A Demographic Logit Model', *Journal of Interdisciplinary History*, 20 (1989), pp. 197-225.

Jensen-Butler, Birgit, 'An outline of a Weberian analysis of class with particular reference to the middle class and the NSDAP in Weimar Germany', *British Journal of Sociology*, 27 (1976), pp. 50-60.

Kaelble, Hartmut, 'Social Stratification in Germany in the 19th and 20th Centuries: A Survey of Research since 1945', *Journal of Social History*, 10 (1976), pp. 144-65.

Kater, Michael H., 'Zur Soziographie der frühen NSDAP', *Vierteljahrshefte für Zeitgeschichte*, 22 (1971), pp. 124-60.

Kater, Michael H., 'Zum gegenseitigen Verhältnis von SA und SS in der Sozialgeschichte des Nationalsozialismus von 1925 bis 1939', *Vierteljahrschrift für Sozial- und Wirtschaftsgeschichte*, 62 (1975), pp. 339-79.

Kater, Michael H., 'Sozialer Wandel in der NSDAP im Zuge der nationalsozialistischen Machtergreifung', in Wolfgang Schieder (ed.), *Faschismus als soziale Bewegung. Deutschland und Italien im Vergleich* (Hamburg, 1976), pp. 25-68.

Kater, Michael H., 'Ansätze zu einer Soziologie der SA bis zur Röhmkrise', in Ulrich Engelhardt, Volker Sellin and Horst Stuke (eds), *Soziale Bewegung und politische Verfassung. Beiträge zur Geschichte der modernen Welt* (Stuttgart, 1976), pp. 798-831.

Kater, Michael H. 'Quantifizierung und NS-Geschichte. Methodologische Überlegungen über Grenzen und Möglichkeiten einer EDV-Analyse der NSDAP-Sozialstruktur von 1925 bis 1945', *Geschichte und Gesellschaft*, 3 (1977), pp. 453-84.

Kater, Michael H., 'Methodologische Überlegungen über Möglichkeiten und Grenzen einer Analyse der sozialen Zusammensetzung der NSDAP von 1925 bis 1945', in Reinhard Mann (ed.), *Die Nationalsozialisten. Analysen faschistischer Bewegungen* (Stuttgart, 1980), pp. 155-85.

Kater, Michael H., *The Nazi Party. A Social Profile of Members and Leaders, 1919-1945* (Oxford, 1983).

Kater, Michael H., 'Generationskonflikt als Entwicklungsfaktor in der NS-Bewegung vor 1933', *Geschichte und Gesellschaft*, 11 (1985), pp. 217-43.

Kater, Michael H., 'Clase social y poder politico el pueblo aleman y el nacional socialismo en la Republica de Weimar y el Tercer Reich', *Opciones*, 10 (1987), pp. 103-21.

Kele, Max, *Nazis and Workers. National Socialist Appeals to German*

Labor, 1919-1933 (Chapel Hill, 1972).

Koehl, Robert, 'The Character of the Nazi SS', (review article) *Journal of Modern History*, 34 (1962), pp. 275-83.

Koshar, Rudy, 'Two "Nazisms": The Social Context of Nazi Mobilization in Marburg and Tübingen', *Social History*, 7 (1982), pp. 27-42.

Koshar, Rudy, *Social Life, Local Politics, and Nazism. Marburg 1880-1935* (Chapel Hill/London, 1986).

Koshar, Rudy, 'From *Stammtisch* to Party: Nazi Joiners and the Contradictions of Grass Roots Fascism in Weimar Germany', *Journal of Modern History*, 59 (1987), pp. 1-24.

Lerner, Daniel, *The Nazi Elite* (Stanford, 1951).

Lipset, Seymour Martin, *Political Man* (New York, 1960).

Löwenberg, Peter, 'The Psychohistorical Origins of the Nazi Youth Cohort', *American Historical Review*, 75 (1971), pp. 1457-502.

Maciejewski, Marek, 'Z badan nad spolecznozawodowa struktura NSDAP w latach 1919-1933', in Karel Jonca (ed.), *Studia nad faszysmem i zbrodniami hitlerowskimi* (Wrolaw, 1985), pp. 141-206, tables.

Madden, J. Paul, 'The Social Composition of the Nazi Party, 1919-1930' (Ph.D. thesis, University of Oklahoma, 1976).

Madden, J. Paul, 'Some Social Characteristics of Early Nazi Party Members, 1919-23', *Central European History*, 15 (1982), pp. 34-56.

Madden, J. Paul, 'The Social Class Origins of Nazi Party Members as Determined by Occupations, 1919-1933', *Social Science Quarterly*, 68 (1987), pp. 263-79.

Mai, Günther, 'Zwischen den Klassen? Zur Soziographie der SA', (review article) *Archiv für Sozialgeschichte*, 25 (1985), pp. 634-46.

Mann, Reinhard (ed.), *Die Nationalsozialisten. Analysen faschistischer Bewegungen* (Stuttgart, 1980).

Manstein, Peter, *Die Mitglieder und Wähler der NSDAP 1919-1933. Untersuchungen zu ihrer schichtmäßigen Zusammensetzung* (Frankfurt a. M./Bern, 1988).

Merkl, Peter H., *Political Violence under the Swastika. 581 Early Nazis* (Princeton, 1975).

Merkl, Peter H., *The Making of a Stormtrooper* (Princeton, 1980).

Merkl, Peter H., 'Zur quantitativen Analyse von Lebensläufen Alter Kämpfer', in Reinhard Mann (ed.), *Die Nationalsozialisten. Analysen faschistischer Bewegungen* (Stuttgart, 1980), pp. 67-83.

Mühlberger, Detlef, 'The Sociology of the NSDAP: The Question of Working-Class Membership', *Journal of Contemporary History*, 15 (1980), pp. 493-511.

Mühlberger, Detlef, 'The Occupational and Social Structure of the NSDAP in the Border Province Posen-West Prussia in the early 1930s', *European History Quarterly*, 15 (1985), pp. 281-311.

Mühlberger, Detlef, 'Germany', in Detlef Mühlberger (ed.), *The Social Basis of European Fascist Movements* (London, 1987), pp. 40-139.

Paetel, Karl O., 'Die SS. Ein Beitrag zur Soziologie des Nationalsozialismus', *Vierteljahrshefte für Zeitgeschichte*, 2 (1954), pp. 1-33.

Rebentisch, Dieter, 'Persönlichkeitsprofil und Karriereverlauf der nationalsozialistischen Führungskader in Hessen 1928-1945', *Hessisches Jahrbuch für Landesgeschichte*, 33 (1983), pp. 293-331.

Reiche, Eric G., 'The Development of the SA in Nuremberg, 1922 to 1934', (Ph.D. thesis, University of Delaware, 1972).

Reiche, Eric, G., *The Development of the SA in Nürnberg, 1922-1934* (Cambridge, 1986).

Rempel, Gerhard, *Hitler's Children. The Hitler Youth and the SS* (Chapel Hill/London, 1989).

Rogowski, Ronald, 'The Gauleiter and the Social Origins of Fascism', *Comparative Studies in Society and History*, 19 (1977) pp. 399-430.

Rothenberger, Karl-Heinz, 'Die NSDAP in der Pfalz. Sozialstruktur der Partei nach der Parteistatistik von 1935', *Jahrbuch Westdeutscher Landesgeschichte*, 12 (1986), pp. 199-211.

Schäfer, Wolfgang, *NSDAP. Entwicklung und Struktur der Staatspartei des Dritten Reiches* (Hanover, 1957).

Schmidt, Christoph, 'Zu den Motiven "alter Kämpfer" in der NSDAP', in Detlev Peukert and Jürgen Reulecke (eds), *Die Reihen fast geschlossen* (Wuppertal, 1981), pp. 21-43.

Stachura, Peter D., 'Who were the Nazis? A Socio-Political Analysis of the National Socialist *Machtübernahme*', *European Studies Review*, 11 (1981), pp. 293-324.

Stachura, Peter D., 'The Nazis, the Bourgeoisie and the Workers during the *Kampfzeit*', in Peter D. Stachura (ed.), *The Nazi Machtergreifung* (London, 1983), pp. 15-32.

Stachura, Peter D., 'The NSDAP and the German Working Class, 1925-1933', in Michael N. Dobkowski and Isidor Wallimann (eds), *Towards the Holocaust. The Social and Economic Collapse of the Weimar Republic* (Westport/London, 1983), pp. 131-53.

Stephan, Werner, 'Zur Soziologie der Nationalsozialistischen Deutschen Arbeiterpartei', *Zeitschrift für Politik*, 20 (1931), pp. 793-800.

Stokes, Lawrence D., 'The Social Composition of the Nazi Party in Eutin, 1925-32', *International Review of Social History*, 23 (1978), pp. 1-32.

Wernette, Richard Dee, 'Quantitative Methods in Studying Political Mobilization in late Weimar Germany', *Historical Methods Newsletter*, 10 (1977), pp. 97-101.

Winkler, Heinrich August, 'Mittelstandsbewegung oder Volkspartei? Zur sozialen Basis der NSDAP', in Wolfgang Schieder (ed.), *Faschismus als soziale Bewegung* (Hamburg, 1976), pp. 97-118.

Ziegler, Herbert Friedrich, 'The SS-Führerkorps. An Analysis of its Socioeconomic and Demographic Structure 1925-1939' (Ph.D. thesis, Emory University, 1980).

Zipfel, Friedrich, 'Gestapo and the SD: A Sociographic Profile of the Organizers of Terror', in Stein Ugelvik Larsen, Bernt Hagtvet, Jan Petter Myklebust (eds.), *Who were the Fascists? Social Roots of European Fascism* (Bergen/Oslo/Tromso, 1980), pp. 301-11.

INDEX

INDEX